AFTERLIVES

**THE HUNGER STRIKE AND THE
SECRET OFFER THAT CHANGED IRISH HISTORY**

AFTERLIVES

THE HUNGER STRIKE AND THE
SECRET OFFER THAT CHANGED IRISH HISTORY

RICHARD O'RAWE

Foreword by Ed Moloney

THE LILLIPUT PRESS
DUBLIN

First published in 2010 by
THE LILLIPUT PRESS
62–63 Sitric Road, Arbour Hill
Dublin 7, Ireland
www.lilliputpress.ie

ISBN   978 1 84351 1 847

3 5 7 9 10 8 6 4 2

A CIP record for this title is available
from The British Library.

Set in 10.5 pt on 14.5 pt Garamond
with Gotham display titling by Marsha Swan
Printed in Spain by GZ Printek, Bilbao

'I have the bad and disagreeable habit of writing the truth as I see it.'
IRA leader Ernie O'Malley in a letter to
republican activist Sheila Humphreys, 1938

Bik McFarlane: Well, Rick?
Richard O'Rawe: I think there's enough there, Bikso.
Bik McFarlane: I agree. I'll write to the outside an' let them
know our thinkin'.
H-Block 3, 5 July 1981

Reporter: Who took the decision to reject that [Mountain
Climber] offer?
Bik McFarlane: There was no offer of that description.
Reporter: At all?
Bik McFarlane: Whatsoever. No offer existed.
UTV News, 28 February 2005

'That conversation did not happen. I did not write out to the [IRA]
Army Council and tell them we were accepting [a deal]. I couldn't
have. I couldn't have accepted something that didn't exist.'
Bik McFarlane, *Irish News*, 11 March 2005

'Something was going down. And I said to Richard [O'Rawe], this
is amazing, this is a huge opportunity and I feel there's the potential
here [in the Mountain Climber process] to end this.'
Bik McFarlane, *Belfast Telegraph*, 4 June 2009

'I confirm what Richard said all along. He is 100 per cent correct. I've no doubts that he's right in what he says.'

Gerard 'Cleaky' Clarke, 23 May 2009

'I think, morally, that the leadership on the outside should have intervened [to end the hunger strike]. This is an army; we were all volunteers in this army; the leadership had direct responsibility over these men. And I think they betrayed to a large extent the comradeship that was there ...

[It was] cowardly in many ways ... to allow mothers and sisters and ... fathers to make these decisions [to allow or not to allow their loved ones to die] ... allowing that to happen was a total disregard of the responsibility that they had to these people ...

I believe that was the reason why the leadership on the outside did not intervene, because of the street protests that were taking place, because of the political party that Sinn Féin was building.'

Brendan 'The Dark' Hughes
—from Ed Moloney, Voices from the Grave (2010)

Foreword

THIS IS quite possibly one of the most important stories to come out of the Troubles in Northern Ireland because it helps to explain how and why they came to an end in a way that is revelatory, deeply disturbing, unprecedented and convincing. But before I explain what I mean by all that, I have a confession to make. As they say in the country where I now live, I have, or rather had, a dog in this fight. I did not want Richard O'Rawe to go down the road that has led to this book.

It was not that I did not want the story of what really happened in the H-Blocks of Long Kesh during the torrid summer of 1981 to be told. Far from it. I am a journalist very much of the 'publish and be damned' school, a firm believer that if you know a story to be true and important and that its publication will not result in physical harm to others, then you should do all you can to get it out to the reading, listening or viewing public. Why be a journalist otherwise?

I also believed Richard's account from the moment I heard it. During much of the hunger strike period in 1981, I was the stand-in Northern Editor of *The Irish Times* and I am pleased to say that the work of the paper's Belfast office during those awful months was in a league of its own. We broke one story after another and got closer to what was going on than any other media outlet.

As a result of what I had learned, I had become extremely sceptical of the official line from the Provos that the prisoners were in charge of the protest. The small bits and pieces of evidence that I had accumulated suggested that Gerry Adams and the people around him were really calling the shots and, by August 1981, I had come to believe that they were not interested in a settlement. It wasn't just that the procession of coffins from the prison hospital in Long Kesh was helping to keep the pot boiling on the streets of Northern Ireland, which it was, but that I had a fair idea of what was really going on in the minds of the Provo leadership.

Long before the hunger strikes happened, I knew that there was a strong view in the group around Gerry Adams (we didn't call it the Think Tank in those days but that is what it was) that Sinn Féin should go political, and stand for elections. But that was a dangerous argument to advocate in a movement that had split from the Official IRA largely in protest at the contaminating effect of conventional politics. The Provisionals were people for whom the gun was the purest and only acceptable expression of political belief, whereas electoral politics, as Irish history bore witness, was the pathway to reformism and compromise.

By 1979 or 1980, those around Adams would talk wistfully to me of how, in five or ten years maybe, they might be able to persuade their other colleagues to stand Sinn Féin candidates for Belfast City Council. But that was as far as their horizons were permitted to expand. Suddenly, just a couple of years later, all had changed utterly. Bobby Sands had been elected to Westminster and Kieran Doherty and Paddy Agnew returned to the Dáil. All three were IRA prisoners. Council elections in the North had in the meantime seen success for anti-H-Block candidates, especially in Belfast, and Owen Carron was poised to take Sands' seat after his death had created a by-election.

It seemed to me that fate had dealt an extraordinary hand to the Adams camp. Suddenly they had an opportunity to fast-forward all their political ambitions in a very real way. Gone was the limited goal of winning seats to Belfast Council in the distant, uncertain future; now it was possible to get into the big game in one go and to do so in a very acceptable way to their grassroots. The dismay and even anger shown by the British and Irish establishments, along with the bulk of the media, at the electoral success of the hunger strikers had, in the eyes of IRA supporters, transformed the mundane process of seeking votes into a worthwhile revolutionary tactic.

So when Richard O'Rawe came forward with a story that strongly suggested that efforts to reach a settlement of the hunger strike in July 1981 had been thwarted by Gerry Adams and those around him, it made complete sense to me. A settlement in July would probably have cost Owen Carron the Fermanagh-South Tyrone by-election and torpedoed Sinn Féin's ambitions to embrace electoral politics.

The key bloc in that constituency, SDLP supporters who normally reviled the IRA, had got Sands elected in order to end the hunger strike but if the protest had ended before the next by-election why on earth would they come out to vote for Carron? Keeping the hunger strike going gave them a reason to vote for Carron and hence the motive for undermining a proposed resolution. Victory in the Fermanagh-South Tyrone by-election made it easier for Sinn Féin leaders to persuade their followers to embrace electoral politics.

I had long suspected that something like this had happened and wrote words to that effect in my study of the peace process, *A Secret History of the IRA*. But I had always focused on events at the end of July when Gerry Adams and Owen Carron had visited the H-Blocks to talk to the hunger strikers but stopped well short of ordering them off the protest as Adams had told Fr Denis Faul he would. What I did not realize, until Richard O'Rawe told his story, was that the key moment had come earlier that month.

There was another reason why I believed his story. By 2001 I had left Ireland and was living in New York. But before I departed, I had set up an oral history archive funded by Boston College designed to collect the life stories of those who had fought in the conflict. These were stories that would be lost otherwise and which could now be safely collected, given that the Troubles were ending. The stories would stay in the archive until the interviewee's death, after which they would be made public; at least that was the plan.

My researcher, Anthony McIntyre, himself a former IRA 'Blanketman', had come across Richard O'Rawe's story and we both agreed that, if possible, he should be interviewed for the archive. That was easier said than done. As with all our interviewees, the decision to participate and how much of their life stories they wished to reveal was entirely a matter for themselves. Interviewees were never put under any pressure. It took weeks and months before Richard finally decided to sit in front of a microphone and as long before he was ready to talk about the events of early July 1981. When he did, it was, I was told, a moment of great emotion with many tears shed, as if a dam had finally burst.

This was not the behaviour of someone who had concocted a slanderous lie in order to cause problems for others but that of a person who knew the great danger he was putting himself in and who had been living with guilt over his part in these events for far too long. These were the telltale symptoms of truth. As so often in journalism, it is features of the story like these, which convince as much as checkable facts.

Then something unexpected happened. I had imagined, even hoped, that the Boston College archive would provide psychological solace for some interviewees. After all, they lived in a world where the rules of *omertà* applied and were enforced sometimes ruthlessly. Perhaps being allowed to tell stories that had been bottled up for too long could give relief. That was certainly the case with Richard O'Rawe but from being a reluctant interviewee he was transformed into someone who now wanted to tell the world his story, to trumpet it from the rooftops. He wanted, he announced, to write a book about what had happened.

I understood and sympathized with this but I also knew that what lay in store for him could be very unpleasant indeed. Those who had the most to lose if the story was made public had been at the top of a very greasy pole for a long time. They had stayed there because they had grown sharp claws that they never hesitated to use against critics, rivals and enemies – or indeed writers who probed too deeply into their affairs. I had some experience of this myself in my journalistic dealings with them, and my researcher Anthony McIntyre had more. Richard and his family lived in the middle of West Belfast, cheek by jowl with people who would now regard him as a traitor. They could and would make his life hell. I tried to dissuade him, to scare him even but to no avail. He had the right to tell his own story and he did.

With hindsight, *Blanketmen* was like the first pebbles to move on a hillside populated with unstable boulders. This book, *Afterlives*, chronicles the avalanche that has followed, the exposed lies, the documentary evidence, the eye- or rather ear-witnesses, the persuasive testimony of participants, and so on. Taken together they provide a compelling, powerful and virtually incontestable case that in the summer of 1981 Gerry Adams and those around him thwarted a proposed settlement of the IRA/INLA hunger strikes that had been put forward by Margaret Thatcher and accepted by the prisoners' leaders.

The rest, as they say, is history. The hunger strike made Sinn Féin's successful excursion into electoral politics possible; the subsequent tensions between the IRA's armed struggle and Sinn Féin's politics produced the peace process and ultimately the end of the conflict. Had the offer of July 1981 not been undermined, it is possible, even probable, that none of this would have happened.

There will be those who will say that the end justified the means, that the achievement of peace was a pearl whose price was worth paying. That may be the case. But it is important to remember that six men died who needn't have died and they went to their graves not knowing they could have lived. One can only wonder how peacefully rest the heads of those who sent them there.

Ed Moloney
New York, October 2010

Prologue

OUTSIDE THE WINDOW on the first floor of Belfast's Europa Hotel the flagpoles swayed precariously in the wind. Across the road, at the entrance to Robinson's bar, a bouncer shuffled in the ear-biting chill, his bulbous form straining against a buttoned, black Crombie overcoat. To his right, outside the Housing Executive offices, stood Scots Mick, his weather-beaten face and outstretched hand appealing to passers-by. I had worked in a hostel for alcoholics and Mick had been a resident. He had been doing well then, off the booze for over two years, but by the looks of his tomato face he was back on the sauce. He called it 'work', scrounging money off people, and he was good at it.

That was in January 2005, and a BBC journalist and I had arranged to meet to discuss a possible documentary on my forth-coming book *Blanketmen: An Untold Story of the H-Block Hunger Strike.* The journalist was concerned that I was aware of what lay before me. 'Believe me, Ricky,' he said, 'come publication day, you'd better have the hatches battened down 'cause you're gonna be right smack in the way of the perfect storm.'[1] I understood that, or at least thought I did.

As a seventeen-year-old student, I had graduated from the

revolutionary class of 1971 with a degree in idealism, and then pursued a career in the IRA. Now, thirty-four years later, having been public relations officer for the protesting prisoners in the H-Blocks with a front-seat view of the unfolding drama inside the prison, I was lifting the veil on the 1981 IRA/INLA hunger strike, during which ten of my prison comrades and cherished friends had died under horrendous circumstances. I was convinced that the last six hunger strikers need not have lost their lives, because the British government, through an intermediary codenamed 'Mountain Climber', had made a substantial offer of settlement on 5 July 1981, before the fifth hunger striker, Joe McDonnell had died. That offer had been accepted by the IRA prison leadership, but rejected by the outside IRA leadership. This rejection came into the jail in a communication 'comm' from Gerry Adams, who said that the outside leadership was 'surprised' that we had accepted the offer, and that 'More is needed.'[2] During the hunger strike Adams headed a steering committee of senior republicans, whose remit was to co-ordinate publicity on the outside, and to liaise with the prisoners on all matters relating to the hunger strike. Throughout this book, I will refer to this body simply as the 'committee'.

I knew that my claims were incendiary. I recognized that by exhuming this particular past, certain republican leaders would bare their teeth. These men, as in 1981, were powerful: they had the authority to bring down on my shoulders the full weight of the republican movement. I expected the poison quills to be sharpened. I knew a chorus of orchestrated indignation and abuse, followed inevitably by character assassination and ostracism, would ensue. An on-side former hunger striker or two would be put on stand-by to lend weight to the campaign. I could almost hear them say: 'He can't argue with an ex-hunger striker.' I could, and I would.

Things became serious when a former Blanketman, reputed to be the then adjutant-general of the IRA, visited my home on

17 July 2003. This man did not threaten me, and he emphasized that he was not there to 'gag' me. He said that he was speaking on behalf of the 'leadership' and enquired if I was writing a book about the hunger strike.

I told him that I was.

Was I writing anything that might hurt Gerry Adams?

I was 'not in the business of hurting anyone'.

What exactly was I writing?

The truth about the hunger strike.

Was I going to say that the 1981 leadership sacrificed the hunger strikers?

No.

Would I speak to Gerry Adams?

No: I would not agree to the book being 'sanitized', and I would not pull out of writing it.

He said that no one was asking me to sanitize or pull it.

It was my turn to become inquisitor.

Did he know what had happened in the prison?

'Most of it.'

Did he know that the prison leadership had accepted the Mountain Climber offer?

'Bad things happen in war, Ricky.'

That gruesome riposte and sidestep was unexpected. The inquisition was over. I made an excuse and we parted as friends.

This encounter told me that Adams and the leadership were fully aware that I was writing a book about the 1981 hunger strike. Yet surprisingly their initial response to *Blanketmen* was one of confusion and contradiction. They would soon recover their composure.

What is undisputable about the 1981 hunger strike is that the last six hunger strikers died in tragic and obscure circumstances. Despite this, and the numerous books written on the subject, we have yet to understand what really happened in the negotiations between the committee and the British government.

The British penchant for secrecy is legendary, and for four years it was my word versus the committee's. Then came a breakthrough. Thanks to a change in the law designed to open up more government secrets to scrutiny, a prominent journalist was given extracts of July 1981 letters from 10 Downing Street to the Northern Ireland Office, in March 2009. The content of these letters reveals that Margaret Thatcher had been closely monitoring the contacts between her intelligence officers and senior republicans Gerry Adams and Danny Morrison. They demonstrate that she had personally authorized significant prison concessions to the prisoners, which were passed on to the Provisional IRA, or at least that was what the British believed. These papers divulge that the Mountain Climber offer had been rejected by the republican negotiators, even though we in the prison leadership had accepted it. These letters will be examined and analysed in this narrative.

The Mountain Climber himself, businessman Brendan Duddy, gave candid and revealing testimony at a hunger strike conference in his native Derry in May 2009. With an audience of over three hundred hanging on his every word, Duddy verified the authenticity of a British statement he had passed on to the IRA leadership on 5 July 1981. That statement, from the then Secretary of State for Northern Ireland, Humphrey Atkins, listed the changes that would be implemented in the prison as soon as the hunger strike ended. The Mountain Climber also confirmed that the IRA negotiators had rejected the offer.

To date, the man in charge of the special hunger-strike committee, Gerry Adams, has had little of substance to say by way of self-defence about his role in the hunger strike, preferring to let others do that for him. Neither had the committee released their papers and comms about the clandestine talks since *Blanketmen* was published in 2005. Had they nothing to hide, they would have mounted a defence and welcomed a forensic examination of their position, but they chose not to do so.

In *Afterlives* I shall be examining the contradictory and

incriminating public stances taken by the committee and their acolytes since *Blanketmen* was published. Evidence will be presented to show that the authority of the IRA Army Council had been usurped by the committee, and that the ruling body of the republican movement had *never* been made aware of British government contacts, much less the offer that Margaret Thatcher had made to end the hunger strike. Naturally, we Blanketmen assumed that our Army Council had its finger on the pulse. It hadn't. Only after the book came out did I learn that the committee had surreptitiously arrogated the Council's authority. As a result, when I wrote *Blanketmen* I mistakenly maligned Army Council members who knew nothing of this episode and who had played no part in it. To these Army Council members, I offer sincere apologies.

It has also become clear that the committee excluded the IRA's junior partners in the hunger strike, the INLA, from the secret discussions with the British, even though three INLA volunteers died on the fast, with the last two being among the last six hunger stikers to die. A spokesperson for the INLA Army Council of 1981 will substantiate that the last two INLA hunger strikers to die, Kevin Lynch and Micky Devine, went to their deaths not knowing that an honourable ending to the hunger strike had been on offer from 5 July 1981 – over four and six weeks respectively before each man passed away.

Two surviving hunger strikers, one from the IRA, the other from the INLA, will confirm that they were never told of any offer when they were on the fast, while another who was hostile to my position, will inadvertently do likewise.

Two further fellow Blanketmen on the leadership wing in the H-Blocks will verify that they had overheard a conversation between Bik McFarlane and myself, during which we accepted the Mountain Climber offer. One is happy to allow his name to be published; the other prefers to remain anonymous, although he has confirmed my account to some of the hunger-striker families.

A representative from the Irish Commission for Justice and Peace (ICJP) will interpret that body's efforts to settle the hunger strike honourably. He will also confirm that the offer the ICJP believed it had secured from the British (before Joe McDonnell's death) was, in every detail, the twin of the offer the British secretly made to the IRA Army Council.

It is now generally accepted that the seed of the Northern Ireland peace process was planted in the prison protests over political status, and was watered by the deaths of the ten H-Block hunger strikers. This was a deeply ironic consequence of the prison sacrifices. Bobby Sands and our nine comrades believed that their actions would advance the cause of socialism in the context of a united Ireland. What emerged was something the IRA had always rejected – an internal 'Northern Ireland' settlement. However, that is not my concern in this book. What *is* my concern is getting to the bottom of the hunger-strike story.

It has been suggested that the committee was responsible for the biggest cover-up and scandal in the history of Irish republicanism. Others believe that the committee, inexperienced in negotiations, made critical errors of judgment. The problem with both scenarios is that no committee member has ever accepted responsibility for *any* decision connected to the hunger strike. Where lies the truth? This narrative will go some way towards answering that question.

Richard O'Rawe
October 2010

PUBLISHER'S NOTE
The title of this book was inspired by Derek Mahon's poem 'Afterlives' from *The Snow Party* (Oxford University Press, 1975).

One

SUPPOSE SOMEONE told you to keep your mouth shut or you could be shot: what would you do? When that happened to me in 1991 I zipped it. In taking this course of least resistance, I felt lousy; it was as if I had betrayed the ten hunger strikers who had laid down their lives for me and for the rest of the Blanketmen in 1981. But I always knew that some day I would find the courage to recount their story.

That day came when my book *Blanketmen: An Untold Story of the H-Block Hunger Strike* was released. It was my account of what happened at leadership level in the H-Blocks of The Maze/Long Kesh prison during the 1981 hunger strike.

From the minute the book hit the shelves, it was fiercely slated by some members of the 1981 IRA leadership. Besides the few individuals who knew what they were talking about, there were other republicans who professed to 'know' things, or to speak 'with authority' about the hunger strike – people whom I had never met in my life. It did not matter. What did matter was putting my dead comrades' story to right. If some people were upset, then so be it – the leadership had floated along on a raft of deceit for far too long.

Tellingly, Gerry Adams, the man at the helm, shunned debate. His self-imposed press exile ensured that he could not be quoted or challenged. Besides the tactical advantages of sending others in to bat for him on the hunger strike issue, Adams was preoccupied with other problems in that winter of political isolation, not least the fallout from the Northern Bank raid in Belfast, during which £26 million was stolen.

Although the IRA denied involvement in the robbery, few people believed them. The Chief Constable of the Police Service of Northern Ireland, Sir Hugh Orde, made it clear that the IRA had been responsible. Most people accepted that no other paramilitary body would have had the expertise to carry off such a complex operation.

On the RTÉ current affairs programme *This Week*, Taoiseach Bertie Ahern pulled no punches: 'This was an IRA job, a Provisional IRA job, which would have been known to the provisional leadership.'[1]

Before the robbery, negotiations between the Reverend Ian Paisley's Democratic Unionist Party (DUP) and Sinn Féin, the political wing of the republican movement, had reached a delicate stage. Paisley, the roaring, granite-like voice of extreme unionism, was demanding to be shown photographs of the IRA's weapons being destroyed before he would go into government with Sinn Féin.

At stake was an *entente cordiale*, an agreement that, if achievable, could end centuries of nationalist and unionist conflict. The bank robbery dampened any enthusiasm within DUP ranks for such an accord.

While this robbery had all the appearances of an act of reckless self-harm, political commentators of note looked around for reasons why the IRA would jeopardize a 24-year peace strategy. Three answers emerged: the first was that the robbery had been an attempt by dissenting elements within the IRA to scupper the peace process. This was an unlikely scenario because by the end of 2004 opposition to the Adams/McGuinness-led peace agenda within the IRA had been obliterated. The second was that the Dublin and London governments had previously ignored intelligence reports that the IRA had carried out other large-scale robberies in the months before the Northern Bank heist, and it was assumed that they would do so again. That possibility could not be so easily dismissed. The third answer was that the robbery had been approved by leading republican politicos so they could finally free themselves from the IRA's straitjacket. The thinking behind this premise was that there would be, inevitably, a profound sense of outrage at the robbery, forcing the IRA to self-destruct – which was what eventually happened.

These theories are unproven because the IRA has said that none of its members had any involvement in the robbery, and to date no IRA member has been convicted for it.

If the IRA had planned and carried out the Northern Bank robbery, they certainly did not plan the horrific murder of 33-year-old Robert McCartney, although it was alleged that their members had carried it out.

Robert McCartney lived in the nationalist Short Strand area of Belfast, along with his partner, Bridgeen, and their two young sons, Conlaed and Brandon. On the evening of 30 January 2005 Robert and some friends got involved in a fight with local republicans in Magennis's bar in the Markets area. The fight ended up outside the bar, where Robert was knifed. He died of his wounds the next day at 8.10 am. His friend, Brendan Devine, was also stabbed and seriously injured.

It was a savage murder, made worse by the revelation that, as soon as the crime occurred, an IRA volunteer apparently announced to the seventy-strong pub patrons, mostly republicans back from the annual Bloody Sunday demonstration: 'This is IRA business. Nobody saw anything.'[2] A forensic clean-up was then carried out, and the bar's CCTV tape was confiscated and destroyed.

Robert's partner and his five sisters tirelessly fought for 'Justice for Robert'. Their protracted campaign garnered support from the European Parliament, the United States Congress and Senate, and President George W. Bush, among others, but it led to no arrests.

The Northern Bank robbery and the murder of Robert McCartney convinced people that the political journey, which had begun with the election of Bobby Sands in 1981, had ground to a halt. It must have seemed so, even to the indefatigable Gerry Adams. And who would have blamed Adams, who many believed to be the primary architect of the peace process, if he had handed over the reins of power to someone else and simply walked away? Had he done so, Adams might have found an opportunity to look back and reflect on the life and times of his old friend, the revolutionary Bobby Sands, and on the aftermath of the prison leader's election to Westminster in the Fermanagh-South Tyrone constituency in June 1981.

Bobby Sands had been a disciple of Gerry Adams, one of the Big Lad's Cage 11 golden boys in the days before the H-Blocks were occupied, when republican prisoners did their time in the compounds, or 'cages', of Long Kesh in the 1970s. It was in Cage 11 that the charismatic Adams, and Brendan 'The Dark' Hughes, preached radical left-wing politics to other prisoners, many of them fresh-faced young republicans. Among those smitten with revolutionary zeal were Bobby Sands, Bik McFarlane and Seanna Walsh. These men, along with Hughes, would become future OCs of the H-Block prisoners.

Of Bobby's election to the Fermanagh-South Tyrone seat, Adams said in 1996: 'I pondered with a certain wry satisfaction the comparison between my first electoral experience, folding leaflets for Liam McMillen in 1964 and suffering lost deposits, and the tremendous impact of Bobby's election.'[3] Some commentators have said that when Bobby died on hunger strike on 5 May 1981, Adams was still pondering, musing whether or not this was the break he had been waiting for to end the IRA's armed struggle and to stride out on the path to constitutional politics.

The election of Bobby's replacement, Owen Carron, occurred on 20 August 1981. On that day Micky Devine became the tenth and last hunger striker to die. On 3 October 1981, on Adams's 'advice', the hunger strike ended.

Within weeks, at the annual Sinn Féin Ard Fheis, the party adopted the 'Ballot box and Armalite' strategy (so called by Danny Morrison) and agreed to contest elections in both jurisdictions of Ireland. In that motion, the first momentous step was formally taken on the road to constitutional politics and the compromises that would inevitably follow. Blinded by the light of Sands' and Carron's electoral success, not many of the delegates who voted for the fresh approach would have realized that they had just slipped the black spot to the IRA.

A year later, three members of the committee, Gerry Adams, Danny Morrison and Martin McGuinness, were elected to the Northern Ireland Assembly, with Sinn Féin gaining over 10 per cent of the popular vote.

Adams's stature as a brilliant tactician grew when, in June 1983, he captured the West Belfast Westminster seat from independent candidate Gerry Fitt, former leader of the Social Democratic and Labour Party. As well as that, Sinn Féin garnered 102,701 votes in the North of Ireland. For many, Adams was the dynamic genius behind the new age of republican enlightenment; he had promised change, and he was manifestly delivering. Suddenly Sinn Féin, the old chestnut of constitutional Northern politics, could no longer be regarded as a joke. Party offices were opened in every nationalist district, and activists, many of them former IRA prisoners, fine-tuned their radicalism to the task of solving the everyday problems of the people. This was Sands's socialism made flesh – and it had all the appearances of a rolling revolution.

It was small wonder, then, that Adams consolidated his power base within the republican movement when Ruairí Ó Brádaigh resigned as president of Sinn Féin in November 1983. Since then historians have portrayed Adams's accession to the presidency as the death knell of 1940s' and 1950s' republicanism. Perhaps, but Adams's *coup d'état*, which had profited enormously from the death of the hunger strikers, was completed only when the then IRA Chief-of-Staff and hard-line socialist, Army Council member Ivor Bell, left the IRA. Bell had been seventeen years old when he was interned during the IRA's 1950s campaign. After the civil rights campaign of 1969, he became a leading figure of the Provisional IRA.

The battle for hegemony between Adams and Bell, former close friends and comrades-in-arms, bore few of the similarities to that which Adams had fought with Ruairí Ó Bradáigh and the traditionalists. There was no democratic vote on Bell's future role in the republican movement. According to Ed Moloney in his book *A Secret History of the IRA*, Bell was charged with 'treachery' and court-martialled. Found guilty, he faced a death sentence, but this was commuted on the advice of Gerry Adams, on condition that Bell remained silent about these events for the rest of his life. To this day he has never broken that silence.

From 1983 until the IRA ceasefire in 1994, Adams and McGuinness led a relentless, often clandestine, drive towards a peace accord with the British.

From the outset the British made it clear that the core republican objective of a British withdrawal from Ireland was not negotiable and that there could not be a united Ireland unless it was voted for by the majority of the citizens in Northern Ireland. In effect the British were reinforcing the unionist veto – the real reason why the war had started. The new republican leadership offered little resistance to this fundamental position.

After internal IRA dissension, the ceasefire broke down in February 1996, but was restored in July 1997. Following the reintroduction of the ceasefire, an IRA Convention narrowly backed the Adams peace strategy.

In 1997 Sinn Féin accepted the Mitchell Principles, the tenets of which committed the republican movement and all the other political parties to 'democratic and exclusively peaceful means of resolving issues', and to 'renounce for themselves, and to oppose any efforts by others, to use force, or threaten to use force, to influence the course or the outcome of all-party negotiations'. This was a public declaration by the republican movement that only peaceful means should be used to pursue political power. It was, *de facto*, an acknowledgment that the armed struggle was over. The signing of the Good Friday Agreement followed in April 1998.

The overthrow of the moderate Ulster Unionist Party by the Democratic Unionist Party in the Northern Ireland Assembly elections of May 2003 led to a hardening of the unionist position, and threatened the collapse of the hard-fought-for peace process. Even before the Northern Bank robbery and the murder of Robert McCartney, the Revd Ian Paisley had said: 'The IRA needs to be humiliated. And they need to wear their sackcloth and ashes, not in a backroom, but openly.'[4]

So if Adams did find time in 2004–5 to look back and reflect, the Sinn Féin president would have seen that he had piloted the republican movement from one side of a political universe to another. Behind him were the days of inviolable republican principle, when Northern Ireland was regarded as an illegal 'statelet' that needed not to be reformed but to be dismantled – by any means. Gone also was the IRA's armed struggle, and those former comrades who still supported its tactical use. Sands's dream of a socialist republic had all but been jettisoned too in the rush to conformity and legitimacy. Had Adams had time to catch his breath in that desolate autumn of 2005, he would surely have wearied of his sorrows and woes.

There was, however, another woe in the wind – *Blanketmen*. In the weeks before the book was to be launched, I had some very difficult decisions to make. My most pressing dilemma was whether or not to inform the families of the dead hunger strikers about the book's contents; if I didn't, I would be exposed to the criticism of being indifferent to, even disrespectful of, their feelings and the memory of their dead relatives. Nothing could have been further from the truth. I wrote the book in good conscience because not only had their loved ones been like brothers to me, but I believed that I had a sacred duty to right a terrible wrong: the untimely and unnecessary deaths of the last six hunger strikers.

There were dangers in disclosure. Undoubtedly the families would have wanted to read the book before giving an opinion. Some family members were Sinn Féin supporters; at least one was a Sinn Féin elected representative. What if, armed with a critical exposé, the republican leaders whom I had criticized convinced even some of the families to oppose the publication of the book at a highly emotive press conference?

(In June 2009, four years after the publication of *Blanketmen*, the same leading republicans gathered representatives from eight families together in a hall in Gulladuff, County Derry, and afterwards persuaded some family members to sign a statement calling on me and others to stop probing into the hunger strike.)

After weighing everything up, I decided against telling the families.

I had another thorny choice to make. The BBC had initially agreed to film a hunger-strike documentary to coincide with the book's release. For reasons never made clear, the BBC sought to change the initial agreement I had with them. This was unacceptable and I withdrew from the project, suspecting that the BBC controllers were concerned about the possible effect the programme might have on the peace process.

Two

BLANKETMEN: *An Untold Story of the H-Block Hunger Strike* was published on 28 February 2005. Most of the book dealt with my experiences of the blanket protest and the rich assortment of characters I met in the wings of H3 and H6. A spontaneous rather than a planned act of defiance, the blanket protest began in 1977 when the British government tried to criminalize the republican armed struggle by forcing IRA and INLA prisoners to wear prison/criminal uniforms and to conform to prison rules.

The first IRA volunteer to refuse to wear the 'monkey suit' was Kieran 'Header' Nugent. He told the screws when they tried to force him to wear the monkey suit, 'You'll have to nail it to my back.' Seeing his strength of character, the screws gave Nugent a blanket to wear. By that act, the blanket protest was born. Hundreds of other determined and committed republicans soon followed Nugent's example.

In a four-year period a bitter war of attrition was fought out in the H-Blocks. At the start of the protest the Blanketmen were locked in their cells for twenty-four hours a day and denied access to everything except food and water, a monthly visit, and a weekly letter. That did not break our spirits, so the British government, through its prison warders, launched a vicious campaign of brutality against us. Men were beaten, and some had their testicles squeezed until they lost consciousness. We initiated a no-wash protest, and for three years we not only refused to wash, but smeared our excrement on the walls of our cells.

Hunger strike ensued.

The first hunger strike ended in December 1980 without loss of life. Unfortunately, it failed to win any of our major demands. That negative result all but ensured a second hunger strike.

The IRA prison Officer Commanding (OC), Bobby Sands, led the second hunger strike, which started when he refused food on 1 March 1981. Sands and nine other republicans were to die on the fast.

Once a prisoner went on hunger strike, he relinquished his rank, and when Bobby refused food his Public Relations Officer, Bik McFarlane, took over from him, becoming prison OC. I was then chosen by Bobby and Bik to take over as PRO. By virtue of this appointment, I became Bik's closest confidante in the prison, and from then until the end of the hunger strike, we were in constant contact on most matters relating to the fast. Therefore I was in a unique position to know what occurred inside the prison leadership during the hunger strike – very different from the version of events that some republican leaders on the outside had put out in the years since it ended. So I wrote *Blanketmen*. In it I asserted:

1. That, rather than the Sinn Féin version of events that it was the prisoners who controlled the hunger strike, it had, in fact, been the IRA Army Council that had had unrestricted control, and that, for us prisoners, the Army Council was the umbrella under which all the other contentious issues sheltered.

2. The British government had made a substantial offer to settle the hunger strike following the release of a conciliatory statement I had written on behalf of the

prisoners on 4 July 1981. This offer, sometimes known as the 'Mountain Climber' offer, was presented on at least two different occasions to Gerry Adams and Danny Morrison by mediators from Derry, who had been in contact with British government representatives. The first occasion had been shortly before the fifth hunger striker, Joe McDonnell, died on 8 July 1981, and the second was after the sixth hunger striker, Martin Hurson, died on 13 July.

3. The then Sinn Féin national director of publicity, Danny Morrison, told Bik McFarlane the details of the offer when they met in the prison hospital on 5 July. Morrison has said, since the book's publication, that he had also made the hunger strikers aware of the offer.

4. When McFarlane returned to our wing, he wrote me out a message outlining what was on offer. Subsequently he and I had accepted it, believing there was enough in it to end the hunger strike with honour.

5. Our agreement to accept the offer was shouted in Irish out of our cell windows, and during our brief tête-à-tête McFarlane said he would write to the outside leadership and let them know of our approval.

6. Shortly after McFarlane had communicated our acceptance to the outside leadership, a comm from Gerry Adams arrived into the prison informing us that there was not enough in the offer to settle the hunger strike, and that 'more was needed'.

7. McFarlane and I accepted what we believed to have been the position of the IRA Army Council.

8. Adams's comm rejecting the offer ensured the prolongation of the hunger strike, with six more hunger strikers dying in its wake.

9. I suggested that there were only two possible explanations as to why the IRA Army Council would reject our

acceptance of the offer. The first was that it believed the British government would make a better offer before Joe McDonnell died, a perfectly understandable, if dangerous, approach, given that the British had not closed down the communication channel.

My second explanation was that the Army Council wanted to accelerate an electoral strategy by getting republican candidate Owen Carron returned for Bobby Sands's old parliamentary seat in Fermanagh-South Tyrone. Since this could not, in all likelihood, be achieved without the hunger strike, I suggested that the Army Council would have had to be prepared to sacrifice hunger strikers in order to achieve that aim.

10. The British government, under Margaret Thatcher, bore responsibility for the death of the hunger strikers.

11. As the controlling body, the Army Council sent in a comm to McFarlane at the end of September 1981, which effectively stopped the hunger strike.

12. The Army Council could have, and should have, intervened to stop the strike sooner.

Danny Morrison was the only one of my protagonists to punch his weight. Danny gave neither refuge nor quarter. That was not unexpected; the naked hatred in his ridicule was.

Bik McFarlane tried to fall in behind Morrison, but being ill-prepared for an inquisitive press, he turned out to be a media asset – for me.

Even though the book's release date had been agreed a year earlier, some of the more exuberant Sinn Féin supporters jump-ed in and suggested that I had timed the book's publication to embarrass the party, coming as it did on the heels of the Northern Bank robbery and the murder of Robert McCartney.

This was pardonable foolishness given the one-for-all, all-for-one musketeer mentality that bonds members of the republican movement. But while fraternal solidarity can be an admirable trait, it also lends itself to myopia. Had the critics read the book, they would have seen that the term 'Sinn Féin' barely received a mention, although, of necessity, the actions of a cabal of republican leaders during the hunger strike did feature heavily in the narrative.

On the day before *Blanketmen* was released, it was serialized in *The Sunday Times*. Journalist John Burns outlined some of the controversial segments in the book. Then he allowed Danny Morrison space to respond. Morrison waxed indignant, saying: 'The prisoners were sovereign; it was their call.'[1] It is impossible to exaggerate the importance of this statement because with sovereignty comes the daunting responsibility of determining not just tactics but also what constitutes an honourable settlement, and how and when the hunger strike should have been ended.

I had not been surprised when Morrison, on behalf of the committee, refused to accept any liability for the conduct of the hunger strike; it had never crossed my mind that he would do anything else. But for the first time a former comrade of Danny's, someone with more than a passing knowledge of the hunger strike, was asking questions: would Danny's denial of responsibility stand the test of objective scrutiny?

I have maintained that the prison leadership had not been in control of the hunger strike. I also stated that we were not given the full details of what was transpiring between the movement's outside leadership and the British government. There are several examples of this.

Gerry Adams, in his book *Before the Dawn: An Autobiography* writes a very revealing passage:

> Margaret Thatcher presented a public face as the Iron Lady who was 'not for turning', yet she was no stranger to expediency. During our [the committee's] contact in the course of the hunger strike, her government representatives approached us in advance of a world leaders' conference [G7] in Canada at which she was due to speak on 21 July. 'The Prime Minister,'

they said, 'would like to announce at the conference that the hunger strike had ended.' They outlined the support that we had and the support we didn't have, and then went on tell us: 'This is what the Prime Minister is prepared to say.' They fed us a draft of a speech which Thatcher was going to deliver in Toronto, and there was no doubt that they were prepared to take amendments to her text from us if it was possible to come to some sort of resolution at that time.[2]

If it was a shock to me to find out that the Iron Lady had allowed her nemesis, the IRA, to see her intended speech, it was an even bigger shock to discover that she had been prepared to allow them to submit amendments to it in order to bring the hunger strike to a close. This was a trait of Thatcher's personality that was unknown to the public; it was the cerebral eclipsing the visceral, the triumph of reason over emotion. Anyone who had lived through the Thatcher era would have witnessed a Churchillean character, one who seemed to revel in the cut and thrust of confrontation; never more evident than when she ruthlessly crushed the coal miners during their strike of 1984–5. It was no different in Ireland; she jumped at every opportunity to polish her 'we-shall-fight-them-on-the-beaches' persona. Yet, far away from public view, Thatcher had no problem with dumping Churchill in favour of the canny Welsh Wizard, David Lloyd George – the greengrocer's daughter could deal when it suited her. Indeed, her private position in relation to the hunger strike has all the appearance of one who had moved considerably to ensure that the IRA was given an honourable way out of the impasse in the H-Blocks.

The prison leadership's acquiescence to the committee was demonstrated in other ways, and the most striking of these was the conduct of the exchanges/negotiations with the British after the sixth hunger striker, Martin Hurson, died on 13 July.

On 22 July Bik McFarlane replied to an important comm from 'Brownie' (Gerry Adams). The background to Adams writing to him had been to tell him of the failure of the latest round of negotiations with the British. The consequences of that breakdown were profound because what resulted from it was that another four hunger strikers subsequently died.

There were several enlightening elements to McFarlane's reply to Adams, but most remarkably Adams and Morrison did not think that McFarlane needed to know the details of what the British had offered before they rejected it. 'You can give me a run-down on exactly how far the Brits went,' McFarlane had written back to Adams.[3] Nothing would ever illustrate the true nature of the command structure more than this sentence because what Bik McFarlane was inadvertently making clear was that he had no input into, or control over, the negotiations with the British. Clearly, he did not know what the committee had rejected on the prisoners' or the hunger strikers' behalf, yet he had been in command of the IRA prisoners. Moreover, the committee never let the prison OC see the draft of Thatcher's proposed Toronto statement; the hunger strikers and the prison leadership were never told of this development. And crucially, no one in the prison, hunger striker or otherwise, was ever shown the full text of the Mountain Climber offer during or after the hunger strike.

Another example of how the committee dictated strategy over the heads of the prison leadership was the circumstances in which the hunger strike was brought to an end.

By late September 1981 four families had intervened to take their loved ones off the hunger strike when they had gone into a coma. Other families had been threatening to follow suit. In terms of the political impact on the British, a blind man could have seen that the hunger strike was on the wane.

For some time I had had reservations about the continuance of the hunger strike, and had come to the conclusion that we stood no chance of attaining our five demands in their entirety (Bik had made it clear that there could be no compromise solution).

With a profound sense of hopelessness, and no small measure of deep sorrow, I spoke to Brendan 'The Dark' Hughes, OC of the H-Blocks before Bobby Sands, and the man who had led the first hunger strike in 1980. The Dark was of a similar mind to me and as the senior IRA officer I agreed to write to Bik on our joint behalf and ask him to call off the hunger strike. I did that, outlining the reasons why The Dark and I felt the fast should be ended. Bik wrote back to me rejecting our request.

That night he wrote to Gerry Adams:

> There is a growing feeling among those with what I would call a bit of savvy that our present troubles may prove insurmountable. I have been asked to consider terminating the hunger strike. Now that I will only consider when I believe we have no chance of regaining the top position and pushing forwards towards a feasible solution. I don't believe we should allow the action of a few clanns [families] to dictate such action by us. We do face a critical few weeks but I believe that we can overcome the problem.[4]

In the same comm, Bik had given him the names of future hunger strikers, the first of whom would have been Gerard Murray, who was pencilled in to begin his fast on 5 October.

Within twenty-four hours, a comm came back from Adams informing Bik that the strike had run its course and needed to be ended. Bik dutifully laid aside his plans to put more prisoners on the hunger strike, and set about arranging meetings with the strikers to tell them that *he* had decided to bring the protest to a close.

On 3 October 1981, two days before Gerard Murray was supposed to go on the fast, the H-Block hunger strike ended.

Even after the hunger strike had been halted, Bik was not averse to performing the odd volte-face if Adams and the committee told him to do so. After agreeing a future strategy with his staff, he wrote to Adams on 4 October saying: 'we must move asap to get ourselves above the present level – i.e. dispensing with Blanket protest and trying to build up'.⁵ By 'build up' Bik meant that we would go into the prison system but still fight for political status through operations such as blowing up the workshops (this was one of a range of options that had been discussed by Bobby Sands, Bik, Jake Jackson, Pat Mullan and me before the second hunger strike had begun).

Bik's comm did not go down too well, and Adams's reply, which I read, left no room for doubting where the real power in the movement lay. In his response Adams told Bik that it was inconceivable that Blanketmen would abandon the protest after ten of their number had died (this despite the British having conceded to us the right to wear our own clothes). Who could have guessed that Bik McFarlane would accept the advice/order and tell his men that the protest would continue ad infinitum?

These are only some of the more conspicuous examples of the committee's control. Despite Danny Morrison's Jesuitical protestations to John Burns, the committee had always been the sovereign party during the hunger strike, and in Brendan McFarlane they had a man who would have charged the gates of hell with his bare hands if ordered to do so. And they were safe hands; they guaranteed no dissent from inside the prison to the decisions taken from outside the H-Blocks. It was unfortunate for Bik that he was tested in this manner; if there had not been a hunger strike, he would never have found himself in such an objectionable position, and on a personal level he and I would have remained the best of friends. But there was a hunger strike, our great men had died, Bik was the committee's ramrod, and it was he who talked the hard talk to the hunger strikers, and who cut off all avenues of retreat.

As well as speaking to Danny Morrison, *The Sunday Times* also contacted Dr Anthony McIntyre. McIntyre, known as 'Mackers', was a former Blanketman who had spent eighteen years in British prisons for his involvement in the killing of two loyalists. When

Burns asked him to comment on the book, he made an interesting statement: 'I don't think the Army Council ran the hunger strike: I think one man did – and that was Adams.'[6]

At the time I thought that Mackers was only rattling Adams's cage – and not for the first time – but, unbeknownst to me, he had not been speculating; he had been speaking from a position of knowledge, having discussed the matter with some members of the 1981 IRA Army Council, who told him that they knew nothing of the secret British contact during the hunger strike.

Burns finally tracked down Gerry Adams and asked him for his view. Unlike Morrison, Adams offered neither froth nor bombast. Instead, his solitary response was: 'I'll comment when I read the book.'[7]

When I read Morrison's strong rebuttal, and saw how easily Adams had fended off the *Sunday Times* journalist, I realized that I was pitted against highly skilled politicos and media operators. Alexander Pope's famous words came to mind: 'For fools rush in where angels fear to tread.'[8] Was that self-pity? Perhaps. One thing was for sure; Danny Morrison was no fool, and Gerry Adams was no angel.

Three

A DAM OF RESERVATIONS, which had been building up in the months before *Blanketmen* appeared, finally burst in a hotel room in Booterstown, County Dublin, in the early hours of 28 February 2005.

With the book hours away from release, little things suddenly became large. I had left my reading glasses at home, and had forgotten to pack Padraig O'Malley's *Biting at the Grave* and David Beresford's *Ten Men Dead*. *Biting at the Grave* was important because not only did it give an in-depth study of the 1981 hunger strike and its political consequences, but it contained some important interviews with former hunger strikers and major republican figures who had been on the outside, people like Pat 'Beag' McGeown, Danny Morrison and Gerry Adams. *Ten Men Dead* was simply invaluable to me because within its pages were some of the actual written communiqués that Bik had written to the outside leadership during the hunger strike. These two books had been my faithful companions for three years, and I felt naked and vulnerable without them.

I spent that night tossing and turning, going through exhaustive question-and-answer sessions in my head. The room seemed like a sweatbox. Had I covered all the angles? What would the leadership's response be? Danny Morrison had given his impromptu response to *The Sunday Times*. There would have been a 'thinktank' meeting (a gathering of Big Gerry's inner circle). Perhaps not. Probably only the members of the committee.

To counterbalance my account of the hunger strike, they would have to persuade Bik McFarlane to oppose me publicly. That wouldn't be hard. Bik's unblushing admiration for Gerry Adams was boundless; he would cross the Atlantic Ocean in a kayak for him. I wondered what he was doing at that moment. Was he lying in bed in Belfast, going through the same question-and-answer session that I was? A small voice struggled to get out:

Tell the truth.

But sometimes the truth isn't enough.

Tell the truth.

But the truth can be twisted.

Tell the bloody truth!

But …

That was that then. Or was it?

Sleep still remained a stranger.

The next morning my wife Bernadette and I were collected by a representative of New Island Books, and driven to the RTÉ studios, where I had been scheduled to speak on the *Marianne Finucane Show*. This was scary. I was new to public speaking, and I had no idea how I would come across.

Before being taken into the studio, Bernadette and I were met by the female producer, who briefly discussed the contents of the book. Then she turned to Bernadette and said that the story of her survival during this traumatic time had more appeal for her than my own story did.

'Tell me, what was life like for you, Bernadette, when his nibs here was off freeing Ireland?'

'Terrible. I was only married six months. I'd no money, I was on the dole, I had to rear our daughter on my own, and do you know what?'

'What?'

'I didn't understand any of it.'

'Did he not explain it to you?'

'Explain it? He didn't even tell me he was back in the IRA. The first I knew of it was when the Peelers raided the house.'

'You're joking? You mean you didn't know?'

'No.'

Lips were pursed. Not mine.

Marianne Finucane was a gem. She took the edge off my nervousness with her warm and friendly manner. Yet even as I went through the detail of the prison leadership accepting the British offer and spoke of the dead hunger strikers, I could feel a lump in my throat. It was as if even naming my dead comrades had the potential to unleash hidden springs of raw emotion from deep within.

No sooner had we left RTÉ and returned to the hotel than I was informed that Bik McFarlane had tried to get on the *Marianne Finucane Show* in order to rebut my account. Good old reliable Bik. Apparently he had been disconcerted by what I had to say. I could not resist a wry smile on hearing that.

UTV wanted an interview with me for the six o'clock news, so we left our hotel and went to another one nearer Dublin city centre. There we met a UTV reporter and cameraman, and went outside to conduct the interview. It was a simple affair; a sentence or two about the book, and the ubiquitous 'walk-past'. Unbeknownst to me, Bik was being interviewed by UTV in Belfast.

It had been arranged that I would be on the BBC *Talk Back* radio show, hosted by David Dunseith. Danny Morrison was to be on the programme with me. For many years Morrison had been Sinn Féin's national director for publicity. He was an experienced public speaker, and in the cut and thrust of debate, a formidable opponent. Would this be his finest hour?

I was fortunate in that I did not have much time to dwell on what Morrison might or might not put to me. Already my publisher was discussing further interviews for the afternoon.

Sitting with the headphones on, in the BBC Dublin studio, I thought there was not much I could say, other than relay my account of the hunger strike without frills or exaggeration. Then a voice came through from Belfast to tell me that I would be on air within a minute or so and that Bik McFarlane was also in the studio. I was asked if I had any objections to McFarlane going live alongside Morrison. Not a word of this had been said to my publisher, who had been in contact with the *Talk Back* team earlier that morning.

I realized immediately that a gun had just been put to my head, because, if I objected, Morrison would have told the listeners that McFarlane had, just minutes earlier, offered to debate the issues with me, and that I had chickened out, stating that McFarlane – not O'Rawe – had been the OC of the prisoners, and McFarlane knew it all, while O'Rawe knew only what McFarlane had told him. Yet if, on the other hand, I did agree to McFarlane's inclusion in the debate, I would have to face down the two of them, rather than one. I did not know if this was standard BBC practice, but I regarded it as an ambush and a dirty trick. There was no wry smile on my face now.

Dunseith opened by asking me to explain why my book was proving to be so controversial. I haltingly outlined the contentious points, the most controversial of which was that Bik McFarlane and I had accepted an offer from the British government before Joe McDonnell had died, and that the outside leadership had written in to us rejecting our acceptance.

When asked if I was shocked that the IRA Army Council had rejected the offer, I said that I wasn't so much shocked as left feeling 'a bit amateurish'.[1] I added that I had personally felt 'clumsy'[2] at having accepted the first offer from the British. I went on to say that I had believed then that Adams and those around him were 'a pretty sharp, pretty *au fait* bunch of guys'.[3]

Dunseith asked Bik McFarlane to respond to what I had said. Bik can sometimes come across as very stern, and on this occasion I thought he sounded like a much-maligned, fire-and-brimstone preacher. He melodramatically stated that he could 'speak authoritatively and with conviction in relation to correspondence that was coming in from outside and back and forward between ourselves and the outside leadership. And, certainly, Richard's recollection is totally inaccurate in relation to that. I mean, I would dispute that with some authority.'[4]

Bik said that the IRA Army Council 'totally and absolutely'[5] opposed the 1980 and 1981 hunger strikes. This was true, but it is not entirely truthful. Once Bobby Sands had got elected, a new political era dawned and the game changed forever. Unheralded and largely unseen by political commentators at the time of Bobby's election, the prospect of an electoral strategy had been opened up, and it has been said that, from then on, the committee had a definite stake in continuing the hunger strike. Following Danny Morrison's line in the *Sunday Times* interview of the previous day, McFarlane also declared, 'The decisions in relation to the hunger strike and what transpired during it were left entirely to the hunger strikers and to the prisoners.'[6]

Monsignor Denis Faul, a civil rights priest who had had a close relationship with us prisoners, was then asked to comment. In a newspaper article that morning, Monsignor Faul had written: 'I had a suspicion at the time, but this book is devastating. It confirms those suspicions.'[7]

The suspicions to which Monsignor Faul had referred were that some members of the outside leadership had been more concerned with getting the republican candidate Owen Carron elected in Fermanagh-South Tyrone than in saving hunger strikers' lives. Monsignor Faul told *Talk Back* listeners of a meeting that relatives of the hunger strikers and he had held with Gerry Adams on 28 July 1981, and how at the end of that meeting he had been hopeful that Adams would go into the prison and find a way to bring the hunger strike to an end. But the next day Adams had phoned Monsignor Faul and said that he wanted to bring Owen Carron in to the prison. On hearing this, Monsignor Faul said, 'My heart sank.'

'Now why did your heart sink at that stage?' Dunseith asked.

'What had Carron to do with this?' Monsignor Faul replied.

'Well, are you implying then that the members of the IRA Army Council, or whoever, felt that there might be an election advantage in these circumstances?'

'Well, I don't know ... I just ... what other business had Mr Carron being there? He had an election coming up on the twentieth of August, and I thought that this had nothing to do with him ...'[8]

Then it was Bik's turn again. He referred to the families of the hunger strikers and how he had spoken to them the previous day and how they had been:

> ... re-traumatized again over this whole article in *The Sunday Times* and the fact that this was coming out and the manner in which it was coming out and they were very hurt. Some of them are very angry as well in relation to this here and others have actually voiced the opinion that, in the current political climate, is it [*sic*] no wonder that anyone is continually trying to do down, you know, people like Gerry Adams, and the republican leadership ...[9]

That last line went to the crux of it: doing down small fry, like me, was acceptable, but 'trying to do down, you know, people like Gerry Adams' was wrong. And if the families had to be used as a battering ram to do me down, then that was okay.

It was not okay. There was something utterly rotten about Bik McFarlane's attitude, because both he and Morrison, given their central role in the hunger strike, knew for certain that I had been wholly accurate in my account of the hunger strike. Steam was coming out of my ears as I sat in that small Dublin BBC studio, listening to McFarlane.

What was emerging was the embryonic outline of 'The Line', the committee's considered media approach to my book. I knew one thing: there would be no on-air confessions and no beating of breasts for members of the committee. Their first priority would be to search for the dirt on me, and to try to discredit me by any and every means possible. They would seek to minimize my involvement in the hunger strike. Then they would maximize Bik's role. He would be the committee's first line of defence; he would 'speak authoritatively', relating his account of the day-to-day running of the hunger strike and his meetings with the hunger strikers. Furthermore, he would promote the subterfuge that the British 'reneged' on a deal at the end of the first hunger strike in December 1980.

The families' vulnerability, perhaps even aversion, to an alternative history of the hunger strike would be a potent weapon: both Bik and Danny had already effectively accused me of being uncaring towards them.

All in all, the committee had a good team and a substantial arsenal.

Danny Morrison, it seemed to me, was beside himself with rage, and he confirmed that this dispute was going to get dirty when Dunseith asked him about his visit with McFarlane in the prison hospital on 5 July 1981, and if he could confirm that there had been an offer:

'Yes, oh, aye … I went in. I mean, I think it's a bit rich, and a bit late for Richard O'Rawe to be turning around and saying we have to get this into perspective.'

Had Dunseith not asked Danny if he could confirm that there had been an offer? Perhaps Danny had not heard the question? He continued:

'I know the British government killed the ten hunger strikers, but after the disgraceful things that were written in that book,

Richard should hang his head in shame for what he has said and the allegations he has made.'[10]

I had never been in this situation before, and I told myself to remain calm, that Morrison's insult was designed to rile me, and throw me off guard.

Morrison confirmed that he had been part of the 'kitchen cabinet [committee] on the outside that was advising the hunger strikers'.[11]

When Dunseith asked him if he had been a member of the IRA Army Council at the time of the hunger strike, Morrison replied 'No.'[12]

He then spoke of being in a house in West Belfast and of 'receiving phone calls via a mediator, an intermediary, through Derry'.[13] This would have been Brendan Duddy, also known as the 'Mountain Climber'. Along with Noel Gallagher, Duddy had been the link between the British government and the IRA, whom the committee represented.

Morrison went on to talk about the first hunger strike in 1980: 'The first hunger strike ended whenever the prisoners went to claim their own clothes as they were promised [by the British] and the authorities turned round and said, "Oh, no. You have to put on prison issue, civilian-type clothing to get your own clothes." So there was a massive degree of distrust, which was why Gerry Adams and myself were to act as guarantors with the prisoners.'[14]

Despite what Morrison said, there simply had not been any agreement with the British to end the first hunger strike in 1980. Brendan 'The Dark' Hughes had been OC of the 1980 hunger strikers, and it was he who ended the fast when he told the prison authorities to feed fellow hunger striker Seán McKenna, after McKenna went into a death coma.

Writing to Gerry Adams on the night the first hunger strike ended, 18 December 1980, Bobby Sands gave his account of the scene that greeted him early that evening in the prison hospital:

I saw Index [Father Toner] and Silvertop [Father Murphy] in the corridor as I walked down the wing. There were three cartons of eggs sitting in a doorway. My heart jumped. Dorcha [Brendan Hughes] came out of Tommy McKearney's room and went into Tom [McFeely's] room in front of me. Tom was in bed. Raymond [McCartney] and Nixie [John Nixon] were sitting beside the bed. They were all shattered. Dorcha said, 'Did you hear the scéal [news]?' I said, 'No.' He said it again. I thought Seán was dead. Then he said, 'We've got nothing, I called it off.'[15]

'We've got nothing.' Could Hughes have put it any plainer? So, despite what Morrison said to Dunseith, and what others later echoed, the British did not renege on a deal to end the first hunger strike. How could they? To have a deal, there must be an acceptance of a mutually agreed set of conditions. Obviously this did not happen. Otherwise, the first hunger strike would not have ended as it did. But the committee seemed to think that there was a defence mechanism with the confusion that surrounded the first hunger strike, and it would crystallize into the definition of what was an offer and what was a deal.

Danny and Bik continued to regale *Talk Back*'s listeners with their well-rehearsed double act: Bik waxes resentful, Danny waxes sarcastic; Bik says nip, Danny says tuck; keep it tight, Bik, and don't forget to get it in about the families now, but don't go into detail about anything. The rest of the committee would all be glued to their radios: Big Gerry, Martin McGuinness, Tom Hartley and Jim Gibney, each weighing up their boys' performance.

It came as no surprise to me that Gerry Adams had picked Danny Morrison to lead the charge: he was crafty, intelligent, and a highly skilled propagandist; an articulate man who could accelerate past weak points and zoom in where he felt strong. As he was answering Dunseith, seamlessly moving from point to point, I had a strange thought: I bet you could have swum two lengths of the old Falls Baths underwater, couldn't you, Danny? Did you ever come up for air, *a chara*?

Four

IT WOULD HAVE BEEN wise for Danny and Bik if they had opted not to comment on *Blanketmen* until after they had read it. That is what most people do whenever they are asked to state their views on a book. Had the two boys stayed their hand, they would have bought themselves time to sharpen up their act and to dig out what they had said in the past in order to maintain consistency. Instead they waded in, ignoring the Roman poet Horace: 'Once sent out, a word takes wings beyond recall.'[1]

Describing to the *Talk Back* audience how he had gone into the prison hospital on 5 July 1981, Morrison said that he 'explained to them [the hunger strikers] what was on offer', adding, 'by the way, the offer that we were being offered through the Mountain Climber was a bigger and better offer than what the ICJP thought they had'.[2] He went on: 'After I had seen the hunger strikers, we all agreed that this [the Mountain Climber offer] could be a resolution, but we wanted it guaranteed.'[3]

This is a significant if exceedingly inconclusive account and one that Danny Morrison would periodically regurgitate – without ever enlightening his listeners or readers as to what precisely had been in the offer. The IRSP/INLA would eventually come to dispute his claim that he had informed their hunger strikers, Kevin Lynch and Micky Devine, of the nuances of the offer, while *Biting at the Grave* author, Padraig O'Malley, had this to say: 'Danny Morrison was allowed into the Maze/Long Kesh to see the hunger strikers on the morning of 5 July – before the ICJP's second meeting – to apprise them of what was going on, although he did not go into detail.'[4]

Whether or not Morrison defined the offer to the hunger strikers, he did break it down to the prison OC, Bik McFarlane, and when Bik returned from the hospital, he in turn outlined it to me.

I believed it to be a settlement, and told him so.

Bik also thought it to be a settlement.

Rather than give the *Talk Back* listeners time to meditate on the wobbly subject of the Mountain Climber offer, Danny Morrison deftly switched the focus to the ICJP, highlighting the difficulties the commissioners had had in their negotiations with the Northern Ireland Office (NIO). What happened next was pure genius: Morrison welded the ICJP's offer to that of the Mountain Climber's, saying that the British had acted in bad faith in both cases, and that the IRA Army Council had not rejected the offer. Then Dunseith asked Bik to comment.

There Bik was, waiting patiently. Danny had been in the thick of it, piloting the debate in the direction in which he had wanted it to go, shying away from saying anything too definitive, in case it would come back to haunt him. Then, just when Danny thought he had steered the ship into calmer waters, Bik almost ran it aground by saying, 'There was no substantive deal at all.'[5]

No substantive deal? Of course there had been no substantive deal! If there had been *any* sort of a deal, then there would have been mutual agreement between the opposing parties and Joe McDonnell and our five comrades who had died after him would have survived the hunger strike.

Without doubt, Bik had been talking gobbledygook, but

that was not to say that it was purposeless gobbledygook, and neither would it be the last time that he would revert to nonsensical responses whenever he was questioned about the Mountain Climber offer.

Yet had Bik made a Freudian slip when he said: 'There was no substantive deal at all?' It seemed to me at the time that he had come perilously close to saying: 'There was no substantial *offer* at all.' If he had said that, then a lot of Danny's withering scorn and hard work would have been flushed down the plughole because how could Danny's assertion that the Mountain Climber offer was 'bigger and better' than the ICJP's stand up, if Bik had said there had *never been* an offer?

Rather than tarry in the danger zone, Bik followed Morrison's lead, and launched into a lengthy discourse about the ICJP's frustrated negotiations with the NIO.

I reckoned that Danny and Bik were taking my good manners and courtesy for weakness, so when asked to comment, I replied:

> Well, this is the boys closing ranks, and that's the bottom line here. The facts of the matter are very, very clear here. Bik went to that hospital, he came back down, and he was two cells away from me. He sent me down a list of stuff that came from this Mountain Climber. I looked at them and I sent them up to Bik and I told him that I believed there was enough there. He agreed there was enough there, and he sent a comm to outside saying that there was enough there. A comm came back soon after that saying the outside did not believe there was enough there, and that effectively scuttled our acceptance of that there. And that's ... I mean, you can dodge this all you want. You can come up with all the nice wee turns and twists. That's the fact of the matter – and Bik knows that. And I'm very, very sorry that me and him are into this here; I'm extremely sorry, because I've a lot of time for Bik – but he knows – and I know what we agreed on, and I'm just sorry that it's come to this here.[6]

Not amused, Bik boomed: 'That's preposterous!'[7] After that, he once again reverted to the safe haven of the feelings of the families.

Morrison came in after McFarlane and once again opened up the ICJP cupboard. I had had enough of this ICJP claptrap:

Never mind the nuances of the ICJP. The ICJP was a totally separate identity. I agree with Bik that the ICJP had nothing. We both agreed there was nothing really in the ICJP thing at all. The substance of where we were looking was this Mountain Climber, and we were both led to believe that he was a substantial person, that he was straight from the British government, that he had Foreign Office clearance, and that what he said was the real McCoy.[8]

The debate ebbed and flowed for at least thirty minutes. McFarlane tried to say that the prisoners and the hunger strikers had been the sovereign authority, to which I retorted: 'Anyone that believes that is very naïve … that the Army Council of the IRA had no real say in this here. C'mon, let's get real.'[9]

Danny Morrison, unable to deliver the decisive blow, said that in the twenty-four years since the hunger strike he had met me many times, and that I had never expressed these views to him. I asked David Dunseith if I could reply to this. He agreed.

Speaking to Danny directly, I invited him to cast his mind back to an occasion, about two years earlier, when, along with fellow committee member Jim Gibney, he had walked into the Rock Bar on Belfast's Falls Road after playing a game of squash in Beechmount Leisure Centre. I then described how I had entered the bar a few minutes before and had joined them in one of the small boxed areas for a pint.

Silence.

I related how Danny told me about a book he was in the process of writing about the H-Blocks, whereupon I had said: 'If you're going to write a book, write the truth.'

Morrison was unusually quiet.

'Do you remember that, Danny?'

'I don't, Richard.'

'Jesus, you have a very selective memory, my friend!'

'Aye, and you're a very selective writer,' he snapped back.[10]

Inexplicably, an unnamed member of the unionist community came on *Talk Back* immediately after the exchange and said that although we were all 'terrorists', it had been obvious that I was telling the truth. That must have smarted.

This was by far the most important exchange I was to be involved in during those hectic first days. Whoever had so shrewdly constructed the *Talk Back* debate, whereby I would be entrapped if I excluded Bik from the debate on the one hand, and overwhelmed if I included him on the other, would also have seen this encounter as vitally important.

From then on, my opponents, short on substance and even shorter on direction, took what was possibly the only course open to them – save coming clean – and endeavoured to close down any attempts to focus attention on the Mountain Climber offer. They did so by clouding the issues, and by following the path lit up by Danny Morrison during our *Talk Back* debate. Crudely put, they scurried behind the ICJP and suggested that the British had treated both the ICJP and the IRA Army Council with equal disdain. Another way of changing the focus of the debate was to attack me and put me on the defensive: the more time and paper space I spent defending my motives and integrity, the less chance I had to question their actions.

All the interviews were over. Bernadette, my daughters, Bernadette and Stephanie, my son, Conchúr, and I returned to our hotel.

As we were about to head out to find a restaurant for an evening meal, the interview that I had given that morning to *UTV News* came on the television.

Bik McFarlane's interview was flashed up afterwards. Bik

looked assured and confident as he stood outside the Sinn Féin headquarters in Belfast, beneath the famous Bobby Sands mural. Reporter Ferghal McKinney asked him about the Mountain Climber offer:

McKinney: Who took the decision to reject that [Mountain Climber] offer?

McFarlane: There was no offer of that description.

McKinney: At all?

McFarlane: Whatsoever. No offer existed.[11]

Had Bik just said that there was no Mountain Climber offer 'whatsoever'? Had he taken leave of his senses? I punched the air and then explained to my family the significance of Bik's remarks. In saying that there had been no offer 'whatsoever', he had contradicted just about *everyone* who had had any involvement with the hunger strike, including David Beresford, author of *Ten Men Dead*, and Padraig O'Malley, author of *Biting at the Grave*. Both had been told of the Mountain Climber offer by none other than Gerry Adams when researching their books.

Adams is acknowledged in *Ten Men Dead* as having told the hunger strikers about the offer when he visited the prison hospital on 29 July 1981. He had also informed Father Oliver Crilly and Hugh Logue of the ICJP of it on 6 July.

During the *Talk Back* interview that very day, Danny Morrison had acknowledged the existence of the Mountain Climber offer, saying that it had been: 'a bigger and better offer than what the ICJP thought they had'.[12]

It is a matter of public record that Morrison had visited the prison hospital on 5 July, and he has been consistent in saying that he had not only made Bik McFarlane aware of the offer, but had outlined to McFarlane exactly what it contained.

I had said there had been an offer; that Bik had sent the offer down to me for an opinion after he had returned from his visit with Danny.

Bik, in saying that there had been no offer 'whatsoever', had just made a liar out of us all – friend and foe alike. In doing so, he had injected a virus into the committee's argument, and there was no firewall to keep that virus at bay.

Adams and Morrison would have known that McFarlane had done serious damage by his assertion. They would have to try to give Bik's words a different meaning from that which he had intended; but getting him out of his predicament would be no mean task – even for someone with Adams's survivalist instinct. It would be intriguing to see what Danny the Magician would pull out of his conjurer's hat on this one.

Five

MY FIRST DAY in the spotlight was nearly over, and I could not say that I had enjoyed a second of it. Even as I sat with my family in a 1950s-style diner in Stillorgan, County Dublin, scoffing a huge cheeseburger without really tasting it, I could not help but rewind in my head what I had said earlier that day. I'd been too mealy-mouthed with Danny and Bik, I told myself. Never mind good manners; I should have jumped in and hammered my points home harder. I should have …

Anthony McIntyre phoned from Belfast. Even when Mackers had been on the blanket protest, he had never suffered from lack of forthrightness. The seconds between the greetings and the hard talk seemed to stretch on a bit.

The first thing that Mackers said was that the debate with Danny and Bik earlier that day had been 'good'. What did that mean? Good for whom? How good for whom?

Continuing, he said that I had won the debate, and that I needed to win it; otherwise I and my book would have been dismissed as inaccurate and irrelevant by now.

'What swung it for me?'

He said there had been two things: firstly, while I lacked the experience and eloquence of Morrison and McFarlane, I came across as 'truthful'.

'And the second thing?'

He said it had been the quip at the end of the debate: 'You have a very selective memory, my friend!'

Mackers went on to say that the revelations contained in *Blanketmen* had sent shockwaves through the republican areas of Belfast, and he recounted that he had been speaking to a former IRA volunteer earlier that day, a man who had no love for Sinn Féin, or their policies, and how this person had told him that he wanted to punch me.

'Why?' I asked.

He said that this republican equated an attack on the hunger-strike decision-making process with an attack on the hunger strikers. I asked Mackers to show me where I had ever done anything other than lionize the hunger strikers.

'It's perception, Richard.'

I had not foreseen this, and worse still, could not comprehend it. The acceptance of newly minted concepts was only one of the dilemmas that confronted me in 2005 …

One of the biggest troubles I encountered when writing *Blanketmen* had been trying to break down into simple terms what was a multi-faceted issue. The hunger strike itself had had many strands: there were the meetings between the prison leaders, and between Bik and the hunger strikers; then there were outside bodies, such as the Catholic Church and the International Red Cross, which had unsuccessfully attempted to mediate between the opposing parties; there were the complications of the Westminster by-election in Fermanagh-South Tyrone, and the southern general election in June 1981, at the end of which hunger striker Kieran Doherty, and a Blanketman from County Louth, Paddy Agnew, had been elected to the Dáil. Besides that, there were comms to and from the outside leadership; the ICJP was engaged in negotiations with the NIO; the Mountain

Climber was secretly mediating between the republican leadership and the British government, and our comrades were dying on hunger strike. Hardly surprisingly, I found it heavy going to keep things simple. Curiously, Bik did not seem to suffer from these complex liaisons, yet undoubtedly he was a complex man.

By disposition, Bik McFarlane was obedient and dutiful. By temperament, he was charming and loyal. But if he had to make a choice between his politics and a friendship, his ruthless instinct would invariably cast aside the latter. Another facet of Bik's character is that he could sometimes pull down the shutter on reality, and that attribute, during the course of our developing dispute, had been like a ball and chain around Morrison's ankle. In practical terms, this wild-card approach could be seen in Bik's seeming inability to grasp the potency of his words when written in 1981 and the adverse effect that they would have on any potential defence on his behalf. How, for example, could he defend the 28 July 1981 comm that he had written to Adams, after he had been on the receiving end of a grilling from the hunger strikers the previous night about the absence of strategy? Here is what he told Adams he had hammered into the hunger strikers:

'We have two options. 1. Pursue our course for the five demands, or 2. Capitulate now. I told them I could have accepted half-measures before Joe died, but I didn't then, and I won't now.'[1]

There is no ambiguity in this passage, no shifting down the gears; Bik understood precisely what he had to do and he took it in his stride. But in order to appreciate this passage fully, it is necessary to return to three events of 5–6 July 1981:

1. Danny Morrison informed Bik McFarlane of the existence and detail of the Mountain Climber offer, or what Bik would call in his 28 July comm to Adams, 'half-measures'.
2. Bik and I accepted the offer.
3. Adams sent us in a comm saying that the outside

leadership did not think the offer went far enough. He said that more concessions were needed to validate the deaths of the first four hunger strikers.

In this comm to Adams, we can see how Bik moulded the facts to suit his objective of keeping the hunger strikers on the fast at all costs:

1. Bik confirms that there had been an offer after all – 'half-measures' – which he says he could have accepted before Joe McDonnell died. This demonstrably contradicts what he had said on the record, that there had never been an offer, or 'half-measures': 'Whatsoever. No offer existed.'[2]
2. Bik writes to Adams to say how he had told the hunger strikers that *he* had rejected the half-measures. According to him, *he – not the hunger strikers –* had decided there was not enough in the offer to end the hunger strike. His self-elevation and use of the singular destroy everything that Danny Morrison and he had promoted about sovereignty resting with the hunger strikers. Patently, the hunger strikers are relegated to third in line in the chain of command – behind Adams and the committee, and himself.

Two overriding points are:

1. McFarlane conveyed to Adams how he had misled the hunger strikers.
2. Adams knew this because he knew that it had been he, on behalf of the committee, who had rejected the half-measures, not Bik McFarlane.

It is important to realize that this comm was never supposed to end up in the public domain. Therefore Bik felt comfortable in relating to Adams the extent to which he had misled the hunger strikers. Truth did not matter; what mattered was the continuation of the hunger strike.

As usual, questions remain unanswered:

a. Why did Gerry Adams never once reprimand McFarlane for misrepresenting the situation to the hunger strikers?
b. Why did Adams not instruct McFarlane to go back to the hunger strikers and put the record straight?
c. Why didn't Adams himself put the record straight and tell the strikers that their prison leadership *had* actually accepted those 'half-measures' when he went in to the prison to see the hunger strikers twenty-four hours after he had received McFarlane's comm?
d. Was there a conspiracy to keep the hunger strike going, at least until the by-election in Fermanagh-South Tyrone?

The evasiveness of the committee to date and the meanderings of Bik McFarlane support a positive response to that last question. One thing is indisputable: four more men went on to die after Adams's visit to the Maze.

When I wrote about this in *Blanketmen*, I said:

> I was taken aback and vexed when I first read this comm in 1985. Clearly Bik is relating to Adams the conversation that he had had with the hunger strikers the previous night and, taken at face value, one would have to assume that Bik was being less than forthright with the hunger strikers because he *did* in fact accept the proposals. I spent a considerable amount of time thinking about this and concluded that Bik was being truthful to the hunger strikers. This is because, in light of the Army Council's rejection of the Mountain Climber's offer, both he and I had unambiguously accepted the view of our peers.[3]

On reflection, I did not want to consider the possibility that Bik McFarlane had deliberately misinformed those dying and starving men. Lest there is any doubt, he and I had had an almost brotherly relationship, and he was a man for whom I had the utmost respect. Now I find it impossible to take a benign view of Bik's actions during the hunger strike, and that saddens me because I am more convinced than ever that, had he been allowed to go on the hunger strike, he would gladly have died. That aside, his obsessive, fanatical drive to keep the hunger strike going – no matter what the cost in comrades' lives – is unpardonable.

As for his use of the word 'capitulate' to these poor men, I find that as pitiless as it was manipulative. In the H-Blocks in 1981 the hunger strikers viewed capitulation as tantamount to cowardice in the face of the enemy, and a betrayal of those dead comrades who had preceded them. As was tragically demonstrated again and again, they would rather have died than let anyone accuse them of either. Yet if they had not been emotionally blackmailed by the use of the word 'capitulate', and if they had been correctly apprised of what was really happening behind the scenes in the discussions between the committee and the British government, might they have taken the fateful decision to abandon the strike? Who knows? At the least, they deserved nothing less than the truth. They never got that.

Six

IT WAS our second day in Dublin, 1 March 2005; twenty-four years exactly after Bobby Sands had started his hunger strike. My first port of call was back to Dublin's BBC studio, where I had been pencilled in to debate the book with former hunger striker Raymond McCartney, whom I presumed would have been in the BBC's Derry studio.

Raymond had been one of my cellmates while on remand in the H-Blocks, and I had always considered him to be a friend. He had volunteered for the first hunger strike in October 1980, and had gone fifty-three days without food before that protest collapsed.

I could readily understand the committee's reluctance to push Bik McFarlane to the fore again, but I was at a loss as to why they would choose Raymond to be their spokesperson. He was a Sinn Féin member of the legislative assembly at Stormont, but that counted for little, given that the subject matter at hand had occurred twenty-four years earlier. Significantly he had not been involved in any leadership capacity during the 1981 hunger strike. If he had been on the leadership wing, McCartney might have overheard McFarlane and me talking out of our cell windows, but he had not even been in the leadership block, so he could not have contributed contemporary witness evidence to the debate. I had few qualms about our forthcoming encounter and gave little preparation to the interview. I suffered from the delusion that my comrade of old would be the same free spirit whom I had known all those years ago. In that belief I was mistaken, even naïve. You do not become a Sinn Féin Member of the Legislative Assembly (MLA) by thinking outside of leadership diktats.

As it turned out, Raymond was a much more formidable opponent than Bik. His opening remark was that Morrison and McFarlane had 'demolished' me during the *Talk Back* debate of the previous day. This was nonsense, but it put me on the defensive and I had to return to what had been said the previous day. While I wanted to say: 'This man wasn't involved; he knows nothing about this,' I never got the opportunity in what was a very short interview.

When the headphones came off, I felt like thumping the table in frustration. McCartney had intimated that he had insider knowledge of these events, when he had not. He would not be alone on that score.

On the way back to the hotel I picked up the morning papers to find that former Sinn Féin president Ruairí Ó Brádaigh had made some comments on the contents of my book.

Ó Brádaigh had republicanism in his marrow and was Chief-of-Staff of the IRA during the failed 1956–62 border campaign. In January 1970 he led a walkout from a Sinn Féin Ard Fheis and subsequently became president of Provisional Sinn Féin, the political wing of the Provisional IRA. In 1981 he had been president of Sinn Féin, with Gerry Adams as a vice-president.

In an *Irish News* article Ó Brádaigh said that it was 'not the policy'[1] of the republican movement to prolong the hunger strike until the by-election that followed Bobby Sands's death. He went on to say: 'I believe then, and still do, that the terms for a final settlement were a matter for the prisoners themselves.'[2]

I found this announcement strange, even disturbing. Ó Brádaigh was not a man known for untruthfulness or mendacity. On the contrary, his honesty was legendary. While many other republicans have watered down their principles to participate in parliaments on both sides of the Irish border over the years, Ó Brádaigh had remained true to his fundamental beliefs. Yet he had come out against me and supported the very people who had so cunningly opposed him as Sinn Féin president in 1983. Why? I asked myself. Ó Brádaigh would never have considered what for him would have been an odious alliance, unless he was convinced that I was irredeemably wrong. I was not, but obviously he did not know that. What I had said in the book had clearly come as a shock to him. His backing of the committee's position was just as shocking to me.

In the same newspaper I read very disparaging remarks about my book from Oliver Hughes, the brother of Frank Hughes, the second hunger striker to die. Oliver had been a Sinn Féin councillor at the time.

Owen Carron, the republican who had won the Fermanagh-South Tyrone by-election after Bobby's death, was living in County Leitrim, where he was working as a school teacher. When asked to comment on my book, he said: 'I am working. I am not going to say anything about this.'[3]

Far from being chastened by our previous encounter, Danny and Bik, sabres drawn, were storming the ramparts, repeating much of what they had said during the *Talk Back* debate.

Bernadette, Stephanie and Conchúr went back to Belfast that morning. My eldest daughter Bernadette and I met an old Gaelic football and business friend, Tom McCusker, at the Great Southern Hotel in Dublin airport, where I was still fielding telephone calls. Afterwards I switched off the mobile phone, went to Tom's home, had dinner with his lovely family, and between us we drank the best part of two bottles of wine.

Earlier that day I had received a phone call from the producer of RTÉ's *Eamon Dunphy Show* asking if I would be prepared to go head-to-head with Bik McFarlane the next day. I had agreed. Then, I received another phone call from the producer saying that Bik could not make it because he was 'sick'.

If I needed the 'cure' after being tipsy on the giddy mix of wine and optimism from the night before, the next day's *Irish News* soon provided it. In a letter headlined 'Book is an outrageous slur on hunger strikers', Oliver Hughes wrote: 'I am outraged by Mr O'Rawe's claims that the republican leadership around the time of Joe McDonnell's death ordered the prisoners not to accept an offer from the British and used the prisoners as "cannon fodder for electoral purposes".'[4]

In an interview accompanying the letter, Hughes said: 'My parents are in their nineties and it is very distressing and hurtful when someone is deliberately distorting the truth. I would appeal to Richard O'Rawe to retract his statement and to let the memory of the hunger strikers rest in peace.'[5]

I cringed as I read that and could not get past the line that I had been responsible for distressing and hurting his mother and father.

Handling the belligerence and guile of McFarlane and Morrison in the media was no picnic; still, I had been a senior republican press officer and could, at least, parry their jabs; but an attack of such ferocity – from a family member of a dead hunger striker? That was something else. Eventually I got around to focusing more fully on the letter.

It appeared to me that Oliver Hughes had dropped a political depth charge by alleging that I was 'deliberately distorting the truth'.[6] How on earth could he have known? After his brother Frank's tragic death, Hughes would have had little contact with the committee. Therefore he would have known nothing about the existence of the secret British offer, which materialized only after the first four hunger strikers had died. And it goes without saying that he would have known nothing of the nuances of the offer, or of the prison leadership's reaction to it, or of the committee's opinion. Could anyone be blamed for thinking that Hughes had cynically used his aged parents to make a cheap political jibe against me?

Equally contemptible was Hughes's appeal for me to 'retract his statement and to let the memory of the hunger strikers rest in peace'.[7] While I had no appetite for attacking a hunger striker's relative, I was fuming at his crass invocation of the memory of the hunger strikers to make his threadbare and barely concealed political argument.

If Hughes had taken the time to read the book (which he had told BBC presenter David Dunseith he would never do) before diving in, he would have known that I held the hunger strikers in the highest possible esteem.

Yet again I could see a familiar skeletal outline in Oliver Hughes's diatribe. As with Morrison and McFarlane, his primary concern seemed to be the exoneration of members of the committee from any blame for the running of the hunger strike.

In the same edition of *The Irish News* there was a contrary headline: 'Dying wasn't their decision.'[8] This was a report from 'a woman connected to one of the hunger strikers'.[9] This person is known to me and to those who had been intimately involved in the hunger strike, but she did not want her name published. She said:

> I want to support the views of Richard O'Rawe and Monsignor Denis Faul.
>
> I went to all the relatives' meetings, and the Sinn Féin meetings and I was there when the families told Gerry Adams to go in to the prison to order the men to come off the hunger strike.
>
> He went in and spoke to the men, but he told them it was up to them. He did not order them to come off the hunger strike.
>
> Those men put their names forward to go on the hunger

strike but when it came to the point of dying it wasn't their decision.

I thank God that at last someone has had the courage to tell the truth at long last. [10]

The lady who made these comments said that she believed the men were 'allowed to die for political gain'.[11] Her account of Gerry Adams being told to 'go into the prison and order the men to come off the hunger strike',[12] relates to a meeting between Monsignor Denis Faul, the families of the hunger strikers, and Gerry Adams, in the Sinn Féin headquarters in Belfast on the night of 28 July 1981. At that meeting, Adams agreed to go into the prison.

In the same *Irish News* edition, Monsignor Faul repeated what he had said on the previous day's *Talk Back* radio show:

I called a meeting on 28 July [1981] in Toomebridge – all the relatives were there and they decided unanimously that they wanted the hunger strike to end.

We headed down to Belfast to meet Adams at 12 midnight and had a long discussion until about 2.30 am. We told him he was to get an order from the IRA [to stop the hunger strike].

We pushed our point and were very blunt about it. The families had a clear-cut request.

They [the republican prisoners] had got their clothes and if they stopped, they would get the rest.

The next day Mr Adams phoned me and said he was bringing someone into the prison with him – Owen Carron. My heart sunk.

I was suspicious; was this for political reasons?

We gave the IRA the opportunity to end it. I went back to the families and told them to take them off hunger strike as soon as the men became unconscious. But by that stage the political aim had been met and the election [for the Fermanagh-South Tyrone Westminster seat] was over.

If these men died for votes, it would be a sad event. I mean, what was important – the votes or the lives?[13]

There was little difference between Monsignor Faul and the female commentator's basic interpretation of what the families had asked Adams to do when he agreed to go into the prison, in that, one way or another, he was to persuade or even 'order' the hunger strikers to abandon their fast. Whether or not he would have succeeded in that charge is not the issue. The point is that *he did not try*. Instead, he left the decision to end the fast to the hunger strikers – in the certain knowledge that this was something they would never do. Ending the fast at this point, with no deal to show for it, would have amounted in their minds to a betrayal of Bobby Sands and his five dead comrades, and Adams knew that.

Revealingly, at the midnight meeting, Adams did not tell the families of the secret British offer, or of his contacts with Margaret Thatcher, even though they were pleading for him to find a way to end the hunger strike and save their sons and husbands. In a world of tears and sorrow, there is something chillingly cold and frightening about Adams's ability to detach himself from the families' anguish.

He was also aware that the prison OC had accepted the 'half-measures before Joe McDonnell died', and that it was he and the committee who had rejected them. Yet when Adams looked the hunger strikers in the eye after his meeting with the families, he did and said nothing to suggest that McFarlane had been less than frank with them. Was he more interested in getting Owen Carron elected than in saving the lives of his comrades in the H-Blocks?

Seven

NO SOONER had I been bombarded by the 2 March 2005 barrage from Oliver Hughes, than I had to contend with yet another cannonade of criticism, hurled at me from Danny Morrison in his weekly *Daily Ireland* column.

I was beginning to think that Danny was taking this personally, that he had been seduced by the challenge of putting me away. From the minute this controversy started, Danny Morrison seemed to be descending into odium and rhetoric without a parachute. That surprised me.

In his article Morrison offered his usual diet of ill-tempered denigration, but he wrote something else that prompted me to think that he was leaving himself very exposed. Recalling his conversation with *Sunday Times* reporter John Burns, he wrote: 'I spent some time on the telephone explaining the exact circumstances of the death of Joe McDonnell and rejecting Richard's claims – though only a sentence or two was actually carried by the paper.'[1]

Casting himself in the role of Defender of the Families, Morrison went on to say: 'After the call I immediately phoned those who had worked in the H-Block office at the time of the hunger strike to alert the families who would be devastated by the allegations.'² Had his priority, in phoning his fellow committee members, not got more to do with putting together a credible counter-argument to what John Burns had just told him about *Blanketmen* than with the welfare of the families? But what if it was established that Morrison had known all along that I had written the truth? What if it was shown that his expressed concern for the families had more to do with saving his and the committee's skin than with protecting them from anything I might say? If that were demonstrated – and it was distinctly possible – Irish history would not forget his contribution to this controversy.

From the start, it was obvious to me that because I had not consulted the families before I released the book, Morrison thought that this was my Achilles heel, that this was where he could outflank me. He was right, in that I did feel emotionally vulnerable at not having made the families aware that *Blanketmen* would be published, although Oliver Hughes's self-righteous public outpourings had eased my discomfiture on that score. That aside, I had nothing to defend other than my account of what happened at leadership level in the H-Blocks in 1981. Meanwhile, every decision of the committee would come under scrutiny, and the more detail they went into, the better for me. I believed then, and still do, that it is only a matter of time before the rotten charade collapses, and that people will see that nothing is *ever* as it seems with the committee.

Morrison, in his article, tried to rubbish my account of the hunger strike by saying that it would have 'fallen asunder'³ if I had consulted Bik McFarlane before *Blanketmen* was published. It was as if he felt lesser mortals than Gerry Adams and himself had no right to be writing books about the republican struggle.

I knew that it was time to get back to Belfast, where the battle of words was being fought; that was where I should be.

There was a knot in my stomach as I drove around Parnell Square, past the Sinn Féin offices, on out towards Drumcondra and the road home. I have always loved Dublin, with its bustling streets and its people. Their native accents may have been earthy, sometimes even gravelly, but that did not make them sound any less melodic. When I was still at primary school, my granda and father would take me down on the train to watch the All-Ireland Gaelic football semi-finals whenever a team from Ulster was playing. On one occasion we had gone to watch the 1968 All-Ireland final between Counties Down and Kerry. Kerry had the mighty Mick O'Connell playing that day, but even Micko could not hold the Ulstermen, and Down won.

As soon as I got across the border, I received a telephone call from Anthony McIntyre. 'I don't think you should be coming up yet, Rick,' Mackers said. He felt that I could be shot dead.

I did not agree with Mackers' assessment, and I told him that I would be in Belfast in an hour.

Back home I tactfully answered Oliver Hughes's criticisms and sent a copy of my reply to *The Irish News*. Hughes did not respond.

Within hours of being back in Belfast I was told of the frantic attempts to suffocate me with rumour and innuendo. One report had me on the run from the IRA and 'hiding out' in Dublin. Another said that I had had a 'mental breakdown'. A third reported that I was an alcoholic, drinking wine with fellow alcoholics in the Dunville Park on Belfast's Falls Road, and had written the book because I had 'hit on hard times'. These are just a flavour of what was being disseminated. It was obvious that the committee had been busy when I had been in Dublin; they had pulled in all the favours to tighten the garrotte around my neck in an orgy of character assassination designed to influence those asking themselves the question: 'Is O'Rawe right?'

At the end of what had been a long day, which had begun in Dublin, I had barely time to gather my thoughts when a relative, who was also a good friend, came to visit me. This man had been a former Blanketman, and was still an IRA volunteer. He understood my feelings in relation to the hunger strike because I had discussed the matter with him often enough over the years.

He began by making it clear that he was speaking for himself and had not been sent by anyone in the republican leadership.

I listened dutifully.

'This boxing match in the press has to stop, Rick,' he said.

I asked him if he had heard the rumours that were circulating, and he said he had not.

We spoke for over an hour. In the end I told him I'd hold off on any press releases on condition that he got back to me with word from the leadership that personal attacks on me would stop. If I did not hear from him within three hours I'd assume that he'd been unsuccessful. He did not get back to me.

No sooner had my relative left than I began to receive phone calls of support. The first came from Monsignor Denis Faul. He recounted the anguish of the hunger strikers' families during the strike, especially the Quinn, Lynch and Devine families, of whom he spoke with great affection and sympathy.

It was Monsignor Faul who had convinced the hunger strikers' families to bring their sons off the fast whenever one of them went into a coma. In response to his intervention, I had, as PRO, penned a cruel statement against Monsignor Faul in 1981. In it, I had called him 'a conniving and treacherous priest'. It was an offensive thing to say about a man whose only concern had been the saving of my comrades' lives, and I deeply regret writing those words.

When Monsignor Faul and I met in a Belfast hotel shortly before *Blanketmen* was published, I was acutely aware that that statement had helped to poison the relationship between the prisoners and him. Such was the antipathy towards the priest after the hunger strike that when he came to Long Kesh/Maze to say Mass, very few prisoners would attend. How painful that must have been for him.

I needed to make amends to this man, and so, with a red face, I apologized to him. 'Denis the Menace', as we prisoners called him even before the hunger strikes, smiled before saying something I'll never forget: 'No matter, Richard. In life, we all must follow the dictates of our consciences. I followed mine, and I don't regret it for a minute. I knew I'd be hated by the prisoners for intervening, but I saved the lives of some of those poor boys, Richard. I saved them.'

Former Sinn Féin MLA (Member of the Legislative Assembly) John Kelly phoned that night to offer his support. Kelly had been a life-long republican, having joined the IRA as a teenager in the 1950s. He had been interned without trial, along with my father, during the failed IRA 1956–62 campaign. After the tumult in nationalist areas of Belfast and Derry in 1969, Kelly became one of the founding fathers of the Provisional IRA. He was charged in 1970 with attempting to import arms into Ireland and became a defendant in what became known as 'The Arms Trial'. Kelly had stood alongside some illustrious co-defendants in the dock, including the then Minister for Finance, Charles J. Haughey, and the Minister for Agriculture and Fisheries, Neil Blaney. Also beside him had been Captain James Kelly of the Irish army. The last defendant was the alleged arms supplier Albert Luykz, a former Waffen-SS soldier and Nazi war criminal, who had escaped from custody in Belgium along a 'rat line', aided by Trappist monks and the Catholic Church, before making his way to Ireland. All five were acquitted. The then Provisional IRA leader, John Kelly and the soon-to-be Irish taoiseach, Charles J. Haughey, maintained a friendly contact for the rest of their lives.

Kelly told me that he had heard my radio debate with Morrison and McFarlane two days earlier, and that he had 'no doubt' I had been telling the truth. This was the first time I had ever spoken to the man, and I found him impressive (John died in September 2007).

Ed Moloney, author of the groundbreaking book, *A Secret History of the IRA*, contacted me and offered his support. Moloney had edited and previewed *Blanketmen* for me, and had robustly tried to dissuade me from publishing it. His view was that I would be 'savaged' by the republican leadership. He was not far wrong.

The irreducible Ruairí Ó Brádaigh also phoned. He sounded perplexed and asked me to carefully recount the events of the hunger strike. Of particular interest to him was my view that the IRA Army Council had had control of the hunger strike. He said that the Army Council had not advised anyone that an offer from the British should be accepted or rejected. That prompted me to ask who had rejected the Mountain Climber offer, because the prison leadership certainly hadn't. Ó Brádaigh repeated what he had already said: the Army Council did not reject an offer from the British to end the hunger strike. Despite this, he implied that he believed my account of the hunger strike. I had never met him but I had always had huge respect for Ruairí Ó Brádaigh and my instinct told me not to pursue the paradox.

Brendan 'The Dark' Hughes phoned me to offer his endorsement. He was laughing as he told me to 'stay strong'. The Dark had known of the contentious issues in *Blanketmen* even before I had been released from Long Kesh in 1983 because I had told him everything. Even as far back as 1981–2, he had not been shocked when I said that the outside leadership had overruled our acceptance of the Mountain Climber offer, and this was made clear in his 2001 interview with Ed Moloney:

> I've always suspected that … there were more reasons than would appear for allowing the hunger strike to go on for so long, political reasons, ambitious reasons … And I have heard stories that I cannot confirm … where people were ignored, parents were ignored, mothers were ignored when they went to the leadership and asked the leadership to order an end to the hunger strike.[4]

Then Brendan made the damning assessment: 'I believe that the reason why the outside leadership did not intervene, because of the street protests that were taking place, because of the political party that Sinn Féin was building. I think that was [the] outside's foremost priority – it wasn't the five demands, I don't believe it was the five demands'.[5] Brendan Hughes died in February 2008.

Tommy Gorman, who had escaped from the prison ship *Maidstone* along with six other republicans in 1972, had already phoned earlier that day to offer me his backing.

I appreciated these voices, but my supporters were few, and my opponents many.

Eight

DANNY MORRISON resigned from the republican movement after being released from prison in 1995, where he had served four years of an eight-year sentence, which was later overturned in the Court of Appeal in Belfast. Since then, he has pursued a successful career as a writer, with at least six books, and a critically acclaimed play that made it to London's West End. Other than the inexhaustible Danny, it appears that the hunger-strike committee of 1981 and the republican leadership of the present are intertwined: the personnel that plotted the course of the hunger strike are still navigating the ship.

While it was these patriarchs, along with a handful of advisors, who developed the laissez-faire political philosophy that came to dominate republican strategy from the time of the hunger strike, it was Gerry Adams who provided the intellectual stimulus. In some respects Adams was the Martin Luther of the republican reformation, the man who challenged the absolutes of the old order. At the centre of this reformation was the thesis that no principle or truth could be allowed to stand in the way of progress. It was certainly divisive in its disregard for what were seen as non-negotiable fundamentals. The most important of these held that republicans could not recognize the authority of any power in Ireland other than that of the IRA Army Council, that body having inherited its mandate from the First Dáil, which sat in 1919, the last time there had been an All-Ireland parliament (a Sinn Féin majority had been returned). To the ideologues and purists, any departure from sacred principle amounted to heresy. To the pragmatic Adams and his reformers, such principles were a burden that had to be offloaded or bypassed whenever the time seemed right.

If this doctrine of ideological elasticity found its natural habitat anywhere, it was in the committee's Machiavellian approach to the hunger strike. Throughout Ireland there had been an unprecedented degree of anti-British sentiment during the 1981 hunger strike, and this convinced Adams and his fellow committee members that the opportunity had arrived to transform Sinn Féin from an insignificant supplement to the IRA into a major political party in both jurisdictions of Ireland. For that to happen, to win over the doubters in their own ranks, they had to get their man in Fermanagh-South Tyrone, Owen Carron, elected to Bobby's old seat. It could be a tipping point in the internal debate. The only problem with this was that hunger strikers would have had to die to get Carron across the line. Carron got across the line; hunger strikers died.

The quintet of men who formed the 1981 hunger-strike committee were Gerry Adams, Martin McGuinness, Danny Morrison, Tom Hartley and Jim Gibney. There may have been others, but these were the only people known to me. Of these, Adams was the most formidable and most senior, even though it has been alleged that Martin McGuinness had been IRA Chief-of-Staff at this time.

I first met Gerry Adams after the funeral of Volunteer Jim Saunders on 6 February 1971, when the then OC of the Belfast Brigade, Billy McKee, directed me to Adams, so that I could give him my name to join the IRA. Nothing came of this, and consequently, to join the IRA, I had to approach a class mate, Jimmy Quigley, whom I knew to be a volunteer (Jimmy was eventually shot dead by a British soldier while out on a IRA 'snipe' on 29 September 1972). I met Adams once more before he and I were interned on the prison ship *Maidstone*. We were later handcuffed together, after a week-long hunger strike over conditions on board the *Maidstone*, when the ship was closed down and we were flown by helicopter to Long Kesh, and incarcerated in Cage 9.

I recognized then that here was someone who was very comfortable with leadership. Even then, I felt that this 23-year-old was destined to become a kingpin within the republican movement.

At the insistence of the IRA leadership, Adams was released by the British government in June 1972. On 20 June, along with senior IRA figure Daithí Ó Conaill, he represented the IRA Army Council at discussions with British government officials Philip Woodfield and Frank Steele, at Ballyarnett, a house near the Donegal border, owned by Colonel Sir Michael McCorkell. On 26 June the IRA announced a 'bilateral truce'. On 7 July Adams, McGuinness and Ivor Bell were part of a delegation that attended truce talks in London with the then Secretary of State for Northern Ireland, William Whitelaw, and other British officials. The talks did not lead to an agreement, and the truce broke down two days later.

It was not until 1983, after I had been released from the H-Blocks and had accepted the job of republican press officer, that I had regular, almost daily, contact with Adams. In 1985 I resigned from the republican movement to spend more time with my family, and our paths rarely crossed after that.

In November 2008 I was walking behind the coffin of a great friend and former Blanketman from the Short Strand area, Cormac MacAirt, with my daughter Stephanie, when suddenly to my left I heard a deep voice: '*Cad é mar atá tú, a Risteard?*' ('How are you, Richard?')

I had not seen Gerry, but he had seen me. *Blanketmen* was

already three years old, and many of those attending the funeral had ostracized me after its release. Gerry Adams did not suffer from such pettiness.

After returning the greeting in Irish, I remarked: 'Jesus, Gerry, the tongues'll be wagging at you an' me walking together!'

'Risteard, can I tell you something? Republicans have never learned to agree to disagree.'[1]

I acknowledged that ingot of wisdom with a nod. He then told me about being in County Sligo the night before in relation to the upcoming European parliamentary election, and I told him of a recent debate in Donegal at which I had spoken about the hunger strike.

Republicans have never learned to disagree? I recounted this later to a well-known republican, whom Gerry allegedly had had silenced when he disagreed with the political direction in which Gerry wanted to take the movement. The man buckled over in a fit of laughter; I think, despite all, he still has a soft spot for The Big Lad.

I do not really know Martin McGuinness, although I had met him once or twice in 1983 in the Belfast republican press office. My impression then was that he was a stoic man. McGuinness had been the IRA leadership's contact with Brendan Duddy during the hunger strike, and when Duddy received the offer from the British on 5 July 1981, he handed it to McGuinness, who delivered it to Adams and presumably the other committee members in Belfast. Deliverer McGuinness would no doubt have known what was happening, but no evidence exists to say that he had played a central part in the committee's strategic thinking.

Danny Morrison is a year older than me. He and I had attended St Peter's Secondary School in West Belfast. My first memory of Danny was of him assuming the role of disc jockey in 'Bubbly Dan's' science room, where the school's O- and A-level students met with their female counterparts from St Louise's. After St Peter's I would bump into him at battalion call-houses in the mid-1970s. He had not changed much – still full of verve.

Within weeks of my being released from Long Kesh in February 1983, Tom Hartley and Gerry Adams had called to my home in Ballymurphy. While Adams sat in the car observing everything, Hartley did the donkey work. He came into the house and asked me to take over the republican press centre. I agreed.

Later that day I met Morrison, who told me, 'Your operating days are over, Ricky. You're leadership now. Republican press officer is a GHQ position, y'know.'

My operating days were over? No more going back to the nick? That was one habit I could live without. Being in the leadership had its advantages.

I worked in the press office for almost a year and had daily dealings with Danny. In those days he was the affable Danny Morrison. After I left the republican movement in 1985, Danny and I had only minimal contact, principally because he, Gerry and their circle were at the pinnacle of the movement, and their status required them to be very security-conscious. A night's socializing for them more often than not would have entailed a meal and a drink in a safe house, but they never invited me to partake in their feasting and revelry. That didn't prevent Danny from extravagantly claiming in a newspaper, 'There have been a dozen occasions when we've [he and I] discussed politics late into the night.'² If there were, I do not remember them.

I did not know Tom Hartley until I was released in February 1983. During the hunger strike, he had assumed the pseudonym 'Liam Óg' and had been a point of contact with the prison leadership. It would not be unkind to say that Tom was an eccentric, opinionated man, someone who could be pleasant in spring and irascible in autumn. After the June 1983 Assembly and Westminster elections, during which Sinn Féin emerged as a serious political party, I let it be known that I was stepping down from the press office job to spend more time with my family. Some time after that, as we drove back from a party workshop in

Derry, Tom tried every tactic in the book to keep me in the job, including invoking the names of the hunger strikers to emotionally blackmail me.

Of all the leaders, I always felt that I could confide in Tom Hartley. He and I had a conversation about the hunger strike in 1991, during which I told him that I was very unhappy about the way the IRA Army Council had rejected the prison leadership's acceptance of the Mountain Climber offer. He warned me never to repeat this assertion, and pointed out that I could be 'shot' for publicly expressing this belief. While he never used the words 'shot dead', I nonetheless felt that that was implicit in his warning. Tom said that he was telling me this as a friend. I believed him. It was surely of great significance that, far from denying what I had said to him about the hunger strike, he had implicitly accepted the truth behind my words.

Jim Gibney and I had been interned together in 1973. I knew little about him in those days other than that he was a very committed republican. Jim was the committee's liaison officer with the hunger strikers in 1981, one of the last people to see Bobby Sands before he died, and in interviews since, he recalls the meeting with great sadness. When asked to explain the significance of Bobby's election, Jim said, 'Well, I think it was probably one of the high points in terms of convincing republicans of the merits of electoral politics.'[3] At the 1986 Sinn Féin Ard Fheis Jim had been the leading lobbyist for urging republican candidates to take up their seats in Dáil Éireann. Many commentators viewed Gibney as a pathfinder for Gerry Adams whenever Adams wanted to exert change on the republican movement.

The principal duty these comrades set themselves during the hunger strike was to determine its course and tenure. In that role, their representatives, principally Adams and Morrison, liaised with the Derry mediators, Brendan Duddy and Noel Gallagher, who were acting as conduits between the committee and the British government.

Other considerations influenced the committee's objectives and options. One was ensuring that the hunger strikers would be psychologically corralled, and kept under the umbrella of their control. In respect of this, they had the benefit of the iron will of Bik McFarlane to curtail any free thinking among the hunger strikers. Bik's two-option ultimatum to the hunger strikers was a perfect example of his ability to temper dissent.

Another illustration occurred before Adams, Owen Carron, and INLA representative Seamus Ruddy visited the hunger strikers on 29 July 1981. Bik McFarlane knew there was disquiet among the hunger strikers; he had experienced it for himself when he'd had discussions with them the day before. He was also aware that the problematic, straight-talking Pat 'Beag' McGeown had the potential to make things difficult for Adams, so he told him, 'Don't make your opinions known.'[4] As expected of a Blanketman and IRA volunteer, Pat Beag obeyed the order and resigned himself to die. With McFarlane preparing the way, Adams did not have to make any reference to the Mountain Climber offer, and avoided answering any of the awkward questions to which the hunger strikers had subjected McFarlane the previous night. Consequently the hunger strike continued, another four hunger strikers died, Owen Carron was elected, and the committee's hands were as clean as the driven snow.

Nine

SOCIAL OR COMMUNAL ostracism is not always predictable, or controllable. History has shown that once baying dogs are released, they are not easily put back into their kennels. Anthony McIntyre found this out to his cost after being made *persona non grata* by many of his former comrades because he had had the temerity to ask questions in 1997 about the direction in which the Adams/McGuinness leadership was taking the republican movement.

McIntyre's seminal book *Good Friday: The Death of Irish Republicanism* is a compilation of articles and interviews that he wrote and compiled after the signing of the Good Friday Agreement in 1998 and his resignation from the IRA. In a piece from April 2002, Mackers summed up his angst:

> The republican struggle is over. The energies expended in it and the structures moulded through it are now being used for a different project entirely. Republicans without republicanism are little different from constitutional nationalists. The blood spilt was a costly fuel with which to power the ambitions of self-proclaimed establishment politicians. The ends have corrupted the means. Genuinely taking the gun out of

Irish politics would be a step forward. Taking the dignity and defiance out of Irish republicanism is a step too far.[1]

Because of his criticisms, Mackers incurred the wrath of the republican leadership. His family home, and that of fellow critic Tommy Gorman, were picketed by members of Sinn Féin in October 2000.

In the land of the saints and scholars, such intolerance is hardly surprising. Since the Irish Civil War republicans have never shown much charity to comrades who entertained alternative thinking.

What had been striking and surprising about Mackers's home being besieged was that a leading Blanketman, a former comrade of ours, had been amongst the red-necked picketers. During the hunger strike, this man had hunkered down behind the canteen hotplate at Mass on Sundays with Bik McFarlane, Pat Mullin and me to discuss strategy. He had been an articulate, free-thinking spirit then – and an elegant rhetorician to boot. Now he was suppressing the ideas of another Blanketman. What had happened?

The same prominent prison leader dramatically turned his head away from me when I made the mistake of greeting him outside a shopping centre in West Belfast at Christmas 2005.

Mackers had told me, on the day I returned to Belfast from Dublin in March 2005, that I would face the same extreme exclusion he had learned to accept as the norm. Deep down, I did not really believe him. Most people think they are good fellows, and I was no different. I would be all right, I thought.

'C'mon now, Mackers, it can't be that bad.'

Mackers went on to say that I had placed a big question mark over the hunger strike, and that that was 'the sacred cow', the one issue that hitherto had been untouchable. Never found wanting whenever an analogy was called for, Mackers said I was 'in the middle of the Bermuda Triangle in a dug-out canoe with a plastic spoon for a paddle'.

I listened as he recounted his experiences.

He addressed no one unless they addressed him first.

'Do you expect me to do that?' I asked.

'Yeah.'

I drew back. I asked about long-time friends: did that include them?

'Especially them. Nobody can hurt you as much as your mates.' Mackers then cautioned me not to expect my close friends to understand why I had stuck out my neck; they would not get it – and they would not want to get it, because to fall in behind me meant going against the republican movement – and the movement has been like an opiate to them, and us, for most of our adult lives. 'And whatever you do, don't lift your hands. You've got to keep control of the situation.'

'So I'm supposed to stand like a dick while some pot-bellied shithead empties his stomach at me?'

'You'll learn to avoid pot-bellied shitheads. And another thing: if I were you, I'd not go for a drink in the local pubs. If you're going to get grief, that's more than likely where it'll come from.'

This all sounded like a prescription for hibernation. Was the infallibility of the leadership never to be questioned? I would soon get my answer.

The next day, 3 March 2005, I went to the local supermarket and noticed a woman shaking her head at me in disdain. She and I had engaged in IRA business many times, and we had been good friends. No more. I stared her down and she walked away, her peacock head tilted defiantly.

I turned into an aisle and coming directly towards me was one of my former cellmates from the blanket protest. This man and I had been good friends even before the H-Block experience. I had gone up to prison to visit him after I had been released. As he saw me, his Sean Connery eyebrows automatically rose. He grinned. I was just about to put out my hand to greet him when suddenly, like a chameleon, his face changed colour from warm plum-red to cold charcoal-grey. Gone was the comradely air. In its place were tight lips and an eagle's gaze, which focused on something behind me. Instinctively I pulled back. He walked right past me. What was it that Mackers had said?

I was bitterly disappointed at the prospect of losing this man as a friend.

We ran smack into each other again at the checkout, but I could not bring myself to break the ice. Neither could he. Instead, we both awkwardly avoided each others' eyes. After finishing his transaction, he walked away and did not look back. A camaraderie and friendship tempered in the revolutionary furnace of Long Kesh had just been extinguished.

That was only a taste of what was to come. I would learn the hard way that things had changed for ever, that no one could be taken for granted.

Sometimes the people I expected to be hostile to me were the most congenial, while others, whom I thought would have been friendly, were remote or antagonistic. Leading republicans Bobby Storey and Gerry Kelly were perfect examples of the two stances.

Kelly was a leading Sinn Féin MLA in Stormont. He and I had known each other from before the Troubles, having gone to the same school and played Gaelic football together. We had also been members of the Ballymurphy IRA unit before he had been arrested for the Old Bailey bombings in London in 1973.

Before *Blanketmen* we would have passed each other in the Falls Park. Kelly liked jogging, while I preferred power-walking. There would have been a bit of banter, usually about us getting 'too old for this', but that changed after my book was published. Even though there was no glint in my eye, and no smile, I still felt obliged to nod hesitantly to Kelly as we drew closer. Like my former cellmate, Kelly's eyes were fixed on a point beyond me. I had become a ghost.

Bobby Storey and his wife passed me in the Falls Park, not long after the Kelly incident. Storey was said to be an IRA general headquarters staff officer, and it had been alleged in the press that he was the mastermind behind the Northern Bank robbery. Not wanting to be bitten again, I determined not to acknowledge Storey, with whom I had been friendly when we had been interned in 1973. To my surprise, he greeted me warmly and we exchanged pleasantries.

This inconsistency appeared often, but that did not make it any easier for me to handle.

I was invited to speak at a literary festival and on the panel was another Blanketman, a shooting star who was carving out a successful career for himself as a writer. I had gone over to speak to him before the event started and found him frosty. After it ended he bolted without saying goodbye. Later I found out that this display of bad manners had been intentional. It irked me.

Despite the perils of being the first to say hello, I did it again and again, sometimes to my cost; but being friendly was my way, and the habits of a lifetime die hard.

In a bar, after the funeral of a cousin in 2005, I almost came to blows with a former friend, a republican whom I had known from the halcyon days of 1972, when he had been my superior officer in the Ballymurphy IRA. This man ignored me when I greeted him, and when I challenged his discourtesy he turned and got cocky, squaring up to me. I did not break Mackers's rule about not lifting my hands; instead, I headbutted him, but I deliberately held back, only slightly clipping him. Bar staff intervened to stop any further trouble. Then I grabbed my coat and stormed out.

I felt a swell of anger, even humiliation, as I walked home: I wanted to walk back into the bar, and pull out that thimble-minded little man. I didn't. But if I needed proof of how I should handle these situations, I'd just got it: I had to become a Rockall and avoid bars in which friction was probable. Sometimes I played hard and fast with that rule – especially if I'd been out for a drink somewhere else beforehand, and ended up on the wrong side of sense and reason.

Although far from drunk, I went into the Rock Bar one night and two republican friends, staunch Adams supporters, offered to buy me a beer. No sooner had the beer arrived than a drunk slunk towards us. This individual had also been in the IRA. He pushed his way into our company, and facing me, asked, 'What are you doing in this bar? We don't allow MI5 agents to drink in here.'

Me? An MI5 agent? This was new territory indeed. Anyone who had known me from my time as an IRA volunteer knew that I had never given a grain of information to the British forces, despite having been on the receiving end of some brutal treatment at their hands.

The two republicans remonstrated loudly with the drunk and a small crowd of onlookers began to gather. How long would I be able to take this constant humiliation? I turned and left. Behind me, in the pub, there was a hullabaloo. I decided to walk home, a distance of half a mile. I should have listened to Mackers's advice and avoided pubs in the area.

As time passed, and I remained unbroken and unapologetic, more thuggish elements emerged – some to directly bully my teenage children. Two burly bouncers from the local republican social club were drinking in a bar, when they found out that the girl buying a drink beside them was my nineteen-year-old daughter, Stephanie. They let loose with a barrage of abuse about me. Stephanie is not a girl to bow to intimidation, and she told them that they sounded like 'fascists'. That was like setting fire to an oil well. Stephanie stood her ground, though, returning insult for insult, before leaving the bar and the salivating browbeaters behind her.

Gerry Adams and I only ever met at funerals, but at least we acknowledged each other. Gerry's civility was infinitely preferable to the childishness that afflicted so many of his supporters. Like him or loathe him, the Big Lad had always been his own man.

Danny Morrison and I rarely met during those early days, but when we did, we would have acknowledged each other, if only with a nod of the head. Later, he greeted me at a discussion during the West Belfast festival as if the old times were still a-rolling, as if there had never been a bitter disagreement between us.

Bik and I did not meet until January 2009, when we both attended the opening night of Martin Lynch's critically acclaimed play *The Chronicles of Long Kesh*. Bik was with his wife and I had invited along an old friend, Gerry Conlon, one of the Guildford Four. Tommy Gorman and his wife, Ann, had joined us. Bik looked at me, and I at him, but nothing was exchanged. It was as if we were strangers.

Ten

ON 3 MARCH 2005 *The Irish News* ran the headline 'Hunger strike claim row deepens', and the man of the moment was none other than the redoubtable Ruairí Ó Brádaigh.

Ruairí started by reiterating his belief that it was 'not the policy'[1] of the republican movement to prolong the hunger strike until the by-election that followed Bobby Sands's death, and that the IRA Army Council did not reject the government offer. However, in a change of emphasis he now signalled that my allegations raised 'extremely serious issues'.[2] Significantly, he added that if any of those who knew of its exact terms had 'invoked the name of the Army Council without authority to support private or personal views, then that is a very serious charge which needs to be answered even at this late stage'.[3] In a sweeping analysis, Ó Brádaigh added that any 'prolongation of the hunger strike and subsequent boost in moderate nationalist support could have been intended to provide the groundwork for the movement's shift towards constitutional politics'.[4]

Ruairí had picked his words carefully and had once more defended the IRA Army Council. His submission had backbone since clearly this republican leader was speaking from a position of knowledge and was beginning to see things through different lenses. Had the Army Council's authority been usurped during the 1981 hunger strike 'to provide the groundwork for the movement's shift towards constitutional politics'? He was unmistakably no longer ruling out such a possibility. It would take me three years, but eventually I would negotiate a path from the abstract to the concrete, and arrive at what Ó Brádaigh had been hinting at.

The communion that unites members of the IRA has been discipline, comradeship and command structure, and the IRA Army Council is the embodiment of all three. Article Five of the IRA constitution says: 'The Army Council shall be the Supreme Authority when a general Convention is not in session.' That is a clear-cut statement of authority enshrined since the birth of the IRA, in the aftermath of the 1916 Irish Rising. While there is no direct mention of communicating with the British government in the IRA Constitution, it follows that, if the Army Council is the 'Supreme Authority', then it – and it alone – has the power to negotiate with the British on all matters relating to policy and the republican struggle. The prison situation, where volunteers had died, and where others had been in imminent danger of death, would definitely have fallen under Article Five. But, if the body of the Army Council had been deliberately kept in the dark on a matter of such magnitude as a contact with the British government in time of war, whether during the hunger strike or otherwise, and if a group of IRA leaders effectively went on a solo run, then they would have been open to the charge of usurping the authority of the Army Council. That would have been, in IRA terms, a court-martial offence – with potentially fatal consequences for anyone found guilty of it.

So, had the 'committee' been acting with the authority of the IRA Army Council, or not? Did they inform the Army Council that they had made contact with the British government? Did they tell the Army Council that the British had made an offer, which the prison leadership had accepted? Did they let the Army Council know that they did not feel the offer could be accepted, and that subsequently they had advised the prison leadership that it be rejected?

We in the prison leadership in 1981 had always believed that when we communicated with Gerry Adams we had been dealing directly with the Army Council and that, when Adams sent us in communications, he wrote with the full authority of the IRA leadership. We believed that he had been on the Army Council – if not the leading figure on it. So it was perfectly reasonable for me to say in *Blanketmen* that 'Gerry Adams was charged by the Army Council to handle communications with the Mountain Climber.'[5]

I have since discovered that the IRA Army Council of that time knew nothing of Adams's and the committee's communications with the British. I found this out from two men who had been 'close' to the 1981 Army Council, after meeting them separately in 2008. Both wanted their identities cloaked and were very guarded in their answers. Neither knew that I had been speaking to the other, and neither had been members of Adams's committee.

I put the following questions to the first man:

RO'R: As someone who was 'close' to the IRA Army Council in 1985, can you tell me if the Army Council was aware of the Mountain Climber initiative, and what was happening behind the scenes in relation to the hunger strike?

Answer: No. Now I want to be very clear about this: it's 1981; you said 1985 ...

RO'R: Yes. Sorry.

Answer: No. I have no knowledge of this Mountain Climber business, that term, which would have been very clear to me. I knew from the papers about the Irish

Commission for Justice and Peace, the Catholic Church, and their initiative, and so on. But about the other? No.

RO'R: So … that's quite astounding … so you wouldn't have been aware that the offer that had been made by the British had been rejected by the outside leadership, who we prisoners assumed was the Army Council? In actual fact, the Army Council wasn't aware of any of the intricacies involved in this hunger strike offer?

Answer: No.

RO'R: Not at all?

A: No. The AC of that time wasn't told about any of this.

RO'R: When exactly did Gerry Adams get around to informing the Council of the Mountain Climber contact?

A: He didn't.

RO'R: He didn't?

A: No, he didn't.

RO'R: Not even after the hunger strike was over?

A: No.

RO'R: So when did you first become aware of the Mountain Climber being involved in the second hunger strike, and his offer?

A: When I read *Ten Men Dead* in 1987.[6]

I questioned this man about Adams's role in the hunger strike and he told me that it was 'understood'[7] at Army Council level that Gerry Adams 'handled'[8] the prison situation.

When asked if he had been aware that a 'kitchen cabinet' or a 'committee' had been formed, he said, 'That would be right,' confirming that he knew some people had been charged to 'help out with publicity'.[9]

I queried the man about Martin McGuinness's role in the hunger strike, and he said that McGuinness would have been a close confidant of Adams and would most likely have been aware of all developments.

But surely Adams had overextended his remit from the Army Council by hiding a contact from the British government? That question elicited only a smile.

The senior republican corroborated that the Derry businessman Brendan Duddy had been a long-standing mediator between the IRA and the British government.

The second man had also been 'close' to the IRA Army Council. He answered many questions for me, but refused to be recorded, although he agreed to let me take some notes.

He confirmed that the MI6 agent Michael Oatley had been at the British end of the negotiation process since 1972, and had a role in establishing the 1972 truce between the IRA and the British. Since then, Oatley had periodically represented the views of the British government to the IRA Army Council. The man said he had known that Oatley had been involved in behind-the-scenes efforts to reach a settlement during the first hunger strike. I asked him to describe the extent of Oatley's connection in the second hunger strike; he could not give me a definitive answer.

Brendan Duddy had been the primary link between the Army Council and the British government. The former IRA leader could not be certain if Duddy had had a role in the 1972 truce, but he had been instrumental in bringing about the 1975/6 IRA ceasefire.

Gerry Adams had been the 'chairman' of the Army Council at the time of the 1981 hunger strike, and Martin McGuinness had also been on the Army Council, but not Danny Morrison. The chairman not only chairs meetings of the Army Council, but he/she is the Army Council's diplomatic representative in discussions with individuals, bodies and governments. In the case where contact had been made with the British government, it would have been incumbent on the chairman to bring this to the immediate attention of the rest of the Army Council.

There had been tensions within the seven-man Army Council, and on controversial issues two distinguishable voting blocs had begun to emerge. The Belfast republican Joe Cahill usually sided with Adams and McGuinness, while the other four men formed an opposing majority.

I asked the second man about the proposition being canvassed by former hunger striker Laurence McKeown and prison OC Bik McFarlane that, because the British had allegedly reneged on any promises during the first hunger strike, the hunger strikers had stiffened their resolve the second time around, and had demanded nothing less than face-to-face explanations from a British government representative. He said that this was 'nonsense',[10] adding, 'The Brits reneged on nothing. The Dark [Brendan Hughes] called the thing off to save Seán McKenna's life. So, no … what Laurence and Bik are saying doesn't make sense; it just doesn't stand up against the facts.'[11]

He said that most members of the Army Council had felt from the start that the hunger strikes would fail, and that this group included Gerry Adams and Ivor Bell. He gave his personal view that the prisoners' best option would have been going into the system in order to wreck it from within. He felt that the prison regime would never have been able to cope with hundreds of volunteers 'wrecking the jail'.[12] When I pointed out that to do that we would have had to wear the prison 'monkey suit', he commented dryly that republicans had worn the suit before.

The Army Council did not unanimously agree to permit the second hunger strike, the second man said, although a majority on the seven-man body had decided to allow it to proceed.

Adams would fulfil the role of liaising with the prisoners on behalf of the Army Council. Since the Army Council met only every three months, he would have a measure of discretion in his dealings with the prisoners, although the Army Council had made it clear to Adams that sovereignty over the hunger strike should always rest with the prisoners, and that they alone should be the arbitrators in all matters relating to the hunger strike. I pushed my respondent on this and he said that it was accepted that the prisoners should decide what would and what would not be a settlement.

The Army Council would have welcomed *any* decision by the prisoners to end the hunger strike at *any* stage. At this juncture I could have been forgiven for thinking that Gerry Adams had briefed this man before we met, because he was reiterating, almost word for word, what Adams said he had told the hunger strikers in the prison hospital during his visit of 29 July 1981.

Gerry Adams did not make the Army Council aware that there had been a substantial offer from the Mountain Climber before Joe McDonnell died. Neither did he inform them that the offer was still on the table after Joe's death.

The alleged chairman of the IRA Army Council did not inform council members that the prisoners had accepted the Mountain Climber offer. Adams did not tell the Army Council that he had written to the prison leadership 'advising' that the offer should be rejected.

Had the prisoners accepted the offer, then the hunger strike 'should have automatically ended', the second man said.[13]

It was clear that I was not speaking to someone of blunder and bluster: this person's demeanour was quiet and matter-of-fact; he picked his words carefully, and I was not in the least surprised when he betrayed little emotion after I made him privy to some of the damning testimony I had gathered since *Blanketmen* was published. He had the same deadbeat expression when I showed him the page in *Ten Men Dead* where Adams had allegedly spelt out in detail the contents of the offer to the hunger strikers, when Owen Carron, Seamus Ruddy and he had visited the prison hospital on 29 July 1981.[14] However, he shook his head and stared at me after he read Bik McFarlane's comm to Adams of 22 July 1981, during which McFarlane had written, 'You can give me a run-down on exactly how far the Brits went.'[15]

Finally he spoke: 'Bik's asking Gerry how far the Brits went? And the Mountain Climber had already gone without Bik knowing what he offered? The AC knew nothing about any of this.'[16]

I then pointed out McFarlane's use of the word 'capitulate' to the hunger strikers, which was in the same comm.

'I noted that.'[17]

When he read McFarlane's comm to Adams of 28 July 1981,[18] during which some hunger strikers had suggested that there be a change of tactics, the source seemed nonplussed. Once again he emphasized that the Army Council had not been told of these developments, and that he had believed the prisoners had always been in the driving seat in relation to tactics. 'Obviously they weren't,' he added.[19]

My interviews with these two republican leaders showed that Gerry Adams did not report back to the IRA Army Council after he had made contact with a representative of the British government and had received a substantial offer to end the hunger strike. It also appears that he and the committee violated an understanding, made clear by the Army Council beforehand, that the prisoners would be the sovereign authority in all matters relating to the hunger strike.

Eleven

I FIRST MET Seán Flynn when he had been OC of the Official IRA prisoners on the prison ship *Maidstone* in early 1972. Before being captured by the British he had been OC of the Markets area, and had been a close comrade of Official IRA legend Joe McCann, who was gunned down by paratroopers on Joy Street, in Belfast city centre, on 15 April 1972.

On 8 December 1974 Flynn was among eighty people, mostly disillusioned ex-Officials, who met in the Spa Hotel in Lucan, County Dublin, to set up a new political organization and secret army. The new political organization was given the title the Irish Republican Socialist Party (IRSP), and its armed wing was called the Irish National Liberation Army (INLA). Flynn was elected to the national executive of the IRSP that morning, and became a leading member of the INLA in the afternoon.

The INLA was responsible for 127 deaths during the conflict. These included the killing of Airey Neave MP in 1979. During World War II Neave had escaped from Colditz Castle, near Leipzig. He was a close political ally of British prime minister Margaret Thatcher, having been her campaign manager for the Conservative Party leadership in February 1975. The INLA was also responsible for the deaths of eighteen people (eleven of them British soldiers) in a no-warning bomb in the Droppin' Well pub in Ballykelly, County Derry, on 6 December 1982. Also of note were the gruesome murders of three members of the Pentecostal Church in Darkley, County Armagh, shot dead while worshipping on 20 November 1983. Although these murders were claimed by a group called the 'Catholic Reaction Force', it is generally accepted that elements within the INLA had carried out the attack. The INLA was notorious for its bitter splits and vicious feuds.

In 1981 Seán Flynn and Seamus Ruddy acted as liaison officers between the INLA hunger strikers, their families and the INLA leadership. I interviewed Flynn in December 2008, and he explained that he had been on the National H-Block/Armagh committee for two years before the second hunger strike, and that Ruddy and he had gone into the prison to meet with the INLA hunger strikers on several occasions.

He said he had visited the INLA prisoners between 4 and 8 July 1981. I asked whether or not the INLA leadership or its prisoners had been told about the Mountain Climber offer.

> SF: No. Regarding our prisoners, including the hunger strikers: they did not know that there were any discussions going on – nor did we in the outside leadership. Nor did, what I might say, the members of the National H-Block/Armagh committee. We were not aware of any deals being done behind our backs.[1]

Seán Flynn's account that the INLA hunger strikers had not been brought up to speed about the Mountain Climber offer is disputed by Danny Morrison:

> It has been known for decades that the Republican Movement and the British were in contact in July 1981 during the hunger strike. As a result of that contact I went into the prison hospital on Sunday July 5th, and told Joe McDonnell, Kevin Lynch, Kieran Doherty, Tom McElwee, Micky Devine, and Brendan McFarlane, the leader of the prisoners, separately, that we were

in contact and the details of what the British appeared to be offering in terms of the five demands.[2]

This is not strictly accurate because Laurence McKeown and Paddy Quinn were certainly at the meeting, and Martin Hurson would most likely have been there also, since he had been transferred to the prison hospital on 24 June. McKeown and Quinn are the only two hunger strikers from that meeting to have survived the fast, after their mothers requested medical attention whenever they went into a coma. Both are strongly supportive of Morrison and the committee's overall position. Yet neither has ever stepped in to confirm Morrison's account – even when it is being severely scrutinized. *Why would they not do that if Morrison was telling the truth?* And why did Morrison name only five of the six remaining hunger strikers who died?

Furthermore, despite what Danny Morrison says, Seán Flynn's recollection that the INLA hunger strikers and their Army Council knew nothing of the Mountain Climber offer has been underscored by an internal IRSP investigation that was carried out from 2006 to 2009. In a statement issued on 2 April 2009, Willie Gallagher, spokesperson for the IRSP executive, said:

> Over the past number of days the IRSP has been speaking to relatives of the three INLA hunger strikers, ex-INLA Army Council members who were involved in the strike, and also to the then OC of the INLA prisoners about these particular documents [British hunger strike documents released under the Freedom of Information Act in 2009]. All have stated to the IRSP that they were not aware of the 'back-channel initiative' or of an 'acceptance of the content of Thatcher's offer but not the tone' by the PIRA in July 8th 1981 which these documents clearly demonstrate.
>
> Both the then INLA Army Council and the INLA prisoners' OC have stated to the IRSP that if they had been made aware of the content of these developments at that time they would have ordered the INLA prisoners to end their hunger strike.[3]

Once more the waters had been muddied, and yet again Danny Morrison is standing knee-deep in it. Even Danny seems reluctant to dispute that the committee did not bring in the INLA Army Council on the Mountain Climber secret. This is unsurprising; after all, according to senior IRA sources from that time, the committee did not inform the IRA Army Council about the Mountain Climber secret either – and they were supposed to be the cardinals of the republican movement.

If we are to believe Morrison when he says he told the INLA hunger strikers Kevin Lynch and Micky Devine the details of the secret offer, it surely follows that they in turn must have taken a decision not to notify their own leadership, or their families. Did Danny elicit from them a promise not to divulge the news? If that promise was not sought, or given, what was to stop Kevin and Micky from letting their own leadership know of this crucial development? Why would they not have let them know?

Jake Jackson had been in the prison leadership at the time. In *Biting at the Grave*, Padraig O'Malley wrote:

> According to Jake Jackson, the only people he could say knew for sure about the Mountain Climber initiative at that point were himself, McFarlane, block OCs Pat McGeown and Sid Walsh and the PRO, Richard O'Rawe, and the hunger striker Joe McDonnell. As for the rest, he says, it would have been a 'need-to-know' basis; the closer a hunger striker was to dying the more likely he was to know. Micky Devine and Kevin Lynch, the INLA members, wouldn't have been informed, one way or the other, nor would the hunger strikers who were still in the blocks.[4]

Most of what Jake said had been news to me when I had first read it. Although I knew that he had been brought in on the Mountain Climber secret, I had no idea who else Bik had, or had not, told about the development.

There is something else salient in Jackson's account. According to him, knowledge of the Mountain Climber initiative was restricted to hunger strikers who would have been at death's door, while others (who were not in the danger zone) were unlikely to have been told of the development. Again I knew nothing of this, and therefore cannot verify or reject it; however, hunger strikers Liam McCloskey of the INLA and Gerard Hodgkins of the IRA have both stated that they had not been admitted to the magic Mountain Climber circle, and their disclosures go a long way towards debunking Danny Morrison's contention that the prisoners were 'sovereign'. How could they have been sovereign if some hunger strikers were not aware of what the British were offering? And where does the McCloskey/Hodgkins revelation leave Bik McFarlane's claim that the hunger strikers 'would decide what was acceptable, and what wasn't?'[5]

Enter Gerry Adams. Trying to circumvent the 'who-was-told-what' minefield, he had a rush of blood to the head and told Padraig O'Malley: 'Any communications which came from the British went to the prisoners. Not a scrap of paper, not a line, not one iota, was held from them.'[6]

This is simply untrue. Adams had read the statement from Secretary of State for Northern Ireland Humphrey Atkins, incorporating the Mountain Climber offer, to be released in the event of the hunger strike ending. The existence of this statement came to light only in May 2009, when it was released to *Sunday Times* journalist Liam Clarke under the Freedom of Information Act. Neither the prison leadership nor the hunger strikers had read it, and we were never shown *any* of the correspondence between the parties.

Here is what Adams said of Duddy's attempts to find a solution: 'There had been a contact which the British had activated. It became known as the Mountain Climber. Basically, I didn't learn of this until after the hunger strike.'[7]

This is bunkum. There is irrefutable evidence, ranging from comms,[8] to his meeting on 6 July 1981 with the ICJP,[9] demonstrating that not only did Adams know of the Mountain

Climber, but that he had been receiving messages through him from Margaret Thatcher in Downing Street. It stands to reason that Gerry Adams would not have wanted the true course of the Mountain Climber negotiations to become public knowledge. He would have understood that were this to happen, he could be exposed to the charge of letting hunger strikers die in order to get Owen Carron elected in the Fermanagh-South Tyrone by-election. That was why, in 1985, he asked me to vet the prison comms in order to remove all references to the Mountain Climber. This task was prompted by the fact that David Beresford was writing his book *Ten Men Dead* and Beresford had been assured by the leadership that he would be given access to the comms. Because of the large number of comms involved, two other IRA volunteers were sent to help me, but somehow a comm containing the term 'Mountain Climber' escaped our attention and Beresford picked up on it. He subsequently confronted the leadership about Mountain Climber and was given a tailored version of the behind-the-scenes negotiations.

So, from the all-or-nothing waffle of Bik McFarlane, to the whiter-than-white guff of Danny Morrison, to the 'it-wasn't-me' twaddle of Gerry Adams, a black-and-white understanding emerges that nothing these men say can be taken at face value.

Twelve

THE PERIOD of maximum controversy occurred between 4 and 21 July 1981. This phase in the hunger strike was marked by a series of crises involving all the relevant parties.

Publicly, the five members of the ICJP were the bridge-builders: Bishop Dermot O'Mahony, auxiliary bishop of Dublin; Father Oliver Crilly, a cousin of hunger strikers Francis Hughes and Tom McElwee; Brian Gallagher, a Dublin solicitor and Commission chairman; Jerome Connolly, Commission secretary; and Hugh Logue, the SDLP's economics spokesperson. The commissioners ventured between the hunger strikers and prison OC Bik McFarlane, and the Northern Ireland Office. They were also briefing the families, the National H-Block Committee, and the Irish government.

Parallel to this activity, but in utmost secrecy, was the Mountain Climber process. In the era before mobile phones and modern communications, the committee had had to split their time between the hunger strikers, the prison leadership, the families, the ICJP, and the National H-Block Committee – as well as the far from inconsequential job of running a revolution. In addition, there was the small matter of communications with the

Mountain Climber, who was talking to an MI6 man, who was talking to a man in a bowler hat from Whitehall, who was talking to the lady from Finchley who occupied No. 10 Downing Street.

While everyone, nationalist and unionist, on the island of Ireland was pondering the Brits' next move, it had already been made, and it was the republican leaders to whom the Brits turned for help to end the impasse. Adams and the committee were the only people who knew what everyone else was doing at any given time of the day, without divulging how they filled their own diary, and they were hell-bent on governing all aspects of the hunger strike, from the prison outwards, a concern mirrored in their sometimes volatile relationship with the hunger strikers' families.

To a great extent, the least of the committee's problems were the people in imminent danger of death, the hunger strikers. When Adams, in particular, gave the prisoners an opinion, it was seen to be a representation of the will of the IRA Army Council, and, as such, tantamount to an order. This gave him incredible influence over the trajectory of the hunger strike. But this reverence for Adams did not extend to the hunger strikers' families. Their primary instinct as parents, wives and siblings was to ensure that their loved ones would not die, which made it much more difficult for the committee to keep them in line.

There are reports that Mrs Sands, Bobby's mother, for example, considered going on television and publicly calling on all the hunger strikers to end their fast, but that she had been dissuaded from taking this course by senior republican Jimmy Drumm.[1] Drumm, a man who had given over fifty years' service to the IRA, had been chosen by the leadership to liaise and provide for the needs of the family of the hunger striker closest to death. It was also his job to remind the families, if necessary, of their son's wishes that they should not intervene in any way to save his life. Mrs O'Hara intended pulling her son Patsy off the strike.[2] Mrs McDonnell suspected that the prisoners were being used by the 'outside leadership'.[3] The Lynch family were scathing in their criticism of Gerry Adams in the days before Kevin died, blaming him for not intervening to save their son's life.[4] Bik McFarlane wrote a comm to Adams on 28 July saying that they intended to issue a statement, along with Monsignor Faul, calling for the hunger strike to be ended.[5] So the families had been difficult, and this was exacerbated by the ICJP's openness with the relatives.

The ICJP was seen by us prisoners as outsiders during the hunger strike. While our lives were being defined by grandiose dreams of finally freeing Ireland from 800 years of British imperalism, and liberating mankind from the yoke of capitalism into the bargain, we viewed everyone outside the republican family as hostile. Bik was particularly antagonistic to the ICJP and, given their links to the Irish government, the Catholic Church and the SDLP – all of them opposed our armed struggle – it was understandable. Adams was also suspicious of the ICJP. I didn't care about the commissioners' political outlooks then simply because I did not see the point of being unfriendly to *anybody* who could to show us a way out of our impasse. It didn't make sense. What mattered was ending the hunger strike with honour. So what if the ICJP was credited with ending the hunger strike? It would have been the hunger strikers who would be remembered and exalted – not the well-intentioned ICJP.

On 6 July 1981 the ICJP, in an attempt to put pressure on the Northern Ireland Office to stand over commitments it had made, was preparing to release a statement outlining what it believed had already been agreed with NIO minister of state, Michael Allison. Gerry Adams heard of this and asked that they send emissaries to speak with him in a safe house in Andersonstown. Father Oliver Crilly and Hugh Logue went to meet him.

In an interview, Hugh Logue told me that Danny Morrison had opened the door to the safe house and let in the two commissioners. Adams came into the house by the back door a short time later. The Big Lad wasted no time: 'It's only after much deliberation that we decided to let you [the ICJP] know what's really going on.'[6]

Hugh Logue said Adams never mentioned the term 'Mountain Climber' at any time during their exchanges, but confirmed that there was a 'contact' with someone from the British Foreign Office:

RO'R: Did Adams give you any indication that this contact was ... weak, or dubious, or might not stand over any commitments given?

HL: No. We were led to believe that the contact was absolutely bona fide. What would've been the point in sending for us to tell us about this contact if the contact's word couldn't be taken, and he couldn't stand by any commitments he'd given? No: at no time did Gerry Adams say to us the British contact's credentials were in question.

RO'R: You're on the record as saying that the Mountain Climber offer was almost, word for word, what you had been offered.

HL: Well, it was. The Mountain Climber offer wasn't any better than we had been given. The offer was exactly the same as ours.

RO'R: Danny Morrison's on the record as telling the hunger strikers that the Mountain Climber offer was bigger and better than the ICJP's. What's your comment on that?

HL: Danny may say that but it was exactly the same. Danny was at a meeting on the fifth of July in the Lake Glen Hotel [Belfast], along with the relatives, and some National H-Block/Armagh Committee people, including Bernadette [McAliskey], and we spelt out the offer. Both offers matched. Danny knew that. Danny left that meeting to go to the prison but did not tell the meeting that that was where he was heading.

RO'R: If both strands of negotiations were reporting back to the same power source, i.e. the British government, that'd be logical, I suppose. I said in *Blanketmen* that the Brits weren't stupid; they knew the Army Council called the shots in the republican movement. So I suppose it'd make sense for them to go directly to the Council. Okay. Did what I believed to be the offer, the one outlined in *Blanketmen*, correspond with what you [the ICJP] had been offered?

HL: Almost to the dot. That's what was on offer.

RO'R: So why did Adams want you [the ICJP] out of the way if he was doing no better than you were with the Brits?

HL: He might've been playing politics; he might have thought that he could add to it. I don't know.

RO'R: After the ICJP's role ended, had you any further contact with Gerry Adams?

HL: Yes, I had. I phoned him from home and asked him why he didn't reveal the Brits had been in touch with him and there had been an offer.

RO'R: And what did he say?

HL: He said he didn't think that would've been good tactics, and that any release of it should be their call.

RO'R: That's been very revealing. Thanks very much, Hugh.[7]

In May 2009, Logue would explain to a journalist: 'We had the impression that Gerry Adams didn't want the ICJP or anyone else to have any credit for resolving it. Credit for church or Irish government was the last thing on our minds ... saving the lives of hunger strikers with honour was all that mattered.'[8]

He went on to say:

When we went back in that evening [5 July], the mood of the prisoners [hunger strikers] had got somewhat tougher and a lot more sceptical about the ICJP. It took us a long time to satisfy them that the deal was on and eventually they said that if a British representative came in and gave the offer they would believe it and that would do it. Kieran Doherty, Tom McElwee, Martin Hurson indicated that there was enough in it for them. The most vehement against us was the newest one on it [Laurence McKeown] and as it turned out he did not die.[9]

The change in mood amongst the hunger strikers is perfectly understandable given that Danny Morrison, during his visit that afternoon, had told the strikers that the ICJP could 'make a mess of it, that they could be settling for less than what they had the potential for achieving'.[10] However, according to Logue, the ICJP overcame the hunger strikers' anxieties, and a deal seemed to be on if, crucially, the Brits would send a representative into the prison to present the offer.

So why did the Brits not do that? Logue suggested the following to Liam Clarke:

It now appears they [the British] were afraid of being stranded, if, having made the offer, the IRA didn't take it. The British feared that it might be used as a basis for getting further elements into the deal.

It is now clear that the British had realized that the ICJP solution to the hunger strike was a runner with the hunger strikers, and with the public, and would take them off the international rack they were on, and their only concern was: would the Provo leadership allow the hunger strikers to prevail? That is what they were checking out with the Mountain Climber.[11]

Tellingly, Logue posed the question: 'Did Adams overplay his hand or misinterpret the intention of the British, believing he could squeeze more? That is something only he can answer. Either way, six more young men's lives were given up.'[12]

If Logue is right in his assertion that the hunger strikers would have accepted the offer, be it called the ICJP or Mountain

Climber offer, then that would have put both the prison leadership and the hunger strikers firmly in agreement that the offer should have been accepted.

That is not how Bik McFarlane saw it, however, in an interview with *Irish News* journalist Stephen McCaffrey on 11 March 2005, less than two weeks after *Blanketmen* had been published:

> Mr McFarlane said he also had fresh memories of July 5 – the day at the centre of Mr O'Rawe's claims. 'Danny Morrison and myself had a visit together,' McFarlane said. 'He informed me that that morning the British had opened up a line of communication to the republican movement in relation to the jail hunger strikes. My eyes widened.'
>
> 'And he said to me: "I am instructed to inform you, do not under any circumstances build up your hopes."'
>
> 'I went back to the block, wrote out a quick note, passed it to Richard, informed him that the British had opened up a line of communication.'
>
> 'We were not to spread the word. I told him and I think I told one other member of the camp staff. I told him again that we need to see what's going to happen here.'
>
> Asked whether was any information passed to Mr O'Rawe on what might have been on offer, Mr McFarlane replied: 'There was no concrete proposals whatsoever in relation to a deal.'[13]

When I read that last line, I cringed for Bik. Why not say there was no offer and be done with it? Why hide behind the gobbledygook once again? One answer stands out: the man who supposedly ran the hunger strike, and whom Danny Morrison and others had held up as *the* expert on the fast, had said, just over a week earlier, that there had been no offer 'Whatsoever. No offer existed.'[14] Against that background, Bik could hardly turn around a week later and say, 'Oops! I forgot. There was an offer after all.'

It wasn't until four years later, under the burgeoning weight of contemporaneous evidence, that Bik McFarlane would be forced to say that the British had to 'expand the *offer* [my italics] and they needed to go into the prison hospital'.[15]

So, as I and Danny Morrison had said, there had been an offer. But what would prompt Bik McFarlane to be so demonstrably out of touch with the facts? What reason had he to avoid admitting that Danny had told him of the offer? There were a few.

Obviously if he had told the *Irish News* journalist that Morrison *did* brief him about the details of the offer, then my account in *Blanketmen* would have been completely vindicated. What wouldn't have made any sense is for the prison leadership to have had in its possession a possible life-saving offer from the British, and *not* to have discussed it, or *not* to have attempted to form an opinion on its merits and defects. And having come to a considered position, we would naturally have had to let our leadership on the outside know of our thinking. How could it be otherwise? After all, eight comrades' lives were in the balance. The crunch factor is this: if Bik had responded honestly to Stephen McCaffrey's question about the existence and details of the Mountain Climber offer, he would have had to answer a number of uncomfortable questions, including these:

- What were the components of the offer that Danny Morrison had relayed to you?
- Did you tell Richard O'Rawe about the offer?
- Did you and he form a judgment on it? If not, why not?
- Did you think the offer was good enough to end the hunger strike?
- Did you inform Gerry Adams of any estimation that the prison leadership may have reached?
- Did Adams write back expressing the committee's or the Army Council's view on the offer's advantages or shortcomings?
- What message did Gerry Adams and Danny Morrison send to the British regarding the prisoners' attitude to their offer?

- What reply was forthcoming from the British?
- Did you enlighten the hunger strikers as to the prison leadership's opinion?

These questions would have been only the tip of the iceberg. That is why Bik McFarlane reverted to mumbo jumbo when he was asked if he had told me about the offer.

The rest of McFarlane's interview with Stephen McCaffrey went down the familiar road of overstatement as he tried to regain lost ground: 'According to Richard, he has a deal done. Richard then says that he shouted down to me that "that looks good". "I agreed" and that I would write out to the Army Council and say that we would accept the deal. That is totally fictitious. That conversation did not take place.'[16]

That conversation did take place and McFarlane knows it, as do other Blanketmen. Later, at least one former prisoner would confirm this publicly, while another would tell hunger strikers' families the same thing privately. What they had to say left Bik McFarlane looking weak and exposed. How could he think that it would end up any other way?

Thirteen

I HAD AN APOLOGY to make to Danny Morrison. In an article in *Daily Ireland* I wrote that he had attended the 28 July meeting in 1981, between the families and Monsignor Faul, with Gerry Adams. I also said he had a potential settlement (the Mountain Climber offer) in his back pocket, which he failed to tell the families about. As he was quick to point out, Danny had been in hospital in Dublin at the time of the meeting.

I publicly apologized in *Daily Ireland* on 14 March 2005. However, a *mea culpa* given with a humble and contrite heart did not impress Danny Morrison. Even though I had been publicly penitent, I nonetheless had unfinished business because of his sarcastic remark that I had 'quickly run out of argument'.[1] It was a gauntlet I had no choice but to pick up.

When Bik McFarlane had said that there had been no offer 'whatsoever', I had not rushed to press home my advantage. Now the time had come.

In the *Daily Ireland* article I referred to the formidable list of influential people – including Adams and Morrison – who had said that there was an offer from the Mountain Climber, finishing the rebuttal thus:

No amount of clever footwork or spin by Danny or anyone else will detract from the fact that Bik's version of events has been holed below the waterline.

After almost two weeks of having to endure a vicious and unprecedented campaign to vilify me, we finally arrive at the point where I'm sitting in my cell reading Bik's comm about the Mountain Climber.

I have said all along that Bik sent me down the offer from the Mountain Climber and that, after considering it for a couple of hours, I called him up to the window and told him in Irish that I believed there was enough there [to honourably end the hunger strike].

He agreed with me.

But Bik says there was no offer 'whatsoever'.

Adams, Danny Morrison, Beresford, O'Malley, Father Crilly, Hugh Logue and I say different.

No doubt Danny will be racking his brain in order to counter what I'm saying to rescue Bik.

I don't relish his task.[2]

As it turned out, Danny did not relish the task of rescuing Bik either because he ignored his plight and the hunger strike controversy in his *Daily Ireland* column of the following Wednesday.

Morrison's tactical withdrawal was a sign for the flying column of letter writers and party hacks to slither silently out of the debate. Gerry Adams had refused to be drawn into the controversy, so Bik could hardly look to him for help. The beleaguered Bik McFarlane issued a holding statement four days later: 'As Officer Commanding in the prison at the time, I can say categorically that there was no outside intervention to prevent a deal.'[3]

Even if the fire had temporally gone out of the debate, smouldering ashes of dissatisfaction threatened to ignite if the wind changed direction. I thought it probable that the twenty-fifth anniversary of Bobby Sands's death, in May 2006, would fuel another conflagration. I was not to be disappointed.

In early May a thorough, two-part RTÉ documentary called

Hidden Lives featured all the major activists in the hunger strike, both inside and outside the prison. This is the programme where Gerry Adams inexplicably said he did not know of the Mountain Climber's involvement until *after* the hunger strike, despite him having been communicating with the British, through the Mountain Climber, during it. This is a truly weird statement because it is accepted by all parties that the Mountain Climber, Brendan Duddy from Derry, gave Martin McGuinness a statement from the British on 5 July 1981 and that McGuinness brought this to Adams in Belfast. Is it possible that Adams did not ask McGuinness for the identity of the person who had handed over the British statement? How could Adams possibly gauge the bona fides of the middleman if he didn't know his identity?

In this documentary, former intermediary Denis Bradley said, 'The memory, and there is some dispute about this, is that there was a phone call on a particular night direct to Maggie Thatcher as she was on her way to a conference abroad. What she was offering that night was basically what the hunger strikers settled for.'[4]

As the tide inexorably turned in my favour, Danny Morrison recommenced his McCarthyite crusade. Setting aside any pretence of manners and decorum, he launched into a vicious denunciation of me.

The most sickening attack came when he wrote about a group of former prisoners and activists who had marked the quarter-centenary of Bobby Sands's death by visiting the prison hospital: 'Richard O'Rawe was everywhere, cheered on by the very people who attempted to criminalize the republican struggle. His book should have been called *On Another Man's Hunger Strike* for he has diminished his own sacrifice as a blanketman. The fool.'[5]

The surrogate title that Morrison proposed for my book derives from the old Ulster proverb, 'It's easy to sleep on another man's wounds', meaning that while heroes suffer, others profit from their pain and valour. *On Another Man's Wound* is also the title of a book by legendary IRA leader Ernie O'Malley's book, a memoir of his leadership role in Ireland's War of Independence.

Despite the bile that Morrison had habitually thrown at me, I tried to retain a modicum of respect for him, as I struggled to comprehend how even he could stoop this low. But he was not finished.

The central problem Morrison and the others faced in their mission to bury me was that, while I could refer to Bik McFarlane's damning comms in *Ten Men Dead* and *Biting at the Grave*, they had nothing similar with which to attack me. Simply put, it had not been my job to write to Gerry Adams during the hunger strike; that was the role of the prison OC, so no private comms existed that could be used to prove that my version of events was flawed or untrue. This put Morrison at a disadvantage because there were major contradictions in Bik's comms, which bulldozed Morrison's customized version of the hunger strike.

How do I patch up the holes in Bik's comms? How do I get to O'Rawe? Those thoughts must have taxed Morrison's agile mind. Finally he came up with a solution of sorts.

In June 2006 he released a detailed article under the title 'Hunger Strike Deal Didn't Exist',[6] quoting extracts from press statements I had written during the hunger strike in my job as Public Relations Officer of the prisoners.

Of necessity, these press statements had to be unyielding and hard-hitting in tone because they were being read not just by the man and woman on the street but by the British government. If they had contained the least hint of weakness, that would have been seen as a crack in our resolve and resulted in a corresponding steeling of the British government's attitude.

I could scarcely make any public reference to the existence of the Mountain Climber process; that was top secret. Therefore all statements were predicated on the very public efforts of the ICJP. As PRO, I was hardly going to send out a press statement saying that leading republicans Gerry Adams and Danny Morrison had rejected the Mountain Climber offer after the prison leadership had accepted it, or that the hunger-strike committee was controlling the strike.

Morrison knew this, yet wrote: 'In his comms from July, August and September 1981, which were released as press statements, Richard makes it clear that there was no deal.'[7]

An independent reader would be forgiven for thinking the comms were somehow clandestine, private letters, addressed to the outside leadership, and that the decision to release them as press statements had been nothing more than an afterthought.

Morrison added: 'Richard's comms – which are contemporaneous accounts of the time – contradict the allegations he is making a quarter of a century later.'[8]

This is a perfect example of a master propagandist plying his trade. Morrison artfully constructs sentences to suit his strategic requirements – without telling any lies. He highlights and repeats the word 'comms', but mentions the phrase 'press statements' only as an adjunct, enticing the reader to subconsciously equate 'Richard's comms' with Bik's. Yet the two could not have been more opposed. My press statements were for public and British government consumption, while Bik's comms were usually addressed to Gerry Adams, and were highly confidential, and therefore explicit and candid.

Morrison finished this article with artful sanctimony:

> I hope this closes this sorry episode and I would like to apologise to the families of the hunger strikers for the suffering and distress that this has perpetuated, but I feel that the false claims have to be answered and settled. It was the British government which withdrew political status, introduced criminalisation, and was responsible for creating the conditions for a hunger strike.[9]

He knew that 'this sorry episode' was far from closed, but it sounded good, and he had apologized to the families for something he claimed was not of his making. Was he apologizing on my behalf, or just polishing his halo? Either way, he was being magnanimous.

Fourteen

COLM SCULLION, my cellmate during both hunger strikes, came from the County Derry village of Bellaghy. The screws decided to move me in with Colm in the summer of 1980 after I had shared a cell with The Dark for six months. Scull was good-humoured and lively. His 'never do today what you can do tomorrow' approach to life suited my own lackadaisical attitude to doing time. On occasion, though, his youthful impishness would cause ructions on the wing – especially when the fancy took him to rib someone from another cell. We became great friends and comrades, and in the twenty months that we shared a cell, we never exchanged an angry word.

When I had almost finished writing *Blanketmen* in 2003, Scull visited my home several times and we discussed the book. He had a sharp memory and he told me of how he had cornered Bik McFarlane after they had both been released and expressed his disquiet at the outside leadership's rejection of our decision to accept the offer. McFarlane had responded irascibly, telling Scull never to speak of the matter again. While Bik may have succeeded in shutting up Scull, he never shut him down: Scull told people what had really happened during the hunger strike.

After I showed Scull the more potentially contentious extracts of my book, he made it clear that he did not want to be publicly drawn into the inevitable controversy that would result from its publication, saying he was 'friends with everyone'. I respected the delicacy of his position and replied that I had no intention of dragging him into the dispute against his will.

However, a tocsin began to ring in my head during telephone conversations that I had with Scull in the first few days after the book's release. This anxiety increased when he told me that soon after *Blanketmen* hit the bookshops, Bik McFarlane visited him and suggested that he not have any contact with me, and that he was not to speak to the press. Scull then informed me that Danny Morrison had made his way to Bellaghy and questioned him closely about what he knew. He said Morrison's reaction was muted when he told him that what I had written was factual. As well as McFarlane and Morrison, Scull revealed that others had called on him, including one outspoken relative of a hunger striker who had quizzed him about my account of the hunger strike. Despite Scull telling him that my account was accurate, it did nothing to dissuade this person from publicly berating me.

I then realized that Scull had become a very important figure in this dispute. As my cellmate during the 1981 hunger strike, he was in the perfect position to stop me in my tracks by simply rejecting my account. That McFarlane and Morrison had taken the time to visit him within days of my book's publication showed that *they* had grasped just how significant Scull could be in this battle over the truth about the hunger strike. While I greatly admired Scull for standing firm, I began to feel the cold wind of vulnerability on hearing of this unholy procession to his door.

Suppose that he could be 'persuaded' to say that I had shown him Bik's comm and that it had not contained a breakdown of the Mountain Climber offer? Or that, even though he had been in the cell with me, he had not heard the conversation between

Bik and myself signalling our acceptance of the offer? Were that to happen, I believed I would have been destroyed.

Colm Scullion is a warm, congenial man, and from our experience together in the H-Blocks I knew that he was courageous. But the pressure likely to be heaped on to him would be nearly impossible to resist, and I have little doubt that he would have been told that my account of the hunger strike was damaging to the reputation of Gerry Adams – which was true – and that, consequently, the peace process could be at risk because Adams represented the first line of defence against those republicans who, mistakenly in my view, believed a military victory over the British was achievable. My instinct told me that, tough as Scull was, he would be vulnerable to this type of remorseless coercion.

I judged that the only way to safeguard my integrity and that of my book would be to get Scull to talk about the issues on tape. The problem was that he was never going to agree. He was so horrified at the prospect of incurring the wrath of the leadership that he had sought and received my promise that I would not reveal the limited amount of help he had given me while I had been researching *Blanketmen*. In the five years since the book was published, Colm has never been back inside my home.

Against this chink in my armour, I felt that I had to secretly tape-record Colm over the telephone because that was the only way we were communicating then. The choice was grim; it was either that or live with the possibility that my position could be eroded and I would be damned as a liar and a fraud.

Surreptitious tape-recording did not come without its problems. I told myself that this was a horrible thing to do to one of my best friends and ex-comrades. I knew Colm would never intentionally do me harm, but I did not think that he could possibly resist the dictates of the leadership – especially if their defence was collapsing in this critical battle. Therefore I captured Colm Scullion in a tape-recording that substantiated everything I had written.

I determined that the recordings would never be made public – unless Scull turned bandit. Even if he did, I was not sure my conscience would allow me to make use of them. It didn't. When Scull did eventually bow to the remorseless pressure and publicly rebuked me in April 2008, I did not release the tapes, and have not done so since.

Surprisingly it was the Mountain Climber, Brendan Duddy, who triggered a sequence of events that led to Scull's public opposition. Brendan Duddy was the subject of a BBC documentary broadcast on 27 March 2008, which revealed that the prominent Derry businessman had been the 'Mountain Climber'. The documentary, entitled *The Secret Peacemaker* described Duddy as 'the link' or 'the contact' between the IRA Army Council and the British government. A former cross-country runner, Duddy claimed that the Mountain Climber codename was bestowed on him because in days gone by he got fit by running up mountains in the neighbouring county of Donegal. Duddy's claim was reinforced by Padraig O'Malley's assertion that 'Mountain Climber was the IRA's code name for the middleman who carried messages between British government officials and the republican movement.'[1]

We in the prison leadership had had the impression that the MI6 agent and British government representative, Michael Oatley, had been the Mountain Climber. However, I spoke to Oatley by telephone in April 2009 and he confirmed that Duddy was the one. Oatley also authenticated his involvement in the first hunger strike, which ended in December 1980, although he said that he had played no part in the second hunger strike, having been in Zimbabwe at the time. He admitted to being defensive about Gerry Adams and Martin McGuinness and gave me the impression that he admired both men for opting to make peace rather than continuing with a futile war. The mild-mannered MI6 agent also said that there had been no secret agreement to end the first hunger strike, although he remembered meeting the Redemptorist priest Father Brendan Meagher, codenamed

'The Angel', at Belfast International Airport, where he furtively handed over what would become known as 'the 18 December document'. Oatley said that the contents of the document had been cleared by the then British prime minister, Margaret Thatcher, who, he alleged, had 'a desire to stop the hunger strike'. It was Michael Oatley's opinion that 'things didn't need to go wrong'. By that he meant that a more liberal interpretation of the 18th of December document by the prison administration might have resulted in there being no need for a second hunger strike.

I gave my view that, in the absence of clearly defined instructions from the British government, most, if not all, prison administrations would inevitably resort to the rulebook. I said I did not think the prison governor in the H-Blocks at that time, Stanley Hilditch, would have felt he had the power to concede on a matter of such importance as the clothing issue (even if he had wanted to, which he didn't) without a directive from the Northern Ireland Office. Understandably, Oatley did not respond directly to this assessment.

Although Oatley is now involved in peace-making in the Middle East, I felt he still had fond memories of his time in Ireland and that his old ties with Adams and McGuinness, and especially with Brendan Duddy, still mattered to him.

In *The Secret Peacemaker* Duddy barely referred to the 1981 hunger strike, concentrating instead on his herculean endeavours from the mid-seventies to the early nineties to bridge the gap between the major warring parties. He did, however, describe how he had broken down when he received a letter from Bobby Sands thanking him for trying to bring about a successful conclusion to the first hunger strike.

His almost total block-out of the 1981 hunger strike during the documentary suggested that he wanted to avoid a similar controversy to what erupted after the publication of *Blanketmen*. While not unforeseen, this was regrettable because he had been the lynchpin between Adams and Morrison and the British government, and ideally placed to shed light on the covert communications exchanged between the parties.

Throughout the documentary, Duddy was candid about his other activities, going as far as to say that in 1993 four IRA leaders (purportedly Gerry Adams, Martin McGuiness, Gerry Kelly and Pat Doherty) had interrogated him in his home about a bogus communication to the British government saying: 'The conflict is over but we need your advice' about ending it. This message infuriated the IRA leadership because it gave the impression that they were desperate to abandon the armed struggle but needed to go cap in hand to their traditional enemy, the British, to get them off the hook.

'Yes, the IRA thought I had sent it,' Duddy told interviewer Peter Taylor. When Taylor asked him if he had been afraid during the interrogation, Duddy replied: 'Let me put it this way: if I'd been guilty of anything, I wouldn't have liked to have been in that room.'[2]

It later emerged that one of Duddy's co-peacemakers, Denis Bradley, along with MI6 agent Robert McLarnon, had written the communication in order to induce movement in the peace process.

Elsewhere in the documentary Duddy revealed that Martin McGuinness had had a two-hour fireside chat with Michael Oatley at Duddy's home in Derry in 1991.

Brendan Duddy patently felt at liberty to broadcast his recollections of these events. So if the veil of secrecy surrounding his position as the Mountain Climber had been lifted, why was he unwilling to divulge what he knew about the second hunger strike in the documentary?

In 2008 I wrote to Brendan Duddy twice to ask him for an interview about his involvement in the 1981 hunger strike. He did not reply to either letter. I persuaded a mutual friend to approach him on my behalf, but he still refused to give me an interview. Whose reputation was he intent on protecting? Certainly not his own. His role in the 1981 hunger strike had been conspicuously honourable; his only motive for getting involved was to provide a mechanism whereby opposing leaders could communicate to reach an agreement that would see no more hunger strikers lose their lives. And Duddy was not shielding me from embarrassing disclosures. So who was Duddy protecting? One, or possibly both of the two major protagonists: the IRA committee and the British government?

While *The Secret Peacemaker* documentary shed no light on the 1981 hunger strike, it did prompt the Mountain Climber's long-time friend, Eamonn McCann, to reveal what he had discovered about the hunger strike.

McCann has lived a colourful, if turbulent, life. Born in Derry in 1943, he devoted his adulthood to the causes of human and civil rights and international socialism. While at sixty-seven, most pensioners would be happy enough to see sixty-eight, McCann still has the self-sustaining energy of the unrepentant activist: in 2006, he and eight militants from the Derry Anti-War Coalition occupied the premises of the multinational arms company Raytheon, in protest at what McCann described as 'Israeli war crimes in Lebanon'. The protesters were charged with destroying property (the result of computers being thrown out of windows), but were acquitted in 2008. A renowned journalist and captivating orator, McCann is respected as someone who speaks his mind and zealously guards his independence. It was McCann, along with another Derry radical, Eamon Melaugh, who organized the 5 October 1968 civil rights march in Derry that was attacked by the Royal Ulster Constabulary. This march is generally accepted as the crossing of the Rubicon, and the starting point for 'The Troubles'.

Knowing that *The Secret Peacemaker* was about to be shown, Eamonn McCann tackled the issue of Brendan Duddy's involvement in the 1981 hunger strike in a *Belfast Telegraph* article entitled: 'Will the IRA ever admit the truth over hunger strike?' He wrote:

Evidence which has now become available helps clarify a dispute sparked three years ago by the assertion by former IRA prisoner Richard O'Rawe that terms for ending the strike, accepted by the prisoners' leadership in the Maze/Long Kesh, were rejected by IRA commanders outside. The implication is that the lives of six of the hunger strikers might have been saved if the prisoners hadn't been overruled.[3]

McCann claimed to have spoken to 'The man who was sharing a cell with O'Rawe in July 1981.'[4] During their conversation McCann said that Scull had told him: 'Richard isn't a liar. He told the truth in his book. I heard what passed between Richard and Bik [McFarlane]. I remember Richard saying: "*Tá go leor ann*" [there's enough there] and the reply: "*Aontaím leat*" [I agree with you]. There's just no question that that happened.'[5]

McCann went on to say: 'O'Rawe's account of the negotiations as seen from "inside" will not be contradicted by the account from a different perspective contained in the BBC programme to be transmitted tonight focusing on the role of the "Mountain Climber", Brendan Duddy.'[6]

He summed up:

> The suspicions that still surround the events and which have damaged the republican leadership in the eyes of many former activists arise, it seems, not so much from O'Rawe's narrative of what happened but from an adamant refusal on the part of the IRA leadership of the time to admit to serious and, in the end, fatal errors in their conduct of the hunger strike and from determined efforts to blacken O'Rawe's name in an attempt to obscure the truth.[7]

In a radio interview the next day, McCann went further:

> I have spoken to people who are certainly in a position to know what happened, who were in a position at that time to know exactly what was going on … Broadly speaking, the information which I now have, I am absolutely satisfied

with, is that, in blunt terms, that Richard O'Rawe, on the key issue between himself and Danny Morrison and others, that Richard O'Rawe was right and that those who were arguing against him were wrong.[8]

When asked if he believed my account, McCann said:

I think that's right ... Richard O'Rawe is telling the truth ... I don't know what the motivation for the rejection, by the outside IRA leadership ... for the rejection of the offer, which was made on 6–7 July, at that time ... I don't know what the motivation was and therefore I can't confirm the motivation, but I can confirm that it happened, that the prisoners' acceptance of the deal was over-ruled by the outside leadership.[9]

McCann concluded: 'I have spoken to the "Mountain Climber". Of course, he didn't know what was going on inside the prison, but the things that he did know, and which he's told me, confirm Richard O'Rawe's account.'[10]

I did not find out about McCann's newspaper article until it was brought to my attention the next day, but the minute I read it I knew that this was the breakthrough I had been waiting on for three frustrating years. The cause of that frustration was in knowing that McCann was not alone in accepting that my version of events in the prison during the 1981 hunger strike had been accurate.

At a chance encounter in the Kennedy Centre on Belfast's Andersonstown Road in early 2006, I met Gerard 'Cleaky' Clarke. Cleaky had been on the leadership wing during the hunger strike and he let me know in no uncertain terms that his cellmate and he had danced with joy when they heard Bik and me endorse the offer.

At the funeral of veteran republican John Kelly in September 2007 another Blanketman told me how he also had listened to the exchange. He did not indicate that he wanted to go public, and I did not ask him to do so.

Yet another laughed when he whispered to me how, along with his cellmate, he had spent hours breaking down all our codes, and how they had known instantly the import of the words Bik and I had spoken.

Possibly the old allegiances still lingered in the psyche of those Blanketmen who knew what had occurred but who had chosen not to come forward. That is understandable. After all, when you have spent a lifetime in the shadow of mighty men and even mightier events, it is no small thing to step out into the sun.

Fortunately, Eamonn McCann's only allegiance was to his conscience. In the light of his testimony, I dared to hope that after three years of being ostracized and ridiculed, my version of events would be generally accepted. In many quarters they had been – even before McCann had buttressed my position. For others, particularly the members of the republican movement, it seemed clear that no amount of evidence would validate the charge that the committee acted deplorably in rejecting the prisoners' acceptance of an offer.

How would Adams, Morrison and Co. respond to McCann's disclosures? Could they say McCann had got it wrong? Were they going to say that McCann was lying when he said that my cellmate, Colm Scullion, told him of the conversation between Bik and me?

Even before Eamonn McCann had put pen to paper, the committee had been finding the going heavy. In the three years since the release of *Blanketmen*, their defence became increasingly suspect. McCann's intervention carried immense weight. He was a staunch anti-imperialist, who did not make a habit of criticizing the republican movement unless it was warranted (he had publicly lambasted the republicans who murdered Robert McCartney on 31 January 2005).

Eamonn McCann had dealt my opponents a body blow.

Fifteen

AFTER EAMONN McCANN'S interview, I felt that the time had come for me to proclaim that my account had been incontrovertibly authentic. As ever, though, it was not that simple.

The winds of change were blowing in from Bellaghy and for some time I'd had no contact with Scull. This was foreboding.

McCann had not named Scull and I had no intention of publicly identifying him either. That said, I was determined to comment on McCann's article.

Three years earlier I calculated that Colm Scullion might play a decisive role in this affair – even though he had made it clear to both sides that he did not want to become involved. As related, I had taken the trouble to tape-record our conversation of 15 March 2005. Now, the moment of truth had arrived: would Scull be strong enough to resist the power and the pressure?

Almost a week had passed since McCann's *Belfast Telegraph* article, and there was still no public response from Danny Morrison or Bik McFarlane. Their options were limited. They could have conceivably challenged McCann directly, but without the solid backing of either Scullion or Duddy, that would have been an unattractive proposition.

On 2 April 2008 *The Irish News* carried a lengthy piece that included a press release I had written and extracts of an interview I gave to a reporter. Under the headline: 'Hunger strike account "vindicated" ', I quoted from McCann where he wrote of how Scull had confirmed that the vital exchange between Bik and myself had taken place (although I did not identify Scull by name). I finished that paragraph by stating, 'My cellmate says it's true and that he heard what I have said,'[1] continuing, 'As far as I'm concerned, it's done and dusted [the dispute] and we can't go back on that, but I hope that more will come forward now and verify what I have said in the past.'[2]

I went on, 'I'm no liar. This [McCann's article] totally verifies my version of events. It removes all particles of contention.'[3] I declared that the new evidence was a 'total vindication of my claims'.[4]

Asked by the reporter what I thought the reaction would be, I said I believed my opponents would be 'keeping their heads down now'.[5] They did, but not from choice.

Unfortunately for us both, Scull raised his.

The silence of Morrison, McFarlane and the others after my 'vindication' statement may have been predictable, but it was ominous. Had Bik nothing to say? Where was the maestro, Danny Morrison? Where had all that melodrama and flaming indignation gone?

On 9 April 2008, precisely a week after the *Irish News* article, Scull had a letter published in *The Irish News* and the *Derry Journal*, trying to limit the damage Eamonn McCann had done to the committee's position. The headline in the *Derry Journal* read: ' "There was no offer to end hunger strike" – ex-prisoner.' Then, inexplicably, the paper quoted this ex-prisoner, Colm Scullion, confirming that there had indeed been an offer.

> There was no deal. I agree with Richard that there was certainly an offer which Richard was made aware of by Brendan McFarlane who was a few cells away. I didn't hear anything like what Richard is saying.[6]

My first reaction was one of blind rage. I had a decision to make.

Release the tape.

Don't release it.

They'd got to him.

Scull wouldn't have done this of his own free will.

But he said he didn't hear the conversation with Bik.

Don't release the tape.

Release it.

In the end, I didn't release it.

Evidently Scull disputed McCann's version of their conversation, but he had gone to great pains to avoid using McCann's name in his letter. This all smacked of frailty and fear, and unquestionably dented Scull's credibility.

When I analysed what Scull said, I concluded that he had come out with more than perhaps those who had cajoled and pressured him would have wanted. For a start, we now definitively knew that Eamonn McCann was speaking about Colm Scullion when he wrote:

> More importantly, the man who shared a cell with O'Rawe in July 1981 confirms O'Rawe's account: 'Richard isn't a liar. He told the truth in his book. I heard what passed between Richard and Bik [McFarlane]. I remember Richard saying "*Tá go leor ann*", and the reply "*Aontaím leat.*" There's just no question of that.[7]

On the other hand, Scull had written: 'I didn't hear anything like what Richard is saying.'[8] If that had been true, it would have contradicted McCann's account (above) of their conversation. So, did McCann make it all up? He told me that he did not pursue Colm Scullion for this interview; Scull sought him out. Had 'they' indeed got to him? A possible answer to this was put forward by another Blanketman, a Tyrone man whom I met in a rural filling station in November 2008, who did not want to be identified in this book. Scull's name inevitably surfaced during our chat. The Blanketman told me that Colm had been put under enormous pressure to come out against me, and that he'd been 'a very worried man'. The Tyrone Blanketman recalled having a telephone conversation with him in the days before the publication of his letter, when suddenly he heard panic in Scull's voice saying, 'Oh fuck! Here come the headhunters!' Scull then slammed down the phone.

'Who were the headhunters?'

'Now, Ó Rathaigh, you know rightly who they were,' the man said, smiling. 'Who did you criticize in your book? Who's been boxing with you?'

On my way back to Belfast I thought about the term 'head-hunters', and it conjured up images of New Guinea cannibals admiring, as trophies, the heads of their enemies. Then it struck me that it had another, quite different, dictionary meaning: 'the recruitment of, or a drive to recruit, new high-level personnel, especially in management or in specialist fields'. How aptly Scull chose his words! Even as he had been talking on the phone to the Tyrone Blanketman, he was being headhunted by the committee, and his letter to the newspaper convinced me that their recruitment drive had been successful. Its absence of detail mimicked the approach of others, who would have told him that straying into specifics can be as precarious as straying into quicksand – once you're in, it is very difficult to get back on to solid ground. And too many specifics can destroy a work of fiction.

I answered Scull:

> Colm Scullion avoids detail and keeps to what is the standard Sinn Féin line in relation to the 1981 hunger strike in his *Irish News* letter (9 April 2008).
>
> However, Colm did contradict Bik McFarlane, the OC of the prisoners, when he said that Bik received the contents of a British offer on 5 July 1981 and that Bik sent that offer down to me on his return from his meeting with Danny Morrison

Bobby Sands's cell in the Maze Hospital Block:
a painting by Hector McDonnell (oil on canvas, 2008).

Left: *Humphrey Atkins (1922–96), Northern Ireland's Secretary of State during the hunger strikes.*
Right: *Eamonn McCann, journalist and civil rights activist.*

Brendan 'The Dark' Hughes (1948-2008), former OC of the Provisional IR of Belfast, and leader of the first hunger strike.

Left: *Jim Gibney, Sinn Féin activist and H-Block committee member.*
Right: *Danny Morrison, H-Block committee member.*

Gerry Adams, Tom Hartley and Martin McGuinness, all members of the
H-Block committee.

Firing party at the Derry funeral of Patsy O'Hara, INLA hunger striker. He was the fourth to die, on 21 May 1981, aged twenty-three.

The ICJP at the Greenan Lodge Hotel, Belfast, 8 July 1981.
Left to right: *Father Oliver Crilly; Jerome Connolly, Dublin solicitor and commission chair; Brian Gallagher, Bishop O'Mahoney; and Hugh Logue.*

The first public hunger-strike debate at Dungloe, County Donegal, 25 October 2008. Left to right: Tommy McKearney, who took part in the first hunger strike; Micheál Cholm Mac Giolla Easbuig, chair of the conference; Laurence McKeown, hunger striker; and author Richard O'Rawe.

The Derry Gasyard Hunger-Strike conference, 23 May 2009.
Left to right*: Richard O'Rawe; Tommy Gorman,* Maidstone
prison-ship escapee; Liam Clarke, Sunday Times *journalist;*
Brendan Duddy, 'Mountain Climber'.

Brendan Duddy at the Derry Gasyard Conference, 23 May 2009.

Gerard 'Cleakie' Clarke, confirming Richard O'Rawe's account of the unger strike from the floor, at the Derry Gasyard conference, 23 May 2009.

Former Blanketmen with hunger-striker's families, June 2009, under the Derry mural of Mickey Devine, the tenth hunger striker to die.
Left to right: *Michael Óg Devine, son of Mickey Devine; Louise Devine, Mickey's daughter; Blanketman Dixie Elliot; Mrs Peggy O'Hara, mother of hunger striker Patsy O'Hara; Blanketman Tony O'Hara, brother of Patsy; Blanketman Willie Gallagher; Blanketman Richard O'Rawe; Blanketman Gerard Hodgkins.*

in the camp hospital. That is progress, because Bik previously said that there was 'no offer whatsoever'.

Now that, I hope, it is universally accepted that there was an offer sent into the prison leadership to consider, perhaps we can get answers to the many questions that it poses. For example:

What was Bik's opinion of the offer?

Did he believe it constituted a settlement?

If so, did he convey this belief to the 'Committee', the caucus of republican leaders who had been designated by the IRA Army Council to advise on the running of the hunger strike?

Did they communicate their opinion to Bik? If not, why not?

Why did Bik, for twenty-six years, deny that an offer had been made?

Suffice to say that, on several occasions, Colm and I had conversations, during which he did accept that (1) there was an offer, (2) Bik and I accepted that offer, and communicated our mutual acceptance in Irish, and (3) a comm came in from outside which rejected the offer. [9]

No one answered my questions, and Scull did not reply to my letter. Had he put pen to paper, I think that the temptation for me to use his own taped words would have been irresistible, and given what Colm and I had come through in the H-Blocks, that would have been a tragedy for us both.

Sixteen

IT WAS SUNDAY, 5 July 1981. Joe McDonnell was on the fifty-ninth day of his hunger strike. A hard Belfast street-fighter, he was now fighting for his life, each laboured breath drawing him closer to death.

Bobby Sands, Frank Hughes, Raymond McCreesh and Patsy O'Hara had already died. These great men were gone forever. The wings were still. Blanketmen spoke in whispers. It was as if a heavy eiderdown had been dropped on the H-Blocks, smothering our spirits.

Our groundbreaking 4 July statement was almost two days old. It had laid out a formula whereby neither the British nor we prisoners would have to lose face. That statement had led to a surge of buoyancy amongst the Blanketmen, but, as the hours passed, and the final countdown began on Joe's life, that earlier optimism began to fade.

That morning at Mass, those of us at leadership level, Bik McFarlane, Jake Jackson, Pat Mullin and me, unanimously agreed that if there was ever going to be movement from the British, it would be on the back of our statement, and it would be before Joe died. But nothing was happening.

The Irish Commission for Justice and Peace had been busy trying to nail down an agreement, but to us it seemed elusive, ungraspable. Certainly, whenever Bik came back from any meeting with the commissioners, he appeared restless and agitated. He wanted them to pack up and go home, since he believed they were encouraging the British to put off talking to the IRA. I was not so sure this was a good strategy; severing the only existing line of communication with the British did not appeal to me.

Scull and I had taken the situation apart and put it back together so many times that we had run out of variables. Then Bik's cell door was opened and he was told that he was being taken up to the prison hospital. Scull nodded to me excitedly: 'Bik's on the move. Something's happenin', Ó Rathaigh.'

I too suspected that this could be a significant development, but I had learned that jumping to premature conclusions usually resulted in bitter disappointment. We would just have to wait until Bik returned.

When Bik did come back, the atmosphere seemed to have changed in the wing: people were chatting at the doors and windows. Bik immediately sent me up a comm in which he said that the British had opened up a line of communication with the outside leadership. Then, point by point, he outlined the British offer. After what seemed like several hours, Bik and I spoke in Irish out of our windows, and we agreed that there was enough substance in the offer to end the hunger strike.

Scull's public denial of hearing this conversation between Bik and myself in his April 2008 letter had been one of the reasons I decided to write this book. As I tossed the prospect about in my head, I realized that *Afterlives* would bear little resemblance to *Blanketmen*. Endearing characters in this drama were few. Of those opposing me, only Danny Morrison had any style; only he could deliver the bons mots with aplomb; the others were dour and grindingly predictable.

In 2006 the journalist Liam Clarke made me aware that he had put in a Freedom of Information request for the release of material relating to the hunger strike. I did not believe anything would come of it. The year 2006 was the twenty-fifth anniversary of the hunger strike, and the boys were out, clogging the airwaves, filling the newspapers, shovelling mediocre denunciations of Richard O'Rawe down people's throats. In the commonwealth of words, I more than held my own. There would be another day, we promised each other. We kept that promise.

In March 2009 Clarke emailed me some documents he had received from the Freedom of Information Office and asked me to study them.

The very title of the first one had my head spinning: 'Extract from a letter dated 8 July 1981 from 10 Downing Street to the Northern Ireland Office'. This was from Margaret Thatcher? I quickly ran my eyes over the document: 'Your Secretary of State said …' Sweet home Alabama! But hold on. Was what I was reading about the ICJP, or about the Mountain Climber? That question was also on Liam's lips when he phoned me after thirty minutes.

'Well?'

'It's Mountain Climber.'

'Are you certain?'

'No doubt. This is Mountain Climber stuff, Liam.'

'I thought that, but I wasn't sure.'

Reading these papers was electrifying. I remember scanning hungrily from line to line, page after page. What did that mean? Is that really what happened? I was mesmerized by this view of the parallel universe inhabited only by moguls and mandarins. Liam and I then had a discussion about the content of the documents.

By far and away the most important one was the 8 July 1981 letter:

> The Prime Minister met your Secretary of State at 0015 this morning to discuss the latest developments in the efforts to bring the hunger strike in the Maze to an end. Philip

Woodfield [one of the two British civil servants who had met Gerry Adams and Daithí Ó Conaill in 1972 to discuss a cease-fire] was also present.

Your Secretary of State said that the message which the Prime Minister had approved the previous evening had been communicated to the PIRA. Their response indicated that they did not regard it as satisfactory and that they wanted a good deal more. That appeared to mark the end of this development, and we made this clear to the PIRA during the afternoon. This had produced a very rapid reaction which suggested that it was not the content of the message which they had objected to but only its tone. The question now for decision was whether we should respond on our side. He [Secretary of State] had concluded that we should communicate with the PIRA over-night a draft statement enlarging upon the message of the previous evening but in no way whatever departing from its substance. If the PIRA accepted the draft statement and ordered the hunger strikers to end their protest the statement would be issued immediately.[1]

It must be remembered that here was an internal letter from one government department to another, released twenty-eight years after the hunger strike, and only then following a Freedom of Information request. This dynamic makes it all but impossible to contest that had the Mountain Climber offer been accepted and the hunger strike ended, the British had every intention of issuing the draft statement that Brendan Duddy had passed on to the IRA committee. That element of British policy was rein-forced when a copy of the statement by the Secretary of State for Northern Ireland, Humphrey Atkins, was later released to Liam Clarke in May 2009: it contained the following precursor:

> The statement [from the Secretary of State for Northern Ireland] has been read [by the IRA leadership] and we await Provo reactions (we would be willing to allow them a sight of the document just before it was given to the prisoners and released to the media).

These documents also showed that the committee at first rejected the offer, saying that 'they wanted a good deal more', and then, after the Brits indicated that they were pulling the plug on the process, they changed their minds, this time saying that 'the content' was acceptable, but not the 'tone'. What is missing from the British documents, relating to the period before Joe McDonnell died, is a request from the committee (not the ICJP) that an official be sent into the prison to explain or to guarantee what was on offer, although that is not to say that such a request was not made in that timeframe. Apparently, the somewhat confused messages from the committee precipitated a gathering of the coven in Downing Street.

I detected a mood in the documents that Thatcher wanted to see an end to the hunger strike, albeit on terms that saved her government's face; it appeared to Bik and me that her terms and ours had not been that far apart, although evidently too far for the committee.

What struck me about the committee's rejection of the British offer was the universal use of the word 'more' over the years. The 8 July 1981 Downing Street letter said: ' ... they wanted a good deal more.'[2] In *Blanketmen*, published four years before the Downing Street documents were released, I wrote: 'If we thought the response from the Army Council would be a formality and that, like us, its members would accept the British offer, we were to be sadly mistaken. On the afternoon of 6 July, a comm came in from the Army Council saying it did not think that the Mountain Climber proposals provided the basis for a resolution and that more was needed.'[3]

At a hunger-strike conference in May 2009 the Mountain Climber, Brendan Duddy, was asked what response the IRA had sent to the British: 'The reply, to the best of my memory and knowledge, to that, was that more had to be added.'[4]

One of the problems with interpreting the documents was that they were incomplete. In an accompanying letter, the

Freedom of Information manager explained that he was still withholding material because, 'To release this information at such a politically sensitive time might have an adverse impact on plans for the devolution of policing and justice [to Northern Ireland].'[5] This was followed by, 'Many of those involved in the original issue are still intimately involved in the ongoing political process.'[6] The implication of that adjunct is that the government was concerned about protecting politicians involved in the 1981 hunger strike because they were essential for the implementation of policing and justice in 2009.

On 5 April 2009 the *Sunday Times* front-page headline read, 'IRA said "No" to hunger strike deal'.[7] I thought this misleading because the leadership of the IRA, as a body, had not been informed of the offer, and therefore they could not be accused of having rejected it (some may say I am splitting hairs here, but it is important to repeat that the committee withheld all information of the Mountain Climber offer from the IRA Army Council).

In an inside page there were photographs of five of the last six hunger strikers, and below them the headline 'Did Adams "sign" their death warrants?'[8] Was the man who could walk on water beginning to look fallible after all? In his explosive article, Liam Clarke succinctly summarized the issues:

Did five, or even six, of the republican prisoners who were in the Maze prison in 1981 die to advance the political strategy of Sinn Féin?

Did Gerry Adams and other members of the IRA kitchen cabinet snub a conciliatory offer from Margaret Thatcher, then the British prime minister, which met the substance of the prisoners' demands, just to ensure that Sinn Féin would win a crucial by-election to Westminster?[9]

Clarke then quoted from an interview I had given to Anthony McIntyre for his website, 'The Blanket', in 2006, where I had said 'the Iron Lady was not so steely'.[10] And she hadn't been. While her public mask never slipped, privately Thatcher appeared to have been remarkably pragmatic in the teeth of international pressure, ordering her subordinates to meet us halfway in the wake of our 4 July statement.

Gerard 'Hodgies' Hodgkins, a former hunger striker, was quoted in the Clarke article. Hodgies was an intriguing character. I first met him in H6 in 1979, when the prison authorities attempted to disrupt the blanket protest by isolating the leadership from the rest of the Blanketmen. Even then, I found Hodgies to be a free-thinking, opinionated individual. In May 2006 he had written to a local paper condemning me: 'The more I see his [Richard O'Rawe] spurious accusations in the media, the more I am inclined to believe that he is following a political agenda …'[11]

Consequently my greeting for him was cool when he and his partner walked into a hunger-strike debate in Dungloe, County Donegal, at which I spoke in October 2008. As it happened, he contributed nothing but his silence, which was appreciated, seeing that I was already outnumbered two-to-one on the panel. Later, he joined fellow panellists Tommy McKearney, Laurence McKeown (both hunger strikers) and me, joking that he did not want to 'start World War III with Ricky'. But the debate opened up a new chapter in Hodgies's life, and after reflecting on the issues I had raised, he converted to my position. He told Clarke: 'It [Thatcher's offer] was something like what we ended up with. If I had had the full facts at the time – that there was a deal on offer – I definitely wouldn't have had anything to do with the hunger strike.'[12]

Now that Hodgies had had the guts to break cover, would anyone follow him? It was no trifling matter for IRA volunteers, past and present, to question the leadership, and most assuredly, it was not encouraged. For an ex-hunger striker to say that he would have had nothing to do with the hunger strike had he known the full facts behind the Mountain Climber offer was breathtaking and courageous. In an interesting post-conflict observation, Hodgies told Liam Clarke: 'The struggle didn't produce the results we had hoped for but the leadership ended up all right.'[13]

INLA hunger striker Liam McCloskey had been on hunger strike for fifty-five days, yet, like Hodgies, Liam had not been informed of the Mountain Climber offer before he ended his hunger strike on 26 September 1981. He too said, when told the substance of the offer, that it would have been enough for him to bring his fast to an end.

At least two hunger strikers did not know of the Mountain Climber offer. Who decided not to share that information with them, and perhaps more importantly, why not? And how many more hunger strikers were not told of the offer? How many hunger strikers died in ignorance of it?

Clarke went on to quote from an IRSP statement saying that its leadership was unaware of the Mountain Climber offer. They also stated: 'Both the then INLA Army Council and the INLA prisoners' OC have stated that if they had been made aware of the content of these developments at that time, they would have ordered the INLA prisoners to end their hunger strike.'[14]

Micky 'Red Mick' Devine was the tenth and last hunger striker to die. His son, also called Micky, commented on the documents: 'These latest disclosures have added substantial weight to claims that the last six hunger strikers' lives could have been saved. Did my father and his five comrades die because a number of individuals didn't like the tone of Thatcher, despite accepting the content of her offer?'[15]

It did not take the services of a soothsayer to predict the initial reaction from Sinn Féin to Liam Clarke's article: 'These documents are not true. They emanate from British Military Intelligence.'[16]

I could not help thinking some demented soul must have sweated long and hard before releasing that. As ever when the committee faced checkmate, the man of letters came to the rescue; he alone could see what others could not, and only he could be depended upon to turn a catastrophe into a reprieve. That man was Danny Morrison.

Danny's first reaction to the Downing Street documents was to say a lot without saying a lot. In an *Irish News* article headlined 'Morrison rubbishes renewed claims of hunger strike deal', Danny asserted, 'a close reading of the documents showed that the British government did not want a settlement on terms acceptable to the prisoners …'[17]

Then it was back to Old Faithful: 'However, Mr Morrison said Mr O'Rawe had confused details of an offer with a deal.'[18]

Later in the week Danny changed from bewailing the release of the documents to trumpeting their disclosure:

> I welcome the release of the documents by the British govern-
> ment under the Freedom of Information Act, though I believe
> that their withholding of one or two particular documents is
> deliberate and mischievous.
>
> The British government documents themselves, far from
> being incriminating, actually corroborate the account of what
> happened at this time by Sinn Féin, surviving hunger strikers,
> OC Brendan McFarlane, the Irish Commission for Justice
> and Peace, and detailed research by authors David Beresford,
> Padraig O'Malley, and Denis O'Hearn.[19]

I didn't see my name on this august list.

Following Danny's bizarre welcome of the Downing Street documents, I wrote to the *Irish Times*:

> There is a fracture running right down the spine of the conven-
> tional hunger strike story and it is this: Brendan (Bik) McFar-
> lane, the commanding officer of the prisoners, has repeatedly
> said that there was no offer from the British to end the hunger
> strike before Joe McDonnell died, while Danny Morrison has
> consistently repudiated this by saying that he told McFarlane
> the details of an offer when they met in the prison hospital on
> the morning of July 5th 1981.[20]

I then posed the following questions:

1. Do Mr Morrison and Mr Adams agree with this interpretation [in the documents]?
2. If they do, why did they not inform the prison leadership, the hunger strikers, the families, and the Blanketmen who stood in the queue waiting to go on the hunger strike, of this enormous volte-face?
3. How is it that the last six hunger strikers died if there was no fundamental disagreement between the IRA intermediaries [Adams and Morrison] and the British on what constituted a settlement?
4. If Mr Morrison and Mr Adams do not agree with the interpretation in the documents, then why did Mr Morrison 'welcome' them in his April 7th statement?
5. Is Mr Adams ever going to break his silence on the hunger strike?[21]

I do not think that Danny Morrison welcomed my letter; he failed to reply to it.

Seventeen

GEORGE BERNARD SHAW said, 'All great truths begin as blasphemies.'[1] *Blanketmen* may not have exactly fallen into the 'great truth' category when published in 2005, but it was certainly denounced as a blasphemous piece of writing, and its author depicted as a blasphemer, a liar, a slanderer, and a traitor. To a degree, that would change.

The Blanketman whom I had met in the Kennedy Centre in West Belfast in January 2008, Gerard 'Cleaky' Clarke, was giving serious thought to confirming publicly that he had overheard the conversation between Bik and me. If Cleaky were to take that step, it would represent a momentous advance and go a long way to removing any lingering doubts about what occurred on 5 July 1981 on our H-Block wing. It was a big decision for Cleaky and one not to be taken lightly. Like me, he too could be drowned in a tsunami of insults. A mutual friend arranged for us to meet in April 2009.

I had seen Cleaky only twice since our time in the H-Blocks, but we nattered away in a shopping-centre car park in Andersonstown like two long-lost brothers. We reminisced about the boys on our wing who had died on the hunger strike: Bobby, Hurson Boy, 'Barrabas' (Kevin Lynch), and Big Tom McElwee. Even as we mimicked Hurson Boy's favourite saying: 'Jaysus, sure she's a great wee protest,' we knew that there was unfinished business. Cleaky had the look of a man who was still in prison, but it was the prison of his conscience. When he said: 'Depend on me, Ó Rathaigh. You depend on me, mo chara,' I knew that Cleaky would break free from his prison. And he did, at a hunger strike conference in Derry on 23 May 2009.

The lead-up to the conference saw a steady increase in activity. On 21 May I clashed for a second time with the Sinn Féin MLA and former hunger striker Raymond McCartney on BBC Radio Foyle. The set positions were laid out, with me telling of the events of 5 July 1981, and Raymond falling back on his favourite theme, which was that my argument had been 'demolished' by Bik, Danny and others.

I pointed out that Raymond had not been on the prison staff at the time of the hunger strike and was not 'a primary source', therefore he could not actually contribute anything of contemporaneous value to our debate. He seemed taken aback by this, but he recovered quickly and agreed with me. I pressed home the advantage: 'Where's Gerry Adams then? Why's he not here instead of you?'[2]

It was a difficult question to answer.

Having nothing fresh to contribute to the debate, Raymond had no choice but to recite the tedious and monotonous mantras of the past. The most significant of these was that no one on our wing had come forward to say that they had heard the conversation between Bik and me.

Knowing Cleaky was on the verge of disclosure, I said, 'I wouldn't be hanging all my clothes on that line if I was you, Raymond,' adding he would 'soon have egg on his face'.

There was a mixed reaction to my performance. Liam Clarke and Willie Gallagher of the IRSP both thought that I had carried the day. Anthony McIntyre and his wife, Carrie, also felt I had won the debate, but were critical of my aggression during the encounter with McCartney, saying belligerence was no substitute for a calm and rational rebuttal of one's opponent's arguments. They were right, but I have always been passionate about the hunger strike, and if I were to be confronted tomorrow with the same verbal compost McCartney had spewed out, I would be just as forceful.

Word had been sent to me that some members of Joe McDonnell's family wanted to see Willie Gallagher and me. Willie had arranged that we would meet them in their home in Belfast a few hours after my BBC radio debate with Raymond McCartney.

I was tense. This would be my first time to meet any family members and I did not know what to expect. Would they be prepared to open their minds to an alternative history of the hunger strike? They had been fed a hotchpotch of propaganda for twenty-eight years, so who could blame them if they were doubtful of my version of the hunger strike? What form of words would persuade them that I – rather than Adams, Morrison and McFarlane – was telling the truth? In the end there was only one form of words that mattered: the facts as I knew them to be.

Joe's sister and brother, Maura and Hugo McDonnell, were waiting on us in their Andersonstown home. I sensed a warmth the minute I came in the door, and that told me they knew this would be difficult for me too. I was offered tea, which I declined, preferring water. We then got straight down to business.

Maura appeared to be as apprehensive as me. She started by saying that, no matter how painful, the family wanted to know the truth about Joe's death.

We all did, I said. In a matter-of-fact manner I told them of how I had first met Joe on the *Maidstone* prison ship in March 1972, and of how we had been released from internment that year, only to both be reinterned in 1973. I outlined how we had ended up together again in the same hut in Cage 3 of Long Kesh, saying I regarded Joe as a friend, as well as a comrade. Then I went through the events of 5 July 1981.

Both Maura and Hugo listened intently and courteously. At the end Maura asked me why I had waited twenty-four years to write my book.

I replied that I would have preferred it if someone else had put pen to paper, but no one else with the intimate knowledge of what had really happened was going to do that, so I felt that I had no choice but to step into the breach.

But why did I wait twenty-four years?

I said I had been warned that I would be shot if I revealed what I knew about the hunger strike, and I had heeded that warning. I went on to explain that I felt that the political climate had changed and that, consequently, the threat against me had diminished. Maura was satisfied with my answer.

After I had finished answering Maura's questions, it was Willie's turn.

He said he had been charged by the IRSP to investigate the matters raised by me in *Blanketmen*. He admitted that he had been 'highly sceptical' of my position at the start of his investigation, but had since become convinced that I was telling the truth. Willie was adamant that neither of the INLA hunger strikers, Kevin Lynch and Micky Devine, had been made aware of the Mountain Climber offer. He said he had met everyone who had been on the 1981 INLA Army Council and not one of them had been told of the offer, either by the IRA, or by their own hunger strikers. Each of the 1981 INLA leaders told him that they would have ordered their volunteers to accept the offer had they known of it. Finally, Willie made references to the Downing Street documents, something Maura and Hugo did not seem to know much about.

After the meeting I tried to examine what had happened. My impression of the Clan McDonnell was that they were decent, down-to-earth people. Like Joe, they would be a formidable force if they thought they had been deceived.

Later that day Willie phoned me to say Cleaky Clarke was

definitely going to the Derry hunger strike conference in two days' time and that after speaking to him he was convinced that Cleaky's baptism of fire – his standing up and being counted – was almost upon him. I hoped others would follow suit.

I received another phone call from John Cassidy of Republican Network for Unity, the group organizing the Derry hunger-strike conference, telling me that Brendan Duddy, the Mountain Climber, would be attending, and that he had said he wanted to 'give the families some closure'.[4] Such a noble sentiment, and one with which I was in full agreement, but coming from the Mountain Climber, it sounded portentous, even exorbitant. How, for example, could Brendan Duddy possibly achieve that goal without endorsing the Morrison–McFarlane line? Alternatively, how could he say that my account was accurate without causing uproar? I had no doubt all involved wanted to give the families and the Blanketmen some closure, but that could never happen if the primacy of truth was to be conveniently set aside, and it struck me that, given Duddy's central role as an interlocutor in both the hunger strike and the peace process, his natural instinct would preclude him from doing or saying anything that might deconstruct a lifetime of fruitful peace-and-reconciliation-work.

Unlike Raymond McCartney, though, Brendan Duddy was a primary source, and an important one at that; his account of the communications between the committee and the British government would be closely studied by the parties in this dispute. I reckoned that I would get only one chance to question Brendan at this conference, and I would have to make it tell.

Liam Clarke emailed me a copy of his latest offering from the Freedom of Information Office – the Mountain Climber offer. He said he intended to introduce it at the Derry conference. The heading at the top of the page was revealing: 'Statement by the Secretary of State for Northern Ireland.' Was *this* what the Mountain Climber had passed to Gerry Adams and Danny Morrison on 5 July 1981? In the twenty-eight years since my ten comrades had died on hunger strike, I had never seen or heard of this document before Clarke had emailed it to me, and now that it was in front of me I was dumbfounded. Why had this document not been smuggled into the Long Kesh/Maze prison for the hunger strikers or the prison leadership to assess? Did someone or some body of people forget to send it in to us? Who took the decision to withhold this crucial statement from the prisoners? Whoever did wanted to keep us prisoners in ignorance of what was truly transpiring with the British. What motivated those who decided to hide this detailed communiqué from us?

When I eventually got around to studying the offer, I realized that it was almost exactly how I had described it in *Blanketmen*.[5]

All in all, I thought the ground had been well prepared, and I was not in the slightest bit perturbed that Morrison, McFarlane and Adams had declined to attend the conference. It spoke volumes about their inability to defend their position.

Eighteen

IT'S PLEASANT to drive from Belfast to Derry on a balmy Saturday night in May. On the way is Toomebridge. Going through it I can always hear the late, great Tommy Makem singing 'Roddy McCorley goes to die on the bridge of Toome today'. Colm Scullion had a great affinity with 'Young Rodaí', as he called him, probably because the United Irishman had hidden from English redcoats in Scull's native townland of Bellaghy during the 1798 Rebellion. Then it's over the Glenshane Pass, with its verdant and rusty heather, gurgling waterfalls and nimble-footed sheep. After that comes the village of Dungiven, where hunger striker Kevin Lynch was reared. *There was a man.*

Finally Derry, city of the thirteen Protestant apprentice boys who in 1688 closed the city's gates on 1200 'Redshanks', soldiers of the Earl of Antrim loyal to King James II (an action that provoked the 105-day Siege of Derry).

The conference where I was to speak was scheduled to take place in the Gasyard Centre in Derry. It was being run by the non-violent and leftist Republican Network for Unity, an organization made up of ex-prisoners and other republicans who opposed the Sinn Féin party. The motion for debate was: 'What is the truth behind the hunger strike?'

I met Willie Gallagher and Thomas 'Dixie' Elliott, a Blanketman who had been on our wing during the hunger strike. Dixie might not have been large in stature at the time of the protest, but what he lacked in size, he more than made up for with heart. He had once been a cellmate of Bobby Sands.

At the Gasyard Centre I met old comrades whom I had not seen for years, particularly Davy Glennon and Jim Gallagher.

The atmosphere was tense, but I had few nerves. Before the conference began, I briefly spoke to Brendan Duddy. He looked rather frail, with his ruddy face, gold-rimmed glasses, thin frame, and once-ginger, now greying, hair. Still, for a 73-year-old he seemed remarkably fresh (all that long-distance running and mountain-climbing must have stood by him). The successful hotelier and publican was quite a character. An affirmed pacifist, his commitment to non-violence had been strong enough to see him fill the demanding role of interlocutor between those giants of Irish history, the IRA and the British government. He reiterated to me what he had told John Cassidy: he hoped that by attending the conference he could give the families some 'closure'. We all shared his hope.

It was only when the five panellists took their seats on the stage that I saw how packed the hall was. There was standing room only at the back and sides of the hall, with perhaps three hundred people in attendance.

The indomitable *Maidstone* escaper Tommy Gorman chaired and opened the proceedings, and Willie Gallagher was the first to speak. Willie read from a prepared paper that outlined how the IRSP leadership had been asked by the families of their hunger strikers to investigate the claims I had made in *Blanketmen*. He told the attentive audience that the IRSP had been reluctant to accept my claims, but that after a period they became convinced that my account was accurate. Then Willie gave some quotes from an anonymous Blanketman about what he had witnessed on 5 July 1981. Willie mentioned speaking to several Blanketmen, one of whom said, 'I can verify it; it fuckin' happened: I don't want anything to do with it. It did happen. O'Rawe's tellin' the truth.'

Willie also referred to a conversation he had had with another Blanketman (Cleaky Clarke) two days after Easter Sunday, who told him that he too had heard the conversation between Bik and me.

Next up was Gerard Hodgkins. The ex-hunger striker related how he had opposed my account at first, even going as far as to write a letter to *The Irish News* in 2006 rubbishing my version of events. Then things changed when he heard me speak at the Dungloe debate in October 2008. Hodgies said that the more he looked at the opposing arguments in the intervening months, the more he had been inclined to believe me, while dismissing the views of Danny, Bik, Jim Gibney and Laurence McKeown. His view was that 'The genie was out of the bottle,'[1] and he requested full disclosure of the facts and an independent republican inquiry into the hunger strike. Here, Hodgies was echoing a call I had made at the Donegal debate.

Following Hodgies was Brendan Duddy, the Mountain Climber. At last!

Brendan did not look comfortable in front of so many people, and that was understandable, given that of necessity he had been a man with no shadow, a ghost who whispered in the ears of spooks and revolutionaries. Through him, communications had been passed that may have had the potential to save the lives of the last six hunger strikers, and that reality meant that Duddy was a veritable reservoir of information. The question was: did he want to open the floodgates and risk drowning those leaders with whom he had undoubtedly built up a rapport over the years? If he really did wish to give finality to the families, then he would have to abandon all thoughts of rationing the facts to save other people's blushes. I suspected that he was not ready to do that.

The Mountain Climber started by saying that Margaret Thatcher did not have any understanding of, nor did she care about, the fate of republican hunger strikers in Irish prisons, or in English ones for that matter.

Brendan Duddy then assiduously described his role in the hunger strike, stressing that his job had been to facilitate contact between the opposing parties and not to give opinion on any aspect of the communications. He said that he could not speak for the 'Provisional IRA, past or present'.[2] Like the MI6 agent, Michael Oatley, Duddy spoke of how the 18 December document had had the potential to end the blanket protest.

Was this a portent of where Brendan Duddy wanted to take this debate? If so, I reckoned that he would be the architect of his own sorrows when it came to answering questions from the floor of the hall.

Brendan's optimistic, perhaps naive view of the 18 December document prompted Tony O'Hara, brother of the dead hunger striker Patsy O'Hara, to interrupt Duddy and describe how Bobby Sands had visited Patsy's H-Block cell on the night the first hunger strike had ended, 18 December 1980 (Patsy had been OC of the INLA Blanketmen at that time). According to Tony, Patsy had told him that Bobby was very open about the fact that the hunger strike had failed and that we had got nothing from it. Patsy apparently then informed Bobby that the INLA prisoners intended to go on another hunger strike with or without their IRA comrades.

When Tony finished, an impromptu question-and-answer session followed, with Brendan Duddy very much in the cross-hairs. There was no mistaking the strength of the anger being voiced, particularly because the INLA leadership of 1981 had been excluded from the secret Mountain Climber process. This animosity was understandable, given that INLA volunteers Kevin Lynch and Micky Devine had been amongst the six controversial hunger strike deaths. Yet I was uncomfortable with the criticism being directed at Brendan Duddy, believing it to be misplaced: it was Adams and Morrison to whom most of the antagonism should have been directed but, shrewdly enough, they had not taken up their invitations to speak at the conference, and the beleaguered linkman had. Even when the chairperson of the conference, Tommy Gorman, reminded people that other panellists were waiting to speak, there were still mutterings of discontent. I felt obliged to come in and defend the veteran Derry negotiator.

I pointed out that he had been only 'a bridging tool' between the IRA and the British government, and that his sole reason for getting involved in the first place had been to save the lives of hunger strikers. I think this cooled people down a bit – albeit temporarily.

When Brendan finished, it was Liam Clarke's turn to speak. Liam produced fresh documents he had received from the Freedom of Information Office. One of these was dated 2 December 1980 (during the first hunger strike). Written by a British bureaucrat, this was a discussion paper that outlined best- and worst-case hunger-strike scenarios. In the worst case (presumably after an unspecified amount of deaths in the prison), the author envisaged major concessions to the prisoners, including all prisoners being permitted to wear their own clothes, segregation from loyalists, an education-based work regime, the restoration of letters and parcels, and the return of a quantity of lost remission.

After that, Liam posed some questions to Brendan Duddy, one of which was whether or not he had given the Provisional IRA an offer from the British government. Duddy replied, 'I delivered a communication from the British government saying what they would do in the event of the ending of the hunger strike on the 5th of July.'[3]

Pressed by Clarke, Duddy confirmed he had received the communication over the telephone, and that he had written down, word for word, what the British had offered. He then gave the communication to a senior republican. He stressed that there had been no direct communication between the parties.

Then Liam produced a copy of the 5 July offer, which Danny Morrison had verbally conveyed to Bik McFarlane in the prison hospital. He read it out:

Statement by the Secretary of State for Northern Ireland

1. In the light of discussions which Mr Michael Alison has had recently with the Irish Commission for Justice and Peace, during which a statement was issued on 4 July on behalf of the protesting prisoners in the Maze prison, HMG has come to the following conclusions.

2. When the hunger strike and the protest is brought to an end (and not before), the government will:

> 1. extend to all male prisoners in Northern Ireland the clothing regime at present available to female prisoners in Armagh Prison (i.e. subject to the prison governor's approval);
>
> 2. make available to all prisoners in Northern Ireland the allowance of letters, parcels, and visits at present available to conforming prisoners;
>
> 3. allow the restoration of forfeited remission at the discretion of the responsible disciplinary authority, as indicated in my statement of 30 June, which hitherto has meant the restoration of up to one-fifth of remission lost subject to a satisfactory period of good behaviour;
>
> 4. ensure that a substantial part of the work will consist of domestic tasks inside and outside the wings necessary for servicing of the prison (such as cleaning and in the laundries and kitchens), construction work, i.e. on building projects or making toys for charitable bodies, and study for Open University or other courses. The prison authorities will be responsible for supervision. The aim of the authorities will be that prisoners should do the kinds of work for which they are suited, but this will not always be possible and the authorities will retain responsibility for decisions about allocation.

3. Little advance is possible on association. It will be permitted within each wing under supervision of the prison staff.

4. Protesting prisoners have been segregated from the rest. Other prisoners are not segregated by religious or any other affiliation. If there were no protest the only reason for segregating some prisoners from others would be the judgment of the prison authorities, not the prisoners. This would be the best way to avoid trouble between groups.

5. This statement is not a negotiating position. But it is further evidence of the government's desire to maintain and where possible to improve a humanitarian regime in the prisons. The government earnestly hopes that the hunger strikers and the other prisoners will cease their protest.[4]

Clarke then asked Duddy if what he had just read out had been the same statement. He replied, 'I think that is a fair version of what's true.'[5]

Here for the first time, we had the Mountain Climber authenticating the British government's offer. Not only that, it was almost a carbon copy of what I had outlined in *Blanketmen* – more than four years earlier.

This conference was turning out to be more than just another skirmish; it was becoming a Gettysburg for the hunger-strike committee.

Nineteen

EVEN THOUGH I had nothing written down, I knew what I wanted to say when it came my turn to speak.

I began by thanking Liam Clarke and Brendan Duddy for attending the conference. Unlike Hodgies, Tommy Gorman, Willie Gallagher or me, these men were not Blanketmen; they had everything to lose and little to gain by being present.

Taking the audience through the events of 5 July, I said Bik and I had accepted the offer, stressing it would have been 'insane' to do otherwise, given that Joe McDonnell was critically ill, and there were seven other hunger strikers whose lives hung in the balance. Then I made reference to Gerry Adams's comm to the prison leadership saying 'more was needed'. Next I examined the ending of the first hunger strike in 1980.

For some reason Brendan Duddy seemed to think that the 18 December document contained a settlement, although he admitted that he had never read it. While it was not my intention to embarrass the man (whom I had instantly taken to when we shook hands for the first time earlier that evening), it was nonetheless incumbent on me to put the record straight. 'There was no deal,' I said, 'and every Blanketman knew it, because Bob

[Bobby Sands] told us there was no deal.'[1] I then relayed how there had been about 350 Blanketmen on the protest at the end of the first hunger strike, and that each and every one of us was told to go out on our monthly visits with a 'smile on our faces – which we did – but in our hearts we were wrecked; wrecked for the boys on hunger strike, but wrecked for ourselves too, 'cause it seemed we were never getting off this thing [the protest]'.[2]

After that, I asked Brendan Duddy if he minded me putting a few questions to him, and he generously replied that he was there to help in any way he could. Going straight to the Downing Street documents, I asked him to comment on the phrase, 'they [the IRA] did not regard it [the Mountain Climber offer] as satisfactory and ... they wanted a good deal more'.[3]

'I think that's a fair version of what's true, yes,' he replied.[4] He later repeated that: 'The reply [from the IRA] to the best of my memory and knowledge was that more had to be added.'[5]

I then enquired about the sentence, 'it was not the content of the message [offer] which they had objected to but only the tone'.[6] Brendan Duddy was quick to answer: 'When I first read that I said: "Where the hell did that come from?" I never heard the word "tone" ever being mentioned in any direction.'[7]

Brendan Duddy later confirmed that he had not been informed of the prison leadership's attitude to the offer.

I needed to be certain that the 5 July offer had never been acceptable to the committee, and on this point Brendan said, 'I never heard anything to suggest that the offer was acceptable.'[8]

After I had finished, Tommy Gorman asked for questions from the floor. Again, these were invariably directed at Duddy, most coming from former or present members of the IRSP. Their anger was palpable and the probing hostile: why had Duddy not consulted with the INLA Army Council on the offer?

Duddy offered – with justification – that he would not have had an opportunity to try to save any lives if he had broken the confidence of the IRA and the British government.

Who selected him for the job of interlocutor?

The interlocutor replied that he had created the role for himself, that he had always believed that the political violence in the North of Ireland was futile, and that consequently he felt conscience-bound to do all in his power to bring the principal antagonists together in order to try to reach a settlement and thus save lives.

If I had liked Brendan Duddy before the conference, I liked him more after that. Under a barrage of criticism, he held to his beliefs. It was to his credit that he stayed to the end of the conference.

There was complete silence when one former INLA leader, Tommy McCourt, rose to describe how he had visited Micky Devine a week before the hunger striker had died. McCourt said that he had bluntly told Micky that the prisoners would not get their five demands. He advised Micky that if he wanted to come off the fast, the INLA would fully support him, but that they 'did not order him on to it, and they could not order him off'.[9] Micky had been adamant, McCourt said; he was staying put, and he changed the conversation to the subject of his funeral arrangements. McCourt finished by saying that he was certain that Micky would have told him if he had known the details of the Mountain Climber's offer, and he was also definite that the INLA leadership would have instructed their men to accept it. For a few seconds, everybody was stunned at Tommy's poignant recollection of his last moments with Micky; it was as if we were having trouble returning to 2009 having time-travelled back to 1981, to the hospital wing in Long Kesh/Maze, where Red Mick Devine lay dying, with Tommy McCourt by his side, supporting him.

Another breakthrough was pending; this time it was Cleaky Clarke. When Brendan Duddy had finished, a megaphone was handed to Cleaky, who stood at the back of the hall.

He started by saying that he was not there to 'lash Sinn Féin, or anybody else'.[10] He then described how he had been in the leadership wing during the two hunger strikes, and how his cell had been 'adjacent to Richard's and Bik McFarlane's'.[11] He was not supposed to hear the conversation, he said, but 'I confirm what Richard said all along. He is 100 per cent correct.'[12] At this, Cleaky was given a round of applause. He later said, 'I've no doubts that he's [Richard] right in what he says.'[13]

Before the conference ended, Carrie Twomey, Anthony McIntyre's wife, summed up and got universal approval from the panel on what had been agreed:

- Liam Clarke had produced a document that contained a British government offer to end the hunger strike.
- Brendan Duddy had authenticated the document, saying that it was a 'fair version of what's true' of the communication he had given to the outside IRA leadership on 5 July 1981.
- Duddy said that the message that came back from the IRA regarding the offer was that 'more had to be added'.
- Duddy said that at no time did the IRA position change during the hunger strike.
- Gerard 'Cleaky' Clarke confirmed that he had heard the conversation between Bik McFarlane and Richard O'Rawe in which it was clear that we had accepted the Mountain Climber offer.[14]

After the conference I was approached by author Joshua Levine, who asked if I agreed with some commentators that the Mountain Climber offer amounted to four of the five demands. My view was that this was an extravagant claim, but that there had been enough in the offer to honourably terminate the hunger strike. Later, in his excellent book, *Beauty and Atrocity: People, Politics, and Ireland's Fight for Peace*, Levine would write: 'I had spoken to Brendan Duddy at his home, where he had said, in reference to the second hunger strike: "Basically, everything that sorted it out was on the table ... This thing could have been sorted." '[15]

Levine went on to say: 'The corollary of this [Richard O'Rawe's assertion that getting Owen Carron elected may have played a part in the committee's assessments] is that, if one accepts that the Good Friday Agreement was made possible by the republican shift from violence to electoral politics, then the current peace can be traced back to the rejection of the offer and the subsequent deaths of the six hunger strikers.'[16]

I was left feeling weary but exhilarated at the end of the conference. Never in my wildest dreams had I anticipated that it would go so well, or that so much would be achieved. And it had been the meek Brendan Duddy who had proved to be the Howard 'Tutankhamun' Carter of the 1981 hunger strike: the Derry pacifist had unwittingly sledgehammered a hole in the wall of the conventional narrative, and allowed a light to shine into the dark recesses of history. And what treasures had been revealed!

I was upset that Brendan taken such an unwarranted amount of criticism, and I phoned him up the next day to see if he was all right. In a fatherly manner, he advised me to let the hunger-strike business go, and to get on with the rest of my life.

Within hours Brendan phoned me back. He told me that he was about to leave home to go on holiday. His attitude had changed; it was sharp, businesslike. 'Richard, listen to me. I have spoken to people who want this to stop. Do you understand?'

I said that I did, as I reached for a pen to write down what he was about to say to me.

'They are not admitting anything,' he said, 'but they want it to stop. There is a desire for this to be ended, and it is extremely strong. Do you hear what I'm saying?'

I heard what he was saying all right, but I could not help thinking how ironic it was that the Mountain Climber should be bringing messages from the republican leadership to me. I told

Brendan that I would not push the issue in the press, providing 'they' reciprocated, and I specifically mentioned Danny Morrison. Brendan said that Danny would not be saying anything.

So that was it then. A concord between former comrades had been reached. Even as Brendan had phoned me, I was putting the finishing touches to a hard-hitting press release which focused on what he had confirmed and on Cleaky Clarke's admission that he had heard the coversation between Bik and me. Now I had given my word to Brendan to remain silent, I did not send out that statement.

Unfortunately, 'they' did not keep their part of the agreement because the next day a fierce battle broke out on Northern Ireland's foremost political internet site, Slugger O'Toole, and it was alleged that Danny was in the thick of it, trying to limit the damage that had been done at the Gasyard conference. Still, I held off from formally breaking the agreement and did not release my press statement.

On 27 May 2009 I brought Bernadette with me to meet Joe McDonnell's widow, Goretti, in her home in Andersonstown, Belfast. Once again I was warmly welcomed. I found it very humbling to tell Goretti what I knew of the hunger strike.

Eight days later an article in the *Belfast Telegraph* caught my attention. Written by the former BBC Security Editor and author, Brian Rowan, the headline quoted Bik McFarlane as saying that the British 'had no intention of resolving the hunger strikes'.[17] In the accompanying interview Bik went on to accuse 'the then Thatcher government of trying to resolve the prison protest "on its terms" while attempting to "wreck" the IRA in the process'.[18]

I took a deep breath, and looked at the photograph of my deceased comrade and friend, 'The Dark', which hung above my desk. 'What's Bikso playing at, Dorcha?' I asked aloud. I could almost hear The Dark laugh! The whiff of retreat was in the air.

Previously, the obdurate McFarlane had said that there was never any offer 'whatsoever. No offer existed.'[19] He followed that up with, 'There were no concrete proposals whatsoever in relation to a deal.'[20] For four years The Whatsoever Man had defended that absurdity: Danny Morrison had not given him the details of the Mountain Climber offer on 5 July 1981; there had been no conversation between us regarding the Mountain Climber offer.

Now, in one small step for Bik, but one giant leap for just about everyone else, all changed. The *Belfast Telegraph* journalist Brian Rowan reported:

> But he [McFarlane] said he also made clear that more was needed – that the British had to expand the offer [at last!] and they needed to go into the prison hospital.
>
> The man from the outside [Danny Morrison] was allowed in to explain the Mountain Climber contacts and the offer the British had communicated.
>
> And the fact that the British were in contact – albeit through a conduit now known to be the Derry businessman Brendan Duddy – was progress.
>
> After meeting Morrison, McFarlane met the hunger strikers. 'We went through it [the offer] step by step,' he said. 'The hunger strikers themselves said: OK the Brits are prepared to do business – possibly, but what is detailed, or what has been outlined here isn't enough to conclude the hunger strike.
>
> 'And they said to me, what do you think?
>
> 'And I said I concur with your analysis – fair enough – but you need to make your mind up.
>
> 'Something had to be written down. Something had to be produced to the hunger strikers, even to the extent that the British were saying, there it is, nothing more, take it or leave it, and that's the way the lads wanted clarity on this.
>
> 'We were never given a piece of paper,' he added. 'We were never given a piece of paper.'[21]

How right Bik was. But something had certainly been written down by Brendan Duddy on 5 July 1981, although a copy of his text was never smuggled in to the hunger strikers or the prison leadership. As we now know, that something was the initial statement that contained the Mountain Climber offer, which the Secretary of State for Northern Ireland, Humphrey Atkins, proposed to release in the event of the hunger strike ending.

It was refreshing, encouraging even, to see that Bik's amnesia had finally been cured. But had it? Perhaps memory loss had never been his problem? It seemed to me that all would be revealed if Bik revealed all. Alas, he did not do that. Still, something cataclysmic had happened to his memory. What could have produced such an awakening?

Twelve days earlier the hunger strike conference in Derry's Gasyard Centre had occurred. During the debate, Brendan Duddy authenticated a copy of the offer that he had sent to the IRA leadership on 5 July 1981. Was the Mountain Climber verification of his offer the trigger that led to Bik's miraculous memory recovery, or was that coincidental?

As if Bik's realignment with Danny and me with regards to the offer was not enough, he had an even bigger revelation to get off his chest.

In four years I have never budged from my original position:

There had been a conversation between Bik and me, during which we had accepted the offer. Bik had not moved either: there had not been an offer, so logic dictated that there could not have been a conversation about it. Now that he was in full retreat, and was admitting that there had been an offer, this is what he told the journalist regarding the pow-wow in the H-Blocks that he once was adamant had never taken place: 'And I said to Richard [O'Rawe] this is amazing, this is a huge opportunity and I feel there's the potential here [in the Mountain Climber offer] to end this.'[22]

So we did have a conversation about the offer after all! And how close we had come to agreeing the essence of our little tête-à-tête! For example, in *Blanketmen* I had written, 'I was amazed at what they were offering.'[23]

Bik told Brian Rowan that he found the offer 'amazing'.[24]

In my book I recorded our conversation thus: 'I think there's enough there, Bikso.'

Bik replied: 'I agree.'[25]

Bik told Rowan: 'I feel there's a potential here to end this.'[26]

Bik's interview with Rowan was a *de facto* confession that he had stretched the facts and that, if necessary, he could be relied upon to turn the truth on and off like water from a tap. The only thing missing from Bik's soulful unburdening is an explanation as to why he had said that there had been no offer in the first place, and why he had been so vehement in his denials that there had been conversation between us about the Mountain Climber offer. Why Brian Rowan did not ask Bik these crucial questions is a mystery to me.

The former prison OC may still deny that he wrote to Adams relaying our acceptance of the offer, but who, outside the blind and the faithful, would believe him? And how could that hold up? Bik McFarlane had been the ultimate authority in the prison, and here he was now admitting that he thought the 'offer' had the 'potential' to end the hunger strike, effectively concurring with me that there was 'enough there'. Would he not have been duty-bound to write to Adams to acquaint him of our joint acceptance of the offer?

Finally, Bik McFarlane shamelessly told Rowan that the responsibility for the rejection of the offer was the hunger strikers' alone, once again exonerating himself and the committee from any blame. Yet, during the 28 February 2005 BBC *Talk Back* debate between Danny Morrison, him and me, Morrison had said: 'After I had seen the hunger strikers, we all agreed that this [the Mountain Climber offer] could be a resolution, but we wanted it guaranteed.' So, if Morrison is to be believed, the offer was very much alive after he had spoken to the hunger strikers and left the prison hospital, but, according to McFarlane, the hunger strikers had rejected it out of hand. Both accounts cannot be right, although the evidence to date suggests that both can be wrong. Perhaps Bik might have thought twice about laying the blame for the rejection of the Mountain Climber offer so firmly at the door of the hunger strikers had he remembered Danny's words.

This attempt at mass absolution is as transparent as it is pathetic, but, rather than making me feel angry, it makes me feel indescribably sad for my poor comrades who trusted these people with their lives, and who, out of a sense of duty and patriotism, died on the hunger strike. What chance had they of survival when Adams, Morrison and the committee did not pass on to them the document/paper on which Brendan Duddy had written down the offer from the British? As for Bik McFarlane: this man knew that the hunger strikers were at the bottom of the decision-making pyramid, yet it did not deter him from brazenly telling the families that their loved ones had been at the top of it. How dare he place the blame for rejecting the offer onto the dead hunger strikers! How despicable is that when he knows in his heart that it was Adams and the committee who had rejected it?

Never one to lament his own contradictions, McFarlane had simply set aside what he had written to Adams on 28 July 1981: 'I [my italics] told them [the hunger strikers] I could have accepted half measures before Joe died, but I didn't then and wouldn't now.'[27] At no time during the course of this interview with Rowan did Bik McFarlane show any cognizance of turning full circle; neither did he offer any explanation for decommissioning the sacred absolutes of the past. Perhaps he thought nobody would notice.

Twenty

WHERE TO GO after the watershed conference at the Gasyard Centre in Derry, and Bik's visit to the confessional? What was left for me to prove? A lot.

I did not like the idea of Bik and the committee getting away with putting the blame on the hunger strikers for rejecting the Mountain Climber offer. I thought that pretty cowardly compared with the heroism of the ten Spartans who had made the H-Blocks their Thermopylae. The truth was that the struggle was far from over. Besides, others had taken up the cause and committed themselves to getting to the truth about what had happened to their comrades on the hunger strike.

Among this group were Willie Gallagher, Gerard Hodgkins, Dixie Elliot, Cleaky Clarke and a Blanketman from Tyrone called Joe McNulty. Likewise, an internet blogger codenamed 'Rusty Nail' continuously championed the issue on the highly influential Slugger O'Toole website. Rusty Nail was Carrie Twomey, the wife of Anthony McIntyre. Her most bitter opponent was 'Blanketman H3', whom Twomey alleged to have been Danny Morrison, despite the fact that Morrison had never been on the blanket protest.

Not long after Bik's interview with Brian Rowan, Willie Gallagher phoned me to say that the McDonnell family had expected us to come back to them after the Gasyard conference. I was a bit surprised to hear this because I was unaware of any request for a meeting.

On 11 June 2009 Willie Gallagher and I again met the McDonnell family only this time we brought along Cleaky Clarke and another Blanketman with us. There were seven members of the McDonnell family, including Maura and Goretti and her two children, Bernadette and Joseph. Cleaky and the other Blanketman described the atmosphere on the wing, and confirmed that they had heard, word for word, the conversation between Bik and me.

There was a brief discussion about the ending of the first hunger strike, during which we told the McDonnell family that there had not been a deal between the British and the prisoners on 18 December 1980. We also told them that the air of optimism that we portrayed in the immediate aftermath of the strike was manufactured to save the blushes of the republican movement.

Willie presented the family with a fact-pack that included a DVD of the Gasyard conference, a copy of the Mountain Climber offer that journalist Liam Clarke had uncovered, copies of the Freedom of Information Act documents, including the Downing Street letters, a copy of Bik's interview with Brian Rowan, and the report that Willie had delivered at the Derry conference.

All in all, I felt that the presentation, if you could call it that, went well. No one had resorted to exaggeration, and the McDonnells had been attentive and courteous.

I did not feel that it was my place or role to try to influence the family into taking any particular course of action as a result of what had been disclosed during our meeting, and I made that clear to them.

That night I had a chance to take stock on where *Blanketmen* had taken me in the four years since its publication. After the initial blizzard of criticism and the icy reception I had received, I was finding that more and more people were going out of their way to contact me or stop me in the street, saying that they believed what I had written was true. A cousin of mine said to Anthony McIntyre after the Derry conference: 'Everybody thought the Richard fella was bonkers when his book came out. They don't think he's so bonkers now.' Undoubtedly there has been a tidal change in public opinion because of fresh evidence recently uncovered. Some influential writers had expressed the view to me that Danny and Bik were the authors of their own misfortune, that their belligerence was their undoing.

Now the balance of probability had swung so dramatically in my favour that I reckoned the committee would be worried about the way the hunger strike debate was going. How could it not be? A copy of the Mountain Climber offer made public after being hidden away for twenty-eight years? The Mountain Climber confirming his offer, and saying that he had relayed it to the IRA on 5 July 1981? Letters from 10 Downing Street saying that the IRA committee's response had been that 'they wanted a good deal more'?[1] Blanketmen coming out to affirm that they heard the conversation between Bik and me? Bik's collapse, to the point where there was barely a cat's whisker separating his newly acquired evaluation of the Mountain Climber offer, and my own, as outlined in *Blanketmen*?

However, I underestimated the innate powers of survival and the ringcraft of Adams and those around him. It never occured to me for a second that they could turn the situation around, but they did, and they did it in such a way that they came out, not exactly smelling of roses, but at least without the stench of surrender in their nostrils.

The soft underbelly of the hunger strike debate was always the families of the hunger strikers. Again and again, Danny and Bik had invoked their authority to attack me; that told me that they had a good relationship with the families and were very confident that they had their support. I had never been asked to explain my position to any of the hunger strikers' relatives until I was approached to meet the McDonnells. After that initial meeting on 21 May, Willie Gallagher indicated to me that some of the McDonnells were contemplating going to the hunger-strike conference in Derry's Gasyard Centre. I later found out that a member of Sinn Féin had approached them and urged them not to attend, that a more important gathering was being planned for June by the Sinn Féin leadership.

I envisaged a public meeting along the lines of the Gasyard conference, but it did not appear that that was what the committee had in mind. Then Willie phoned me to say that Gerry Adams had invited all the families to a private meeting on 17 June and that Bik McFarlane and Danny Morrison would also be in attendance. According to a letter from Adams, the meeting had been called in response to a request from some family members who had expressed concerns about the continuing controversy.

This event reeked of a set-up. If a family or two had voiced unease at the issues I had raised, Adams, McFarlane and Morrison could have visited them privately, but they did not take that option; instead, they had called a meeting of the families. This reinforced my previous suspicion (when the McDonnells had been urged not to attend the Gasyard conference) that they were thinking tactically. Willie Gallagher informed me that Sinn Féin in Belfast had made it clear to him that no one, except relatives, would be allowed to attend the meeting. The triumvirate wanted a clear run at those families, with no one from the opposite camp about the place.

My instinct told me that I could look forward to some kind of statement of censure at the end of the meeting.

On 17 June 2009 in Gulladuff community hall in south Derry, some of the families of ten dead hunger strikers met Gerry Adams, Danny Morrison and Bik McFarlane. The Hughes, McCreesh, O'Hara, McDonnell, Hurson, Doherty, McElwee and Devine families were represented. The Sands and Lynch families were absent.

I did not think it appropriate for me to go to Gulladuff. Some friends and Blanketmen did travel to the venue, however. Outside the hall in which the meeting was taking place were former hunger striker Gerard 'Hodgies' Hodgkins, Jimmy Dempsey, whose sixteen-year-old son, John, had been shot dead by a British soldier hours after Joe McDonnell's death, and Willie Gallagher and Carrie Twomey, both of whom Tony O'Hara and Michael Devine junior had selected to be their advocates at the meeting. When these republicans tried to gain admittance to the meeting, Danny Morrison closed the door in their faces. According to Twomey, Morrison said that they were not wanted, and that they had had their chance to speak to the families at the Gasyard conference and that the families had chosen not to attend. No one was to be allowed to get in the way of the committee's strategic imperative of getting the families to fall into line.

A family member who had attended the meeting later gave me a run-down on what was said. Nothing was presented to counter the new evidence that had come to light at the Gasyard conference, he said. Instead, it was a back-stabbing session of epic proportions – with my back being the biggest target of all.

The family member told me that Danny Morrison's dagger was the sharpest. Apparently Morrison resurrected the beaten-down arguments of old: I had written the book for money; not once during all the years since my release from prison had I mentioned my reservations to him. He even produced the press statements I had written during the hunger strike on behalf of the prisoners, and presented them to the families as my personal 'comms'. In case anyone in the hall should retain a modicum of respect for me, he said he would not sit in the same room as Richard O'Rawe, 'the man who accused me of murdering six hunger strikers'.

That was the tone of the meeting; I was demonized, and described as a 'liar' and a 'scumbag' amongst other things.

I had anticipated that there would be a motion of censure of some sort coming my way, and such a motion was proposed, but there was no show of hands and it did not pass.

Adams put the controversy down to a conspiracy theory, and asked some family members: 'Do you think I killed the hunger strikers?' He was entitled to ask that question given how central he was to the controversy, but how could any of the families have possibly said 'Yes'? Faced with this gathering of emotionally scarred people, Adams's question was designed to evoke sympathy. I would have been surprised if it had not achieved its objectives.

Then I was told that Bik had been close to breaking down as he said that it had been the hunger strikers, not he, and not Adams, who had told the British they 'wanted a good deal more'.

If Adams's less-than-subtle appeal did not quite strike the right chord, and McFarlane's theatrics did not hasten a heart-wrenching meltdown, Morrison's penchant for histrionics and weaving and bobbing did.

The meeting ended amid emotional scenes, with some family members openly weeping as they left the hall. This was terrible news. Had I generated such misery amongst these poor people? Was I partly responsible for this distress? There was no resistance to that thought in my mind. I went to bed in a state of moral and mental collapse, and wallowed in self-deprecation.

Only the next day did I recover when I heard how much these three men had stirred up the families during their meeting. The contrast between these guys' approach to the families, and mine and Willie's could not have been starker.

We had met members of the McDonnell, O'Hara and Devine families and presented our position in an honest, no-frills manner. We had brought along Blanketmen who affirmed that they heard the acceptance conversation between Bik McFarlane and me. Questions were asked and answered. The families gave no indication that they were dissatisfied with the answers. Willie gave each family a DVD of the Gasyard conference and a fact-pack. No person or political party was vilified. It was emphasized to each family that it was up to them what they did with the information we had given them.

There were no tears.

Twenty-one

ON THE FACE of it, Adams, Morrison and McFarlane were in trouble. They had come away from the Gulladuff meeting without a motion of censure against those of us who were searching for the truth about the deaths of our hunger strike comrades. That was a dreadful result, given their carefully constructed, 28-year relationship with the families. Had all that contrivance and hand-wringing been for nothing and those crocodile tears wasted? Well, no.

The Lynch family, who did not send a representative to the meeting, sent word that they would support the call for an end to any further investigation into how the hunger strike was handled. That, when added to the fact that six of the eight families at Gulladuff also wanted an end to our investigation, would have been very encouraging for the three politicos. These leaders could build on that, although what they really needed was a plausible excuse to draw up a statement signed by the seven families who supported a call for us to be muzzled. That excuse presented itself when Willie Gallagher posted an inaccurate account of the meeting on the IRSP website, saying, amongst other things, that Michael Devine junior had stormed out after being shouted down. As soon as Willie was made aware of his factual errors, he removed them from the website, but by then it was too late. Someone else had spotted it.

Willie phoned me up to tell me that the families' statement had been posted on the pro-committee, Bobby Sands website. He blamed himself for allowing the committee to get out their message. It was misplaced guilt because this statement would have found its way into the media whether Willie had inadvertently had a hand in it or not; its publication was the real reason why Gerry Adams had invited the families to the meeting in the first place.

Riding on the wings of Willie's mistake, members of Sinn Féin were dispatched to the families throughout the North to inform them of his misleading description of the Gulladuff meeting. Fortuitously, the Sinn Féin members had come armed with a ready-made rebuttal of Willie's internet post, which, unsurprisingly, also included the statement of censure of Willie and me that had not been passed at the meeting. As expected, the seven pro-committee families signed the statement. The O'Hara and Devine families did not; neither did the Sands family.

While the statement was released within hours of being signed by the families, it soon appeared in Sinn Féin publications throughout Belfast and other parts of the North, under the headline, 'Hunger Strikers' families hurt by false and offensive allegations'. The 19 June statement read:

> Wednesday evening's meeting was a very emotional and difficult occasion for all of us, particularly in light of the allegations coming from Richard O'Rawe and the IRSP. All the family members who spoke, with the exception of Tony O'Hara, expressed deep anger and frustration at the ongoing allegations created by O'Rawe.
>
> Tony O'Hara's suggestion that we should meet with Richard O'Rawe and Willie Gallagher got no support and we asked Tony to express to Richard O'Rawe and Willie Gallagher our

wish for them to stop what they are doing and give us peace of mind.

The account of the meeting published by Willie Gallagher is inaccurate and offensive.

Our loved ones made the supreme sacrifice on hunger strike for their comrades. They were not dupes. They were dedicated and committed republicans. We are clear that it was the British government which refused to negotiate and refused to concede their just demands.

The seven families' statement had been crafted by someone of exceptional cunning. Its relevance lay not in safeguarding the families but in protecting the committee's backs; it was, in effect, their oblique invocation of the spirit of the Fifth Amendment, refusing to answer any further questions on the hunger strike on the grounds that it might incriminate them.

When looked at, what had been omitted was as revealing as what had been admitted. It said, for example, 'Tony O'Hara's suggestion that we should meet with Richard O'Rawe and Willie Gallagher got no support …'[1] Tony told me that there was no show of hands on his suggestion, or any other suggestion for that matter.[2] The statement does not register Tony's proposal that Adams, Morrison and McFarlane should support a public inquiry into the hunger strike, nor does it reveal that his words were met with stony silence.

It must surely have crossed some of the families' minds that there was a reason why these men wanted to avoid an inquiry. Surely someone in that hall was thinking: What are you boys hiding? A family member who signed the statement against us was later heard to say: 'Something terrible happened here, but I don't want to know about it.' If only it was that simple.

Following the publication of the Sinn Féin-sponsored statement, the O'Hara and Devine families issued a statement of their own on 30 June:

We, the families of hunger strikers Patsy O'Hara and Michael Devine, support the call by former hunger striker Gerard Hodgkins for an independent inquiry into the 1981 hunger strike.

We cannot understand why any republican would have anything to fear from such an inquiry, or why they would not support it.

The Gulladuff meeting between the Sinn Féin leadership and eight of the hunger strikers' families was very emotional, and we were not unaffected. However, at that meeting, the Sinn Féin delegation refused our request for an independent inquiry. Why?

We call on Gerry Adams, Danny Morrison, Bik McFarlane and Richard O'Rawe to publicly support our call for an independent inquiry. We call on each of these principals to submit themselves to a judicial process, which would include not only giving evidence but cross-examination. Only then, and not before, will any of the hunger striker families get to the truth about what happened to our loved ones. [3]

This was a very strong statement, and particularly embarrassing for Adams, Morrison and McFarlane. How could they justify rejecting the call for an independent inquiry without looking like men with dirty secrets? It was not as if Sinn Féin had an aversion to independent inquiries: they had called for independent inquiries on numerous occasions during the conflict, most noticeably over the loyalist murders of the human rights solicitors Pat Finucane and Rosemary Nelson. Why not support these families in their call for an inquiry?

In answer to the statement requesting me to stop probing into the committee's handling of the hunger strike, and the O'Hara/Devine one calling on Adams, Morrison, McFarlane and me to respond positively to their demand for an independent inquiry, I issued a reply:

Following a call from the families of Patsy O'Hara and Micky Devine to Gerry Adams, Danny Morrison, Bik McFarlane and myself to support an independent inquiry into the 1981 hunger strike in the *Derry Journal*, 30 June 2009, I wish it to be known that I pledge my full support for such an inquiry. I am prepared to give evidence, and submit myself to cross-examination, in order to hopefully get to the full facts of what happened during the hunger strike. It is my fervent hope that the three republicans mentioned by the O'Hara and Devine families pledge their support also.[4]

The three republicans did not respond. Instead, the Sinn Féin leadership spent the summer trying to repair the damage done at the Gasyard conference in Derry by holding meetings with their supporters and assuring them that the leadership's hands were clean.

The party also distributed in nationalist areas leaflets that contained the Gulladuff families' statement. Commenting on this, an unnamed Sinn Féin member wrote: 'Families of those IRA and INLA Volunteers who died during the 1981 Hunger Strike have issued a statement condemning those who have relentlessly hurt them by making false allegations that their loved ones died needlessly.'

The more I looked at that sentence, the more I suspected that its author had also composed the families' statement. I first read the leaflets when I picked up one that was thrown over our front gate in the middle of the night. The contents did not particularly annoy me, but what did jar was hearing that some of my former comrades and good friends had handed them out in Ballymurphy. Some of these men had often listened to me complaining about the way in which the outside leadership had conducted the hunger strike. These men *knew* me; they knew I was telling the truth, but it did not matter. What did matter was that Gerry Adams and his committee were losing the hunger-strike debate and they needed their troops to fall in behind them. The problem with this is that a few can lead all to ignominy.

Twenty-two

THE CARIBBEAN-AMERICAN author and poet Audre Lorde wrote in 1984, 'Your silence will not protect you.' I am not sure that is strictly true: the Royal Ulster Constabulary and the British army had arrested me dozens of times when I was an IRA volunteer, and I always found that keeping my mouth shut was a more rewarding policy than talking. I have no doubt a younger Gerry Adams would have shared that sentiment with me. Perhaps he still found succour in silence because for over four years he had doggedly resisted the temptation to enter the hunger-strike argument. But could he keep this up, especially when *The Irish News* had indicated it was running a multi-page hunger strike special edition some time in July/August 2009? Part of me felt that there was still fire in the Big Lad's blood; perhaps he would deliver an intellectual *coup de grâce* by submitting an article of such passion and prose that I, and his other opponents, would wither before his brilliance.

I sent my 800-word article to *The Irish News* in early July. It contained little that was new, but I spent time ensuring that I had all angles covered. Then I waited for the big day ... and waited ...

Word got back to me that the Irish taoiseach at the time of the 1981 hunger strike, Dr Garret FitzGerald, had agreed to be interviewed, but that he was abroad, and so the date of the special edition was delayed. The 83-year-old FitzGerald was known for his anti-IRA stance while in office, and if he were to support my position, my opponents would say here was an anti-republican agenda. However, FitzGerald had been democratically elected as taoiseach in the June 1981 election, and as such he was an important figure in the hunger-strike story.

I also heard that Gerry Adams was on holiday for three weeks and could not be disturbed. Rumours abounded; the paper wanted to conduct an interview with Adams, but he was opposing this, preferring instead to offer a platform piece; Danny Morrison and Laurence McKeown had contributed articles; Bik McFarlane did not intend to comment.

In July the sun blinked before going into its autumnal hibernation. In August it never stopped raining. The committee members, and the clever fellows who would've been advising them, wouldn't be too concerned; they had heavy weather of their own with which to contend. The question was: would they mount a defence?

On 28 September 2009 I was up and out at 5.30 am to buy the first part of *The Irish News'* two-day special edition. During the previous week, the paper had announced that Martin McGuinness, Dr Garret FitzGerald, Laurence McKeown, Hugh Logue, and I would be submitting articles. There was no mention of Adams, Morrison or McFarlane. What was going on? Was the committee's B team being made ready? It seemed that Martin McGuinness had decided to try his hand at staunching the haemorrhage. Perhaps he had something, maybe a manuscript or a document of great evidential value, which would disprove everything I had said?

Still, Martin McGuinness's involvement was strange. The Deputy First Minister at Stormont had said nothing of substance about the hunger strike before.

The newspaper's headline read: 'The hunger strike: was there a deal?' and Dr Garret FitzGerald was the first contributor. Dr FitzGerald had received his seal of office from President Hillery only five days before the Mountain Climber offer was made. He said that the Irish government had had a mole in the H-Blocks: 'They [the prisoners] were keen to accept that [the ICJP offer]. We knew that. We had our sources within the prison. As well as the commission [ICJP], we knew something was happening in the prison from other sources.'[1] FitzGerald felt that if the British had not made contact with the IRA committee through the Mountain Climber, a deal could have been concluded on the basis of the ICJP offer. FitzGerald admitted that the hunger strike had led directly to the Anglo-Irish Agreement of 1985, which was a pact between the London and Dublin governments designed to counter the political rise of Sinn Féin since the ending of the fast. He went on: 'O'Rawe's account seems to me to be, within his framework of knowledge, honest and accurate.'[2] Finally he said that he would co-operate with any official inquiry, but he did not think that the leadership of the IRA would provide an accurate account of what had taken place.

Martin McGuinness's article was peppered with the usual indignation and innuendo, but he did admit for the first time that it was he who had received the British offer from Brendan Duddy on 5 July 1981, and who had relayed it by telephone to Gerry Adams in Belfast: 'Out of the five demands the only thing the British were offering to the hunger strikers after four men had died was that they could wear their own clothes.'[3] This assessment was a long way from Bik McFarlane's appraisal, given in the *Belfast Telegraph* to reporter Brian Rowan on 4 June 2009 when he described the offer as 'amazing', adding that 'this is a huge opportunity and I feel there's the potential here [in the Mountain Climber offer] to end this.'[4]

When the hunger-strike controversy first erupted in 2005, Laurence McKeown responded with a series of polemics as poisonous as they were hateful. His *Irish News* article was more of the same. He began by labelling anyone who questioned the committee's version of events as 'an assortment of disaffected former members of the republican movement and political opponents of Sinn Féin'.[5] Then he launched into a tirade against Margaret Thatcher and her rigidity, citing the sinking of the *Belgrano* during the Falklands War in 1982, and the ruthless way in which she set about breaking the mineworkers' strike in Britain in 1984–5, as examples of her obduracy.

He wrote about his conversation with an unknown BBC producer who felt that there would have been a revolt in the upper echelons of the prison service had the Mountain Climber offer been granted. What both Laurence McKeown and the BBC producer failed to appreciate was that, within two days of the hunger strike ending, all prisoners in Northern Irish jails had their own clothes, and within two months most of the Mountain Climber offer was implemented without as much as a murmur of protest from the prison administration. Unfortunately, and I have no doubt intentionally, McKeown's article was bereft of detail; he did not confirm or deny that Danny Morrison had elaborated on the Mountain Climber offer when visiting the prison hospital on 5 July, and he made no mention of ever having set eyes on the actual offer that Martin McGuinness had taken from Brendan Duddy. Why would McKeown – one of my most vociferous opponents – not take this golden opportunity to back up Morrison's story?

Members of three families were interviewed in *The Irish News* on 28 September 2009. Mrs Margaret Doherty spoke movingly of her son, Kieran: 'He was a great son, he had a very strong faith; he never missed his Mass no matter what. When he knew he was near the end he told his father not to worry.' Mrs Doherty said that Kieran tried to console his mother by telling her: 'It's only a wee step over to the other side.'[6] Representatives of the Doherty family issued a statement: 'These totally untrue allegations have caused untold hurt and anguish to our family and we feel sully the proud memory of Kieran and his comrades.'[7]

Patsy O'Hara's brother Tony expressed concern that 'the Sinn Féin version of events has changed too often since Richard O'Rawe published his account of a possible deal in 2005'.[8] Tony again called for 'a full inquiry, chaired by an international human rights figure'.[9]

Michael Óg Devine, Micky Devine's son, said that, although he was only eight years old when his father died, he still remembered visiting him in his final days. Michael Óg said he believed his father had not been made aware of the Mountain Climber offer, and he also called for an independent public inquiry into the hunger strike.

Hugh Logue, who had been part of the ICJP negotiating panel, wrote a moving article entitled 'Honour of those who died needs explanation'. His description of first meeting the hunger strikers on 4 July suggested that he had been deeply touched by the hunger strikers:

> The image of those eight hunger strikers for me has never dimmed. Clothed predominantly in the white attire of hospital, the weakest sitting at a table, water jugs and mugs in hand, the strongest seated on higher tables, or standing behind.
>
> That scene has stayed with me over the last 28 years and will remain imprinted on my brain as long as I live. They had been brought together as a group from their hospital beds to meet us in the canteen of Long Kesh.
>
> Bright articulate young men, some reserved and quiet spoken, others defiant and inquisitive, eyes accentuated, all in various stages of physical decline, eager to live, ready to die.[10]

Logue outlined the ICJP's role during the hunger strike. Referring to the Downing Street documents and the Mountain Climber offer:

> Was British secretary of state [Humphrey] Atkins able to sign off if he got an affirmative answer from the IRA? It now

appears he was. Did the republican leadership understand that? Parallel republican writing that Margaret Thatcher wished a settlement suggests they did.

This exchange was at least a day before the hunger strikers were told to demand, via the ICJP, verification from the British authorities. If the IRA had the British offer, why were the hunger strikers being put through this ritual? The hunger strikers, on the instructions of the IRA, were demanding that the ICJP deliver the British to deliver an offer statement. And the British, whilst agreeing to deliver the statement, apparently were waiting on the okay from the IRA before delivering the statement to the hunger strikers that had already been delivered to them.[11]

Logue's article contained other questions: 'Did the IRA genuinely overplay their hand believing that once the British were into dialogue more could be extracted?'[12] 'Did "the long game" [the development of the Sinn Féin party through the election of Owen Carron in Fermanagh-South Tyrone] focus come into play on this occasion?'[13] Forlornly casting his thoughts back on the hectic comings and goings of those dark days in early July, Logue reflected:

And all the while, a hunger striker [Joe McDonnell] was slipping in and out of consciousness, edging closer to death. Too grotesque to contemplate. But it happened. Why? Truly, in the name of honour and the dignity of the hunger strikers, explanation and clarification is needed.[14]

Hugh Logue's plea was to hit the same stone wall as Tony O'Hara's; the committee ignored them and in so doing sent out the message that they would not be cajoled, pushed, or frog-marched over the edge of a cliff.

Twenty-three

MEDIA SOURCES and some friends from West Belfast agreed that the first day of the *Irish News* special series had been dreadful for the committee. A friend from Ballymurphy, known for betting on the horses, said that Martin McGuinness and Laurence McKeown had 'refused to leave the stalls'. Yet their rubber-legged performances had little to do with an ability to write good prose, or with a glaring desire to rebut my assertions, and had everything to do with the moral and evidential deficit that restricted their ability to mount a credible defence. The next day's *Irish News* confirmed this.

On the front of that newspaper was a photograph of hunger striker Gerard Hodgkins. Inside was another photograph of 'Hodgies', standing alongside Danny Morrison after their convictions for falsely imprisoning a suspected IRA informer called Sandy Lynch were overturned in the Belfast Court of Appeal in 2008. Danny was smiling as he sported a broad, black-brimmed hat. I liked it; it gave him an air of bohemian decadence (and it took some balls to wear it).

The headline of Hodgies's article ran: 'All evidence points to dark dealings'.[1] He wrote that *Blanketmen* had been 'uncomfortable' reading for many republicans. Then he declared:

A prima facie case exists that Richard's assertion has validity: Gerry Adams (writing in one of his books) previously referred to a happy ending narrative rather than a tell-all story now, yet he won't elaborate on what this cryptic sentence means.

Gerry Adams referred to the British coming back with the deal again around July 18/19 1981.

Gerry Adams has referred to how he got into the habit of catching sleep during the daylight hours during that summer of 1981 because the British would contact him via telephone late at night.

Yet Adams refuses to put meat on these statements. What is he hiding? What was the true extent of contact between the leadership and the British?[2]

In a memorable summing up, Hodgkins wrote:

On the face of it the evidence points to dark dealings going on in the background of the hunger strike, dealings of which nobody on hunger strike was aware.[3]

Below Hodgies's article there were extracts from an interview between an *Irish News* reporter and Ruairí Ó Brádaigh. The headline misleadingly read: 'Deal claims "completely wrong": Ó Brádaigh'.[4] While these words were said by the 1981 Sinn Féin president regarding Dr Garret FitzGerald's claim that a deal had been 'scuppered' by the outside leadership, Ó Brádaigh, in reality, was only being his usual concise self. Commenting further on Dr FitzGerald's claim, he said, 'I must reject what is being said. Sinn Féin at the time were not involved in making settlements.'[5] He went on, 'I don't believe either that the [IRA] army council was aware that there were terms on offer either.'[6] Although Ruairí Ó Brádaigh had taken the circuitous Cape Horn route rather than the much shorter Panama Canal, he nevertheless reached his destination and confirmed that neither the Sinn Féin leadership nor the Army Council knew anything about the Mountain Climber offer or any of the intricacies involved with it. Despite the obvious intent in Ó Brádaigh's words, some of the committee's supporters clung like limpets to the disingenuous interview headline, contending that Ó Brádáigh had reinforced their position to the detriment of mine.

To clear up this important matter, I spoke to members of Republican Sinn Féin in Belfast, of which Ruairí had been president, and asked them to let him know how his words were been interpeted and misused. A message came back saying he was 'livid' at the way in which *The Irish News* had portrayed his views and had written a letter to the newspaper to put the record straight.

This letter appeared on 20 October 2009 and in it Ó Brádaigh made clear that the 1981 Sinn Féin leadership and the Army Council knew nothing about negotiations with the British. However, once again he clouded the issue, this time by prefixing the word 'alleged' whenever he referred to the Mountain Climber offer. Having been at the apex of a fragmentary republican movement for almost sixty years, Ruairí Ó Brádaigh had learned the value of the spoken word, although that did not make his concision any less irritating.

Willie Gallagher, on behalf of the IRSP leadership, demanded 'answers as to why the 5 July Mountain Climber offer – which was accepted by the IRA jail leadership – was rejected and who outside rejected it'.[7] In addition, he said:

We also want to know why the INLA jail leadership and their outside representatives were kept in the dark about the Mountain Climber negotiations and the offer.[8]

Other contributors included the author and journalist Ed Moloney, who described the hunger strike as 'the Provos' Easter Rising'.[9] He remarked, 'There have been changes to some people's stories that are so significant it begs the question, why?'[10]

What emerged from this bruising two-day public encounter? Probably it was what had *not* been included in the *Irish News* coverage that captured people's attention. Laurence McKeown's reluctance to lend his support to Danny Morrison's claim that he had told the hunger strikers the details of the Mountain Climber offer on 5 July 1981 was striking. And Morrison's assertion began to look even more threadbare when McKeown refused to answer an appeal for clarity from Michael Óg and Louise Devine. In a letter published in the *Derry Journal* on 6 October 2009, Micky Devine's children asked McKeown:

> Tell us publicly exactly what did happen in the prison hospital [on 5 July 1981] and what exactly was my father told, if anything, that he felt he couldn't share with his family or movement.
>
> We would also like to ask Laurence [McKeown] did he see a copy of the offer which Duddy [Brendan] gave to McGuinness [Martin] who in turn gave it to Gerry Adams.[11]

McKeown's barely concealed prevarication was not the only thing missing from the *Irish News* special edition. The question was being asked: why did Adams, Morrison and McFarlane not fight their corner? These were politically astute men and they must surely have known that opting to say nothing would have been viewed as damning. What made their silence all the more puzzling was that Martin McGuinness, in presenting his article for publication, had scuttled any chance that Adams, Morrison, and McFarlane might have had of hiding behind the families' 19 June 2009 statement. Why did McGuinness commit the cardinal sin of breaking with the policy line? Was he seeking to put distance between himself and his three colleagues by admitting that he had handed over the Mountain Climber offer to Gerry Adams – thereby hoping to remove himself from the hunger-strike decision-making process? We may never know, but we do know that the committee's approach to the *Irish News* special edition series was little short of disastrous and their position had now become acute.

I discussed the situation with Willie Gallagher and Carrie Twomey, amongst others, and Willie put it to me that he believed the committee would do nothing; he felt that they had been forced from their original 'prove it' stance, to one of 'so what?' I was not so sure. As it turned out, we all got it wrong.

News that something was stirring came from a friend of Carrie Twomey. Carrie phoned me on 8 October 2009 to say that Gerry Adams had written an article about the hunger strike and that it had appeared on a Sinn Féin press officer's Twitter feed. Later the article was removed. It was then displayed on the party's *An Phoblacht* website, only once again to be removed.

So was the honourable Member of Parliament for West Belfast, fountainhead of knowledge regarding the hunger strike, about to put some manners on those insubordinates who had questioned his version of events in 1981? He hinted as much; on 27 February 2005, the day before *Blanketmen* was due for publication, he had balefully told a reporter, 'I'll comment when I read the book.'[12] Now, after almost five years, it seemed that he was up for the battle. Yet, judging by the swift withdrawal of his article from the republican websites, I was beginning to think that Adams might have been having second thoughts. I tried to buy a copy of the Sinn Féin weekly *An Phoblacht* to see if his commentary was in it, but, strangely, none of the usual outlets had the paper in stock. Throughout the North, people told me they were experiencing the same difficulty, leading some to conclude that the paper had been withdrawn from sale. Eventually I was able to buy a copy of the paper.

As I read Adams's article, the words of Winston Churchill sprang to mind: 'History will be kind to me for I intend to write it.' Like Churchill, like all political leaders, Gerry Adams's hope would undoubtedly be that history will be kind to him, and, rather than leave anything to chance, he has written twelve books about his 43-year involvement with the republican struggle – without admitting to ever having been an IRA volunteer. So it came as no surprise that most of Adams's article was uncannily reminiscent of his predecessors' contributions to the debate (he even went so far as to imitate Danny Morrison by attributing to me personally a paragraph from a press statement that I had written on behalf of the republican prisoners in the H-Blocks in 1981). Flailing wildly at Dr Garret FitzGerald, *The Irish News* and myself, Adams wrote:

> Twenty-eight years ago, ten Irish republicans died over a seven-month period on hunger strike, after women in Armagh prison and men in the H-Blocks (and several 'on-the-blanket' in Crumlin Road Jail) had endured five years of British Government-sanctioned brutality.
>
> The reason for their suffering was that, in 1976, the British Government reneged on a 1972 agreement over political status ('special category status') for prisoners which had actually brought relative peace to the jails.
>
> You would not know that from reading this series in *The Irish News*.
>
> Nor would you know from reading Garret FitzGerald's newly-found 'memory' of 1981 that in his 1991 [sic] memoir he wrote:
>
> > 'My meetings with the relatives came to an end on 6 August when some of them attempted to "sit-in" in the Government ante-room, where I had met them on such occasions, after a stormy discussion during which I had once again refused to take the kind of action some of them had been pressing on me.'
>
> This came after a Garda riot squad attacked and hospitalised scores of prisoners' supporters outside the British Embassy in Dublin only days after the death of Joe McDonnell.
>
> It is clear from FitzGerald's interview and from his previous writing that his main concern – before, during and after 1981 – was that the British Government might be talking to republicans and that this should stop.
>
> With Margaret Thatcher he embarked on the most intense round of repression in the period after 1985. Following the Anglo-Irish Agreement of that year, the Irish Government supported an intensification of British efforts to destroy

border crossings and roads and remained mute over evidence of mounting collusion between British forces and unionist paramilitaries.

The same FitzGerald was portrayed as a great liberal, yet every government which he led or in which he served renewed the state broadcasting censorship of Sinn Féin. This denial of information and closing down of dialogue subverted the rights of republicans. It also helped prolong the conflict.

The Irish News played an equally reprehensible role.

As far as I am concerned, this newspaper is a 'player' in these attacks on Sinn Féin. Oh, but had *The Irish News* given a series to the Hunger Strikers when they were alive! Instead, at the same time as *The Irish News* decided to publish death notices for British state forces, this paper refused to publish a death notice from the Sands family because it carried the words 'In memory of our son and brother, IRA Volunteer Bobby Sands MP'.

The men who died on Hunger Strike from the IRA and INLA were not dupes. They had fought the British and knew how bitter and cruel an enemy its forces could be, in the city, in the countryside, in the centres of interrogation, and in the courts.

But you would not know that from reading this series in *The Irish News*.

The prisoners – our comrades, our brothers and sisters – resisted the British in jail every day, in solitary confinement, when being beaten during wing shifts, during internal searches and the forced scrubbings.

The Hunger Strike did not arise out of a vacuum but as a consequence of frustration, a failure of their incredible sacrifices and the activism of supporters to break the deadlock, to put pressure on the British internationally and, through the Irish Establishment, including the Dublin Government, the SDLP and sections of the Catholic hierarchy – although you would not know that from reading this series in *The Irish News*.

In December 1980, the republican leadership on the outside was in contact with the British, who claimed they were interested in a settlement. But before a document outlining a promised, allegedly liberal regime arrived in the jail, the Hunger Strike was called off by Brendan Hughes to save the life of the late Seán McKenna. The British, or sections of them, interpreted this as weakness. The prisoners ended their fast before a formal 'signing-off'. And the British then refused to implement the spirit of the document and reneged on the integrity of our exchanges.

Their intransigence triggered a second Hunger Strike in which there was overwhelming suspicion of British motives among the Hunger Strikers, the other political prisoners, and their families and supporters on the outside.

This was the prisoners' mindset on 5 July 1981, after four of their comrades had already died and when Danny Morrison visited the IRA and INLA Hunger Strikers to tell them that contact had been re-established and that the British were making an offer.

While this verbal message fell well short of their five demands, they nevertheless wanted an accredited British official to come in and explain this position to them, which is entirely understandable given the British Government's record.

Six times before the death of Joe McDonnell, the Irish Commission for Justice and Peace (ICJP), which was engaged in parallel discussions with the British, asked the British to send an official into the jail to explain what it was offering, and six times the British refused.

After the death of Joe McDonnell, the ICJP condemned the British for failing to honour undertakings and for 'clawing back' concessions.

Ex-prisoner Richard O'Rawe, who never left his cell, never met the Hunger Strikers in the prison hospital, never met the governor, never met the ICJP or Danny Morrison during the Hunger Strike, and who never raised this issue before serialising his book in that well-known Irish republican propaganda organ, *The Sunday Times*, said, in a statement in 1981:

'The British Government's hypocrisy and their refusal to act in a responsible manner are completely to blame for the death of Joe McDonnell.'

But you would not know that from reading this series in *The Irish News*.

Republicans involved in the Hunger Strike met with the families a few months ago. Their emotional distress and ongoing pain was palpable. They were intimately involved at the time on an hour-by-hour basis and know exactly where their sons and brothers stood in relation to the struggle with the British Government.

They know who was trying to do their best for them and who was trying to sell their sacrifices short.

More importantly, they know the mind of their loved ones. That, for me, is what shone through at that meeting. The families knew their brothers, husbands, fathers. They knew they weren't dupes. They knew they weren't stupid. They knew they were brave, beyond words, and they were clear about what was happening.

All the family members, who spoke, with the exception of Tony O'Hara, expressed deep anger and frustration at the efforts to denigrate and defile the memory of their loved ones. In a statement they said:

'We are clear that it was the British Government which refused to negotiate and refused to concede [the prisoners'] demands.'

But you would not know that from reading this series in *The Irish News*.[13]

Twenty-four

WHAT YOU would not know from reading Gerry Adams's piece is whether or not he was supporting Danny Morrison when Morrison said that he had told the hunger strikers the details of the Mountain Climber offer. On the contrary, you would be forgiven for thinking that Adams's intention had been to cut Morrison adrift: 'Danny Morrison visited the IRA and INLA Hunger Strikers to tell them that contact had been re-established and that the British *were* [my italics] making an offer.'[1] These were not the words of a major political leader unreservedly standing by his point man. After all, Morrison had gone 'all-in' on his assertion that he had told the hunger strikers the details of the offer – not that 'contact had been re-established'. And the British were not 'making an offer' – they *had* made an offer. So what was Gerry Adams's game? Was he lining Morrison up to be the fall guy?

And you would not know from reading Adams's article anything about the secret negotiations that Danny Morrison and he had conducted with the British government during the hunger strike. Nor did he give a reason why the committee and he had rejected the prison leadership's acceptance of the Mountain

Climber offer, or why a copy of the offer had never been sent into the prison, either to the hunger strikers, or the prison leadership.

However, he did say that I had never raised the hunger strike issue until *The Sunday Times* serialized *Blanketmen* in 2005, conveniently forgetting that, on 17 July 2003, a former Blanketman, reputed to be the IRA Adjutant-General at that time, came to my home and said he had been sent by 'the leadership' to find out if I was writing a book about the hunger strike, and what would be in it. This man had suggested that I meet Gerry Adams. Did Adams not know anything about this?

He certainly knew what he was doing when he wrote: 'The men who died on hunger strike from the IRA and INLA were not dupes.'[2] And in case anyone missed the point the first time, he returned to this theme, 'The families knew their brothers, husbands, fathers. They knew they weren't dupes. They knew they weren't stupid.'[3]

The term 'dupes' first raised its loathsome head in the Sinn Féin-sponsored 19 June 2009 statement, which the families who had attended the Gulladuff meeting had been asked to sign. Since then this term has been widely used in Sinn Féin papers, and by their spokespersons, such as Pádraic Wilson.[4] This is despite the fact that none of us who sought answers from Adams and his committee – and that included some hunger strikers' family members – had ever written or uttered that word. The question thus arises: why introduce the word 'dupes' at all? Why was it so important to Adams and his group?

The answer, as ever, is self-preservation: the person who created this monstrous vista did so because, firstly, he/she wanted to promote the premise that, if the committee's version of the hunger strike was proved to be one big lie, then by extension, the hunger strikers must have been dupes; like putty in the committee's hands. The second reason for the introduction of this word was that it sent a not-too-subtle message to any family that may have been entertaining rebellious thoughts: your brother, husband, father will be forever branded a dupe, because of your actions; is that really what you want? This was old-fashioned emotional blackmail and I determined to deal with it in my response to Adams's article.

How I would respond to his attack was the least of his or *An Phoblacht*'s problems at that particular time though because Adams had furiously slated *The Irish News* for running the hunger strike special series, stating: 'As far as I am concerned, *The Irish News* is "a player" in these attacks on Sinn Féin.'[5] In an act of unbridled loyalty, *An Phoblacht* had decided to reflect the Sinn Féin party leader's anger in the preamble to Adams's article:

> Sinn Féin asked *The Irish News* for a full right of reply [to the special series] and the newspaper agreed. When the response from Gerry Adams was harshly critical of *The Irish News* itself, the article was blocked.
>
> *An Phoblacht* carries the article below. We are waiting for *The Irish News* to do the same.[6]

At face value, this had all the appearances of a declaration of war, and if that was so, it was a war that I did not think *An Phoblacht* would win. *An Phoblacht*'s charge was that *The Irish News* had treated Gerry Adams badly by denying him a right of reply to the hostile opinion pieces in the paper's special series. Yet I had phoned *The Irish News* on at least three occasions from mid-July to mid-September to find out why the special series had been delayed, and one of the reasons I was given was that the paper had been keen to interview Adams, or at least get a platform article from him, but it appeared that he was hesitant about whether or not he should participate. So *The Irish News* waited while Adams dithered. In the end he contributed neither interview nor article.

Having read the Adams commentary in *An Phoblacht*, I phoned *The Irish News* to find out if they would be printing it because I wanted the right of reply. When I asked about *An Phoblacht*'s accusations, I was informed that *The Irish News* had not blocked Adams's right of reply, and that they rejected the

Sinn Féin paper's version of events. On 10 October it was brought to my attention that the editor of *The Irish News*, Noel Doran, had laid out the newspaper's position on – of all places – Gerry Adams's blog. Doran wrote:

> Everything which *An Phoblacht* said about *The Irish News* was untrue. We approached Gerry Adams over a seven-week period in advance of our hunger strike coverage, asking him for either an interview or an opinion article, but he was always unavailable. After the coverage appeared, we approached him again to see if he could comment on the issues arising. At no stage did Sinn Féin seek a right to reply, as *An Phoblacht* claimed. The article which we had requested eventually arrived, and we immediately agreed to publish it. As it was much longer than expected, and would require a response from the paper, we told the party [Sinn Féin] in writing that it would appear within a matter of days. The party then changed its mind, withdrew the original article from Mr Adams and said it would submit a revised version shortly.
>
> *An Phoblacht* made no attempt to check any of this with *The Irish News*, and instead proceeded with the false allegations against our paper. We have since received a series of private apologies from Sinn Féin representatives, and we are expecting an on-the-record statement from the party shortly. We have also, today, finally received the revised opinion article from Mr Adams, which we intend to publish tomorrow. We further expect that *An Phoblacht* will issue an apology to *The Irish News* in its next edition.[7]

Whether or not the humiliating publication of Doran's account on Adams's blog was the price that Sinn Féin had to pay for the party's vilification of *The Irish News* is unclear, but on 12 October *The Irish News* carried an apology from *An Phoblacht*:

> We claimed that *The Irish News* had refused to publish it [Adams's article]. This is untrue. *An Phoblacht* regret this and are happy to clarify the point.[8]

Happy? I doubted that. Still, this was certainly a jigsaw puzzle for sure. Adams's article was withdrawn from *The Irish News*: *An Phoblacht* accused *The Irish News* of blocking it; the *Irish News* editor accused *An Phoblacht* of misrepresenting the facts – on Gerry Adams's blog; *An Phoblacht* apologized to *The Irish News*; Adams's article was finally published – minus any criticism of *The Irish News*!

No matter how much I peeled away the layers of this conundrum, I always found the same answer underneath – Gerry Adams had not written the original platform piece to which his name had been so recklessly attached. *He*, more than anyone, knew that *The Irish News* had been chasing him for seven weeks for an interview or an article, and *he* knew that he had stalled them to the point whereby they had little choice but to say that enough was enough, and out of duty to everyone else who had contributed, the paper published the special series. So why then would Adams, a man renowned for his cool head and shrewd judgment, launch such a self-destructive attack on *The Irish News*?

It only made sense if someone else had written the article and had not shown it to him before it was sent to *The Irish News* and before *An Phoblacht* had published it. Then, when Adams eventually did set eyes on it, he withdrew it from *The Irish News*. It is also likely that he ensured that copies of *An Phoblacht* were recalled.

The *An Phoblacht* charge that *The Irish News* had 'blocked' Adams's article is not so easily explained, although it is possible that someone on the paper's editorial staff, after seeing the misplaced passion in the Adams article, had come down with a bout of over-exuberance.

No matter who was responsible for this comedy of errors, I suspected that they would have been on the receiving end of the Big Lad's wrath.

I was not displeased with the way things had turned out. After five years, Adams had been forced to comment.

By 14 October I had sent an 800-word piece to *The Irish News* in answer to Adams's attack on me. By 16 October my reply had still not been published, but that did not unduly worry me; I knew from experience that the paper rarely rushed these things. Then, that night, I received a phone call from Carrie Twomey, who pointed out a very important passage that she had discovered while reading the 1994 book, *Nor Meekly Serve My Time*,[9] which Laurence McKeown had co-edited with Blanketmen Brian Campbell and Felim O'Hagan. I instantly knew that this passage was important, so important that I worked until 3 am on a fresh *Irish News* article. At 9 am the next morning I phoned the paper and asked if I could withdraw my original reply to Adams. They agreed. Two days later, after much redrafting and fine-tuning, I submitted my new platform article.

On the day before it was due for publication, 22 October, the paper's subeditor phoned me to ask if he could replace a couple of words that he thought might have been too inflammatory. There was no loss of emphasis, so I agreed.

The next day my answer to Gerry Adams's harangue appeared under the headline 'There was an offer on the table – but the prisoners weren't told'. In it I wrote:

> There is now no room for doubting that the hunger strikers, by their sacrifice and courage, melted the iron will of Margaret Thatcher.
>
> In doing so they tore asunder the British government's policy of criminalisation. Not only that, but the hunger strikers forced the British to make a substantial offer, which was passed to Brendan Duddy (the Mountain Climber) on 5 July 1981.
>
> Martin McGuinness said in his 28 September *Irish News* article that he took the offer from Duddy and passed it on to Gerry Adams in Belfast.
>
> I believe that, had that offer not been rejected by those republican leaders on the outside who ran the hunger strike, it would have spelt victory to the Blanketmen, proved to be

a massive propaganda coup for the republican struggle and, most importantly of all, saved the lives of six hunger strikers.

I also believe that while other accounts of the period have crumbled under the weight of damning contemporaneous evidence, my version of events has been vindicated: there was an offer; Bik McFarlane and I did accept it; a comm from Gerry Adams came in to the prison leadership which said that 'more was needed'. A similar message was sent to the British government.

Besides Martin McGuinness, the former hunger striker Laurence McKeown contributed an article to the *Irish News* special edition.

In it Laurence made no direct reference to this offer, preferring instead to write about a conversation he had had with a BBC producer in the 1990s. That prompts the question: had Laurence and the hunger strikers been made fully aware of the details of the Mountain Climber offer?

I do not think that they were and Laurence McKeown's own book, *Nor Meekly Serve My Time*, demonstrates this.

For example: on 29 July 1981, at the request of the families and Monsignor Denis Faul, Gerry Adams, Fermanagh and South Tyrone election candidate Owen Carron, and INLA leader Seamus Ruddy visited the hunger strikers, ostensibly to give them their assessment of the situation.

Thirteen years later, in 1994, Laurence recorded the visit in his book. On page 236 he wrote of Gerry Adams having visited hunger striker Kieran Doherty:

> *On their way out of his cell Doc's parents met and spoke with Gerry, Bik and the others. They asked what the situation was and Gerry said he had just told all the stailceoirí [hunger strikers], including Kieran, that there was no deal on the table from the Brits, no movement of any sort and if the stailc [strike] continued, Doc would most likely be dead within a few days. They just listened to this and nodded, more or less resigned to the fact that they would be watching their son die any day now.*

Kieran Doherty TD passed away four days after Adams's visit, believing that there 'was no deal on the table from the Brits, no movement of any sort'.

What Adams seemingly did not tell Kieran's dignified parents, Alfie and Margaret, was that, actually, there was a deal on the table from the Brits, and it had been there from before Joe McDonnell died.

Moreover, he did not tell them that there had been movement [there had been the Mountain Climber offer].

Adams did not tell Mr and Mrs Doherty – or their noble son – about the Mountain Climber offer.

According to Laurence McKeown, Adams did not tell any of the hunger strikers about the Mountain Climber offer. Worse still, he told them the opposite of what he knew to be the facts of the situation.

I believe that Adams misrepresented the situation and Bik McFarlane did nothing to correct him. That is hardly surprising since before Adams had even set foot in the prison McFarlane told Pat 'Beag' McGeown, 'Don't make your opinion known,' at the forthcoming meeting. Subsequently Pat Beag said, 'When Gerry was in I didn't say anything to him.'

In the face of all the evidence Sinn Féin has sought to demonize anyone who criticizes their version of the hunger strike by representing that any condemnation of them automatically means that the hunger strikers had been dupes.

The hunger strikers were never dupes. In reality, like Pat Beag, they were very astute and politically-aware individuals, people who would not 'easily be deceived or cheated' by anyone.

Yet, like most of us, they could only make decisions on the basis of the information they had.

If those they trusted withheld vital information from them, their judgements would obviously have been impaired.

Besides Gerry Adams not having told them of the Mountain Climber offer, when he visited them on 29 July, Bik McFarlane never told them that he and I had accepted the Mountain Climber offer.

Furthermore, like McFarlane and the rest of the prison leadership, the hunger strikers were never shown a copy of the British government's offer.

In fact, none of us prisoners in Long Kesh were told that the offer came in the form of a statement from the secretary of state for Northern Ireland, Humphrey Atkins, which the British, as documents recently disclosed under the Freedom of Information Act made clear, would have released if and when the hunger strike ended.

So, why was this offer not sent in to the hunger strikers so that they could properly evaluate the attitude of the British?

Who took the decision to withhold it from them?

And the biggest question of all – why?[10]

Below this article in *The Irish News* there was an interview with former hunger striker Bernard Fox. Bernard had spent thirty-two days on the fast, but he had had to abandon it because of an obstructed kidney. While Bernard's tone was unreservedly defensive of Bik McFarlane and the committee, he nevertheless reinforced what I had written on the same page about the hunger strikers not knowing the details of the Mountain Climber offer:

> I wasn't in the hospital at the time [when Danny Morrison visited the hunger strikers] and I don't know what the men were told or not but I do know that there was no deal.[11]

Bernard is right in saying that there had been no deal; if there had been a deal, he would not have been on the hunger strike. That aside, Bernard said, 'I don't know what the men were told or not …' If he did not know what the men were told or not, then, quite simply, *he* had not known the details of the Mountain Climber offer, and, while he had been given every opportunity to die on the hunger strike, he had never been given an opportunity to form an opinion on an offer that promised victory over defeat and life over death.

In the same edition of *The Irish News* Tony O'Hara had a letter published under the heading, 'The truth about the Hunger

Strike'. Recalling the 17 June 2009 meeting between some hunger strikers' relatives and Gerry Adams, Danny Morrison and Bik McFarlane, Tony wrote:

> It should also be clarified that there was no family statement at Gulladuff.
>
> The following day Sinn Féin members took a SF-composed statement around to some family members for them to sign.
>
> My mother and I never signed it.
>
> Neither did Michael Devine (who was also at Gulladuff) or Louise Devine.[12]

Tony went on to write:

> At Gulladuff I suggested that we invite all concerned into a room together to thrash things out.
>
> Gerry Adams didn't reply.
>
> That suggestion is still there, only now I ask for it in public, with an agreed international humanitarian chairperson. Only that will end it.
>
> Richard O'Rawe has agreed to attend; former Taoiseach Garret FitzGerald has also said that he would cooperate with an inquiry.
>
> Will Gerry?[13]

Gerry did not bother to answer Tony O'Hara's question. Nor did he answer the damning indictment that I had levelled at him in my latest *Irish News* article, which was that he, on 29 July 1981, 'misrepresented the situation' to the hunger strikers and to Mr and Mrs Doherty. His supporters would probably say that silence does not necessarily equate with guilt, and that is true; but why, if they had nothing to hide, would Adams and his committee *not* agree to the public inquiry that Tony O'Hara and others have asked for, and in doing so, remove any misgiving there might have been that they wilfully allowed the last six hunger strikers to die in order to get Owen Carron elected in Fermanagh-South Tyrone?

On 15 November 2009 Ruairí Ó Brádaigh finally removed all doubts about the thorny issue of who knew what about the Mountain Climber offer. In an interview for New York's WBAI radio station to mark his stepping down from the presidency of Republican Sinn Féin, and also his remarkable sixty years of involvement with the republican movement, Ó Brádaigh was asked:

> In the *Irish News* special edition series on the hunger strike Martin McGuinness confirmed that he received an offer from the British government on 5 July 1981, which he said he passed on to Gerry Adams in Belfast. This is known as the Mountain Climber offer. As President of Sinn Féin at the time, did Gerry Adams, Martin McGuinness, or anyone else on the hunger-strike committee, make you aware of the existence of this offer?

Ó Brádaigh, whom many believed to have been on the IRA Army Council at that time, was unhesitant in his answer:

> I had no knowledge of any such offer, nor had Sinn Féin in general, and not alone that, I believe that the Army Council of the IRA were not aware of this offer either and I have gone on the record as saying that.[14]

The former hunger striker Gerard Hodkins had also gone on the record and perhaps it is fitting that he has the last word on these matters:

> Whether we ever will know the truth of those times is doubtful. The acquisition of any level of power and maintenance of that power is rarely a tale of honour alone.[15]

Epilogue

ON 28 FEBRUARY 2009 Roger Spottiswoode, who directed the James Bond movie *Tomorrow Never Dies* and the Arnold Schwarzenegger movie *The 6th Day*, interviewed me for his latest cinema release about peace and reconciliation in trouble spots throughout the world. Before coming to Ireland, Spottiswoode and his team had been to Rwanda, and afterwards they were going to Palestine and Israel. Our interview was conducted at The Maze/Long Kesh prison.

When we arrived at the gates of the prison, I was surprised to find that it had been practically demolished. Where once had stood mighty concrete walls of containment, there was now only space and speckled shrubbery. This was visible proof that all things must pass, no matter how permanent they may seem in the moment.

A security man approached us from the gatehouse, where, during the 1983 'Great Escape', ten republican prisoners, disguised as guards, held over twenty prison officers hostage. Thirty-eight republican prisoners had escaped, including Bik McFarlane, who had played a leading part in the planning and execution of the escape. The security man walked away after a brief conversation with Spottiswoode.

The interview eventually proceeded at the site of the old British army barracks, situated just outside the prison, where, fortunately for the documentary-makers, a part of the outer wall had not yet been knocked down.

Later that night I was walking briskly along the Glen Road, and, as usual when exercising, I churned over the day's events. As a result of the interview, my emotions were pulling in opposite directions. Why did I feel a sense of loss at the prison being demolished? In real life, it had been a hell-hole. The world would be a better place without it, I told myself. But a whole generation of republicans, loyalists and prison officers had learned to co-exist on this anthill of inhumanity. Above all, ten Blanketmen had died on hunger strike within its walls.

I had just about conquered the mile-long Monagh Link, when my mind turned in a different, if not altogether unrelated, direction: why did Vietnam War veterans visit the Vietcong tunnels? After all, it was from these tunnels, deep beneath the jungles of South Vietnam, that the Vietcong had launched horrific attacks that resulted in thousands of young Americans losing their lives. It then struck me that breaking with the past – especially when that past held indelible memories of lost comrades – was almost impossible. Like the Vietcong tunnels, Long Kesh was a bridge to the past, to the brave men who never came back.

I have said repeatedly that the history of the 1981 hunger strike should be a living testimony to the astonishing courage of the hunger strikers, and in that sense it does matter what motivated certain leaders on the outside to act as they did. What also matters is that injustice is not perpetuated by allowing the hunger-strike story to be polluted by the demands of political expediency. As I wrote in *Blanketmen*: 'Justice demands that the facts be told without prejudice or favour and not submerged in half-truths, which are also half-lies.'[1] Given what we now know about the hunger strike, is there not a case for saying that the hunger-strike committee has submerged itself more in half-lies than in half-truths? Eamonn McCann put this in perspective: 'When the republican movement began its decisive shift away from a United Ireland or nothing … that made it imperative of the leadership of that time to keep control of the memory … to keep control of the hunger strike …'[2]

So has the committee kept control of the hunger strike? Certainly no one could accuse them of being found wanting in their endeavours to do just that. They suffered, however, because their leader, Gerry Adams, did not want to get his hands dirty.

Undoubtedly things have changed since the publication of *Blanketmen*. Mine is no longer the voice of one person crying in the wilderness. Other republicans, many of them Blanketmen, and some families, are demanding an independent inquiry into the hunger strike. I have stated that I support such an inquiry. At the time of writing, the committee has not.

There are many matters of dispute between the opposing parties, but the events in the prison on 5–6 July, and 18–21 July, 1981 are of central importance in discovering where the truth dwells. The issues have been clearly defined during the course of this narrative:

1. I said that Bik McFarlane had brought back a detailed offer from the British government, after he had met Danny Morrison in the prison hospital on 5 July 1981. For four years McFarlane vehemently denied that there had ever been an offer.
2. I said that McFarlane and I had accepted the British offer, and that we communicated our decision in Irish out of our cell windows. McFarlane also denied that.
3. I put forward that the hunger-strike committee rejected our acceptance of the British offer. McFarlane denied this as well.

So has this account provided evidence that on 5 July 1981 Bik McFarlane brought back the details of the Mountain Climber offer and sent them up to me for consideration? I say that it has:

a) Danny Morrison has always said that he gave McFarlane the details of the Mountain Climber offer during their 5 July 1981 meeting in the prison hospital.

b) Colm Scullion, in his 9 April 2008 letter to the press, said he was aware that Bik McFarlane had sent me a comm containing the offer.

c) In his 4 June 2009 interview in the *Belfast Telegraph* with Brian Rowan, McFarlane openly admitted to there having been an offer, and that he discussed it with me.

Has this account provided evidence that there was a conversation in Irish between Bik McFarlane and me, during which we accepted the Mountain Climber offer? I say that it has:

a) Gerard 'Cleaky' Clarke bore witness to this exchange when he attended the Gasyard conference in Derry in May 2009.

b) Another Blanketman, who has met three of the families of hunger strikers, has also said that he heard this conversation.

c) In the Rowan interview, Bik McFarlane reflected: 'And I said to Richard [O'Rawe], this is amazing, this is a huge opportunity and I feel there's the potential here [in the Mountain Climber process] to end this.'[3] That is an admission that we did, after all, have that conversation and it is tantamount to an acceptance of the offer.

Has this narrative provided evidence that the hunger-strike committee rejected our acceptance of the offer? I say that it has:

a) There is no evidence to show that the prison leadership voluntarily changed its mind after accepting the Mountain Climber offer. As McFarlane's Rowan interview and my account in *Blanketmen* show, we were 'amazed' and delighted with the offer.

b) McFarlane's testimony has been discredited. He has been

shown to be factually incorrect in saying that (i) there was no offer 'whatsoever', and (ii) there had been no conversation between us whereby we accepted the offer. Would he be any less factually incorrect in promoting the notion that the committee did not reject our acceptance of the offer?

c) My testimony has held up. Nothing has been said or brought forward to refute my account of the hunger strike.

d) Gerry Adams has not put up any meaningful defence to my assertion that he sent in a comm that 'advised' that the offer be rejected.

Has this book provided evidence that the committee deliberately misled the hunger strikers? I say that it has:

a) The committee hid the document containing the Mountain Climber offer from the hunger strikers, and the prison leadership. Only after twenty-eight years, and only as a result of a Freedom of Information request, was it uncovered.

b) Gerry Adams did not reveal anything about the Mountain Climber involvement or offer when he visited the hunger strikers on 29 July 1981.

c) The committee hid from the IRA Army Council both the Mountain Climber involvement in the hunger strike and the document containing the offer.

d) McFarlane has always advocated that it was the hunger strikers who rejected the Mountain Climber offer, not he or the committee. This is discredited, because: (i) it is McFarlane who is saying it, (ii) Danny Morrison is on the record as saying that he 'did not go into detail' about the offer, (iii) no living hunger strikers – even those who have vehemently supported the committee – have ever confirmed that they were informed about the Mountain

Climber offer (although at least three have stated that they knew nothing of it), (iv) the hunger strikers were never shown the document containing the Mountain Climber offer, and (v) the 1981 INLA leadership is adamant that its volunteers, Kevin Lynch and Micky Devine, knew nothing of the offer.

In all this, Gerry Adams has adopted the persona of a barely interested observer, the white swan gracefully gliding over the sea of misery. The reality, though, was very different: he was, in the words of Tim Pat Coogan, the shogun-like figure; it was he who had unleashed his Dobermans to savage me in the media in the aftermath of the publication of *Blanketmen*.

A crucial part of that media onslaught had been McFarlane and Morrison's continuous use of the hunger strikers' families to isolate and undermine my position. Nothing had vexed me more than this cynical play on the emotions of those innocent people.

As ever, readers are entitled to make a judgment for themselves about these issues. In considering the matter, it may be prudent to recall the words of former US president John Adams: 'Facts are stubborn things; and whatever may be our wishes, our inclinations, or the dictates of our passion, they cannot alter the facts and evidence.'[4]

So, did errors of judgment on the committee's behalf, coupled with plain bad luck, inadvertently result in the deaths of the last six martyrs? On balance, the evidence against this being the case is very damning; there are just too many indicators pointing to the committee having decided that Owen Carron's election to the Fermanagh-South Tyrone Westminster seat held precedence over the lives of hunger strikers. Plain bad luck played no part in the gagging of Pat 'Beag' McGeown by Bik McFarlane during Adams's meeting with the hunger strikers. Nor does it provide any cover for the fact that when Adams visited the prison hospital on 29 July 1981, he went through that meeting without referring to the reservations that some of the hunger strikers had expressed to Bik McFarlane previous day.[5]

Likewise, ill fortune would not explain why Gerry Adams told Mr and Mrs Doherty and the hunger strikers that there was nothing on offer from the British when he knew that he had received the Mountain Climber offer for a second time just ten days earlier and had sent the British back a message saying that 'more was needed'. And finally, for some reason, Gerry Adams did not bring in to the hunger strikers a copy of the statement from the Secretary of State for Northern Ireland, Humphrey Atkins, which contained the Mountain Climber offer so that they could judge for themselves whether or not they should continue with their fast. Instead, he and his committee have ensured that this offer has remained hidden for twenty-four years: that particular subterfuge had nothing to do with lady fortune not smiling on them.

One thing has changed since *Blanketmen*: it is no longer sustainable to blandly blame Margaret Thatcher for refusing to countenance any attempts to end the impasse. Demonstrably, what I said in 2006 holds up: 'The Iron Lady was not so steely in the end. She wanted a way out.'[6] Or, as Gerry Adams himself put it: 'Margaret Thatcher presented a public face as the Iron Lady who was "not for turning", yet she was no stranger to expediency.'[7]

Adams and the committee were no strangers to expediency either when it came to dragging the republican movement in from their political Siberia and moulding the Northern Ireland peace process. Of those who made up the committee, it was Gerry Adams who provided the intellectual stimulus that led to the republican movement abandoning armed struggle in favour of constitutional politics. At the moment he is the MP for West Belfast, an MLA for West Belfast and has been president of Sinn Féin for the last twenty-seven years. Arguably, he is recognized throughout the world as the face of change in Northern Ireland politics. He still lives in West Belfast and is a successful writer.

Danny Morrison remained as the press officer for the republican movement until he was convicted of false imprisonment and received an eight-year sentence. After his release from prison in 1995 he allegedly severed his ties with the republican movement, although he has remained their point man on the hunger strike. Morrison pursued a career as a writer and journalist. He is still a close friend of Gerry Adams and is presently the secretary of the Bobby Sands Trust, on which he sits with fellow hunger-strike committee members Gerry Adams, Tom Hartley and Jim Gibney. Bik McFarlane is also a member of the Trust. In October 2008 Morrison's conviction for false imprisonment was overturned on appeal.

Martin McGuinness, reputed to be IRA Chief-of-Staff during the 1981 hunger strike, is now Deputy First Minister in the Northern Ireland Assembly, and works alongside the unionist First Minister, Peter Robinson. McGuinness has stridently renounced those still engaged in armed struggle, and has led the calls for Sinn Féin supporters to inform on these republican rebels.

Tom Hartley, chairman of the hunger-strike committee, emerged as chairman of Sinn Féin in the early 1990s, becoming a Belfast city councillor in 1993. He made good a pledge he had given to one of my family members, at the height of the hunger strike, when he became Lord Mayor of Belfast in 2008. Hartley is also a writer and a local historian.

Jim Gibney is a newspaper columnist, and an advisor to a Sinn Féin MLA in the Northern Ireland Assembly.

All the members of the 'committee' survived the conflict and are now approaching retirement age. They seem to be living fruitful lives. None has ever expressed the slightest regret for the way in which they handled the hunger strike. None has ever admitted playing any part in orchestrating what may well be the biggest cover-up in the history of Irish republicanism.

Thirteen hunger strikers survived the 1981 fast. Of these, Brendan McLaughlin, who had a perforated ulcer and was bleeding internally, was ordered to end his fast on 27 May after thirteen days. Brendan was confined to a wheelchair after a stroke in 2000.

Paddy Quinn's mother intervened to save his life after he lapsed into a coma on 31 July, after forty-seven days on hunger strike. Paddy still has medical problems associated with his time on the hunger strike.

Matt Devlin's family agreed to medical intervention when he went into a coma on 4 September. He had been fifty-two days on the fast. Big Matt died in December 2005 at the age of fifty-five in County Westmeath.

Laurence McKeown's family stepped in to save his life on 6 September, after Laurence had been on the hunger strike for seventy days. Considering his length of time on hunger strike, he has made a remarkable recovery. He is now a playwright and an author.

Pat 'Beag' McGeown's wife, Pauline, asked doctors to save his life when he lost consciousness after forty-two days on hunger strike. Pat Beag was only forty years old when he died from a heart attack in October 1986. Because he suffered from heart disease induced by his hunger strike, Pat Beag is often referred to as 'the eleventh hunger striker' to die.

Bernard Fox's hunger strike ended after thirty-two days when it was discovered that he had an obstructed kidney. Newspaper reports have said that he resigned from the IRA in 2006, after thirty-seven years of dedicated service. It is no secret that Bernard had disagreements about policy with former comrades on the Army Council.

Liam McCloskey ended his hunger strike after fifty-five days when his family told him that they would be requesting medical intervention as soon as he went into a coma. Liam embraced religion after being released from prison.

When the hunger strike was called off, Pat Sheehan had gone fifty-five days without food. He is a Sinn Féin activist.

Jackie McMullan spent thirty-four days on hunger strike. He

is an advisor to the Sinn Féin Minister for Education, Catriona Ruane.

Gerry Carville spent thirty-four days on hunger strike. He is not politically active.

John 'Pickles' Pickering refused food for twenty-six days. He is still thought to be involved with the republican movement.

Gerard 'Hodgies' Hodgkins was on the hunger strike for nineteen days. He is not a member of any political party, but he has supported the campaign to get to the truth behind the deaths of his comrades who lost their lives on the hunger strike.

Jim Devine was the last person to go on hunger strike. His fast lasted twelve days. Jim is not politically active.

Ten great Irishmen died on the hunger strike: Bobby Sands MP, Francis Hughes, Raymond McCreesh, Patsy O'Hara, Joe McDonnell, Martin Hurson, Kevin Lynch, Kieran Doherty TD, Tom McElwee and Micky Devine.

As I was wrapping up an interview with Eamonn McCann in Derry in 2008, he remarked: 'Y'know, I think that the hunger strike was the last flowering of ... the indomitable spirit of republicanism.'[9] Certainly, while other great Irishmen gave their lives in the struggle for Irish freedom, it is fitting that the hunger strikers should be held in the highest esteem because their selflessness represented nothing if not the triumph of the human spirit over death. And if death had no sting for the hunger strikers, then it was Bobby Sands who put into words what his comrades were feeling when he told Monsignor Denis Faul before the start of the hunger strike: 'Greater love hath no man than to lay down his life for his friends.'[9]

Appendix 1

EXTRACT FROM A LETTER DATED 8 JULY 1981 FROM
10 DOWNING STREET TO THE NORTHERN IRELAND OFFICE

The Prime Minister met your Secretary of State at 0015 this morning to discuss the latest developments in the efforts to bring the hunger strike in the Maze to an end. Philip Woodfield was also present.

Your Secretary of State said that the message which the Prime Minister had approved the previous evening had been communicated to the PIRA. Their response indicated that they did not regard it as satisfactory and that they wanted a good deal more. That appeared to mark the end of this development, and we made this clear to the PIRA during the afternoon. This had produced a very rapid reaction which suggested that it was not the content of the message which they had objected to but only its tone. The question now for decision was whether we should respond on our side. He had concluded that we should communicate with the PIRA overnight a draft statement enlarging upon the message of the previous evening but in no way whatever departing from its substance. If the PIRA accepted the draft statement and ordered the hunger strikers to end their protest the statement would be issued immediately. If they did not, this statement would not be put out but instead an alternative statement reiterating the government's position as he [the secretary of state, Humphrey Atkins] had set out in his statement of 30 June and responding to the discussions with the Irish Commission for Justice and Peace would be issued. If there was any leak about the process of communication with the PIRA, his office would deny it.

The meeting then considered the revisited draft statement which was communicated to the PIRA. A copy of the agreed statement is attached.

The Prime Minister, summing up the discussion, said that the statement should now be communicated to the PIRA as your Secretary of State proposed. If it did not produce a response leading to the end of the hunger strike, Mr Atkins should issue at once a statement reaffirming the government's existing position as he had set out on 30 June.

Appendix 2

As you know Philip Woodfield came in here this evening to brief the Prime Minister on the situation in regard to contacts with the hunger strikers in the Maze prison. He explained to the Prime Minister the sequence of events in the last 36 hours leading up to this afternoon's statement by the PIRA about the need for an official to go to the Maze to meet the hunger strikers.

Mr Woodfield told the Prime Minister that Mr Atkins felt that the government had to respond to the PIRA statement either with a statement of its own along the usual lines refusing any negotiation or by sending in an official to clarify the position to the hunger strikers yet again. The official would set out to the hunger strikers what would be on offer if they abandoned their protest. He would do so along the lines discussed with the Prime Minister last week. He would say that the prisoners would be allowed to wear their own clothes, as was already the case in Armagh prison, provided these clothes were approved by prison authorities. (This would apply in all prisons in Northern Ireland.) He would set out the position on association; on parcels and letters; on remission; and on work. On this last point he would make clear that the prisoners would, as before, have to do basic work necessary to keep the prison going: there were tasks which the prison staff could in no circumstances be expected to do. But insofar as work in the prison workshops was concerned, it would be implicit that the prisoners would be expected to do this but that if they refused to do it they would be punished by loss of remission, or some similar penalty, rather than more severely.

Mr Woodfield emphasised that the official would not be empowered to negotiate. He would simply be making a statement about what was on offer to the hunger strikers if they abandoned the hunger strike. The statement would be spelling out what had been implicit in the Government's public statement and explicit in earlier communications. We would aim to avoid argument on the conditions under which the meetings had been arranged. We would simply say that we had done it on our own terms. There could be no guarantee that acting in this way would end the hunger strike. However there had been one or two indications that the hunger strikers were hoping to come off their strike.

The Prime Minister agreed that a further effort should be made to explain the situation to the hunger strikers. The official who went in should stick closely to the statement which had been drafted last week. He should go in to the prison early tomorrow morning.

However, following further discussions, in the course of which it was drawn to the Prime Minister's attention that any approach of the kind outlined above to the hunger strikers would inevitably become public whether or not it succeeded, the Prime Minister reviewed the proposal on the telephone with the Secretary of State for Northern Ireland. Mr Atkins confirmed that it would not be possible to keep the initiative quiet once it had been communicated to the hunger strikers. The Prime Minister said that she thought the approach could be made on the same basis as before and that therefore nothing would be lost by trying. However it seemed that this was not the case. She was more concerned to do the right thing by Northern Ireland than to try to satisfy international critics. Mr Atkins observed that, from a purely Northern Ireland point of view, he would rather do nothing.

The Prime Minister asked whether it would not be sufficient for the official to repeat the Secretary of State's previous statement. Mr Atkins said he did not think this would do the trick.

The Prime Minister asked whether if a detailed offer along the lines set out above were made and failed, he could hold the prison officers [get them to not obstruct the government's policy]. Mr Atkins thought that this would be just about possible. The Prime Minister pointed out that once the offer of own clothes had been made publicly, it would have to be implemented whether or not the hunger strikers called off their strike. Mr Atkins agreed. After further discussion, the Prime Minister decided that the dangers in taking an initiative would be so great in Northern Ireland that she was not prepared to risk them. The official who went in to the prison could repeat the Government's public position but could go no further. The Secretary of State agreed.

The Second Hunger Strike: A Chronology

18 December 1980   The first IRA/INLA hunger strike collapses after fifty-four days when the Officer Commanding the hunger strikers, Brendan Hughes, intervenes to save the life of fellow hunger striker Seán McKenna.

1 March 1981   Bobby Sands, age twenty-seven, from Belfast, goes on hunger strike for 'political status'.

15 March 1981   Francis Hughes, age twenty-five, from south Derry, joins the hunger strike.

22 March 1981   Raymond McCreesh, age twenty-four, from south Armagh, joins the hunger strike.

22 March 1981   Patsy O'Hara, age twenty-four, from Derry city, joins the hunger strike.

9 April 1981   Bobby Sands is elected Member of Parliament for Fermanagh-South Tyrone.

5 May 1981   Bobby Sands dies on the sixty-sixth day of his hunger strike.

9 May 1981   Joe McDonnell, age thirty, from Belfast, replaces Sands on the hunger strike.

12 May 1981   Francis Hughes dies on the fifty-ninth day of his hunger strike.

14 May 1981   Brendan McLaughlin, age twenty-nine, from north Derry, replaces Hughes on the hunger strike.

21 May 1981   Raymond McCreesh and Patsy O'Hara die on the sixty-first day of their hunger strike.

22 May 1981   Kieran Doherty, age twenty-five, from Belfast, replaces Raymond McCreesh on the hunger strike.

23 May 1981   Kevin Lynch, age twenty-five, from north Derry, replaces Patsy O'Hara on the hunger strike.

27 May 1981   Brendan McLaughlin ends his hunger strike after suffering from a perforated ulcer.

29 May 1981   Martin Hurson, age twenty-four, from east Tyrone, replaces Brendan McLaughlin on the hunger strike.

3 June 1981   The Irish Commission for Justice and Peace (ICJP) begins attempts to find solution between the prisoners and the British government.

8 June 1981   Tom McElwee, age twenty-three, from south Derry, joins the hunger strike.

15 June 1981   Paddy Quinn, age twenty-eight, from County Armagh, joins the hunger strike.

22 June 1981   Micky Devine, age twenty-seven, from Derry city, joins the hunger strike.

29 June 1981   Laurence McKeown, age twenty-four, from County Antrim, joins the hunger strike.

30 June 1981   The British government issues a tough statement saying that they will not grant political status to the prisoners and will keep control of the prison.

3 July 1981   ICJP have eight-hour meeting with the British.

4 July 1981   The prisoners issue a conciliatory statement saying that all prisoners should be allowed to wear their own clothes. This statement is warmly received in political and media circles.

               The ICJP meets the British again; believe that they have secured a set of concessions that could end the hunger strike.

               A secret intermediary, codenamed 'Mountain Climber', makes contact with an IRA committee, led by Gerry Adams.

5 July 1981 Mountain Climber presents the IRA committee with a set of concessions from the British government.

IRA leader Danny Morrison visits the prisoners and the prison OC, Bik McFarlane. Morrison tells McFarlane what the British are offering.

McFarlane returns to H-Block 3 and tells Richard O'Rawe what is on offer. During a conversation, McFarlane describes the offer as 'amazing'.

McFarlane and O'Rawe accept the offer. McFarlane agrees to inform the committee of this decision.

6 July 1981 Communiqué comes into the prison leadership from Gerry Adams saying that the British offer did not go far enough and that 'more was needed'.

6–7 July 1981 The British government is told by the committee that 'They [the PIRA] wanted a good deal more.'

8 July 1981 Joe McDonnell dies on the sixty-first day of his hunger strike.

10 July 1981 ICJP leave Belfast. They play no further part in the hunger strike.

Pat McGeown, aged twenty-four, from Belfast, replaces Joe McDonnell on the hunger strike.

13 July 1981 Martin Hurson dies on the forty-sixth day of his hunger strike.

15 July 1981 Matt Devlin, age thirty-one, from County Tyrone, replaces Martin Hurson on the hunger strike.

19 July 1981 The British re-activate the Mountain Climber link and send the committee a lengthy statement that contains little new, but which is placatory in tone.

21 July 1981 The secret talks between the British government and the committee break down again.

28 July 1981 The families of the hunger strikers and Monsignor Denis Faul meet Gerry Adams in Belfast in the hope that he can bring about an end to the hunger strike.

Adams agrees to go into the prison to meet the hunger strikers.

29 July 1981 Gerry Adams, republican candidate for Fermanagh-South Tyrone, Owen Carron, and IRSP representative, Seamus Ruddy go into Long Kesh and meet the hunger strikers. Adams tells the hunger strikers and some of their families that there is nothing on the table from the British.

31 July 1981 Paddy Quinn's mother instructs doctors to save her son's life after he goes into a coma.

1 August 1981 Kevin Lynch dies on the seventy-first day of his hunger strike.

2 August 1981 Kieran Doherty, TD, dies on the seventy-third day of his hunger strike.

3 August 1981 Liam McCloskey, age twenty-seven, from north Derry, replaces Kevin Lynch on the hunger strike.

8 August 1981 Tom McElwee dies on the sixty-second day of his hunger strike.

10 August 1981 Pat Sheehan, age twenty-three, from Belfast, joins the hunger strike.

17 August 1981 Jackie McMullan, age twenty-five, from Belfast, joins the hunger strike.

20 August 1981 Micky Devine dies on the sixtieth day of his hunger strike.

Pat McGeown's wife asks doctors to save her husband's life after he goes into a coma.

Owen Carron is elected in the Fermanagh-South Tyrone by-election, called after the death of Bobby Sands.

23 August 1981 Sinn Féin announces that in future it will contest all elections in Northern Ireland.

24 August 1981   Bernard Fox, age thirty, from Belfast, joins the hunger strike.

31 August 1981   Gerry Carville, age twenty-five, from south Down, joins the hunger strike.

4 September 1981   Matt Devlin's family ask doctors to save his life after he goes into a coma.

6 September 1981   Laurence McKeown's family ask doctors to save his life after he goes into a coma.

7 September 1981   John Pickering, age twenty-five, from Belfast, joins the hunger strike.

14 September 1981   Gerard Hodgins, age twenty-one, from Belfast, joins the hunger strike.

21 September 1981   Jim Devine, age twenty-four, from County Tyrone, joins the hunger strike.

25 September 1981   Bernard Fox ends his hunger strike because of an obstructed kidney.

26 September 1981   Liam McCloskey ends his hunger strike after his family tell him that no matter what, they will ask doctors to save his life if he goes into a coma.

3 October 1981   The hunger strike ends.

Notes

PROLOGUE

1. Conversation with member of the BBC *Spotlight* documentary team.
2. Communication (comm) from Gerry Adams to prison leadership, 6 July 1981.

ONE

1. An Taoiseach, Bertie Ahern, RTÉ programme, *This Week*, 9 January 2005.
2. Catherine McCartney, *Walls of Silence* (Dublin: Gill & Macmillan Ltd 2007), p. 10.
3. Gerry Adams, *Before the Dawn: An Autobiography* (London: Heinemann 1996), p. 294.
4. Revd Ian Paisley in a speech in Ballymena, 7 November 2007.

TWO

1. *Sunday Times*, 27 February 2005.
2. Adams, *Before the Dawn*, p. 305.
3. David Beresford, *Ten Men Dead: The Story of the 1981 Irish Hunger Strike* (London: Grafton Books 1987), p. 324.
4. *Ibid*, p. 330.
5. *Ibid*, p. 418.
6. *Sunday Times*, 27 February 2005.
7. *Ibid*.
8. Alexander Pope, *An Essay on Criticism* (1710).

THREE

1. BBC Radio Ulster, *Talk Back*, 28 February 2005.
2. *Ibid*.

3. *Ibid.*
4. *Ibid.*
5. *Ibid.*
6. *Ibid.*
7. *Irish News*, 28 February 2005.
8. BBC Radio Ulster, *Talk Back*, 28 February 2005.
9. *Ibid.*
10. *Ibid.*
11. *Ibid.*
12. *Ibid.*
13. *Ibid.*
14. *Ibid.*
15. Denis O'Hearn, *Bobby Sands: Nothing but an Unfinished Song* (London: Pluto Press 2006), pp. 299–300.

FOUR

1. Horace, *Epistles* Book 1, no. 18, 1, 71.
2. BBC Radio Ulster, *Talk Back*, 28 February 2005.
3. *Ibid.*
4. Padraig O'Malley, *Biting at the Grave: The Irish Hunger Strikes and the Politics of Despair* (Belfast: The Blackstaff Press 1990), p. 96.
5. BBC Radio Ulster, *Talk Back*, 28 February 2005.
6. *Ibid.*
7. *Ibid.*
8. *Ibid.*
9. *Ibid.*
10. *Ibid.*
11. *UTV News*, 28 February 2005.
12. BBC Radio Ulster, *Talk Back*, 28 February 2005.

FIVE

1. Beresford, *Ten Men Dead*, pp. 335–7.
2. *UTV News,* 28 February 2005.
3. Richard O'Rawe, *Blanketmen: An Untold Story of the H-Block Hunger Strike* (Dublin: New Island 2005), p. 220.

SIX

1. 'Hunger strikers' lives not sacrificed: family', *Irish News*, 2 March 2005.
2. *Ibid.*
3. *Ibid.*
4. 'Book is an outrageous slur on hunger strikers', *Irish News*, 2 March 2005.
5. 'Hunger strikers' lives not sacrifice – family', *Irish News*, 2 March 2005.
6. *Ibid.*
7. *Ibid.*
8. *Ibid.*
9. *Ibid.*
10. *Ibid.*
11. *Ibid.*
12. *Ibid.*
13. 'Monsignor Faul regrets his late intervention', *Irish News*, 2 March 2005.

SEVEN

1. 'Hunger Strikers story brought to book', *Daily Ireland*, 2 March 2005.
2. *Ibid.*
3. *Ibid.*
4. Ed Moloney, *Voices from the Grave* (London, Faber and Faber 2010), pp. 251–2.
5. *Ibid.*

EIGHT

1. The funeral was held on 3 November 2008.
2. 'O'Rawe's attacks untrue', *Daily Ireland*, 9 March 2005.
3. *Frontline Online*, The IRA/Sinn Féin interviews.
4. O'Malley, *Biting at the Grave*, p. 83.

NINE

1. Anthony McIntyre, *Good Friday: The Death of Irish Republicanism* (New York: Ausubo Press 2009), p. 73.

TEN

1. 'Hunger strike claim row deepens', *Irish News,* 3 March 2005.
2. *Ibid.*
3. *Ibid.*
4. *Ibid.*
5. O'Rawe, *Blanketmen*, p. 174.
6. Interview with IRA leader, September 2008.
7. *Ibid.*
8. *Ibid.*
9. *Ibid.*
10. Interview with second IRA leader, November 2008.
11. *Ibid.*
12. *Ibid.*
13. *Ibid.*
14. Beresford, *Ten Men Dead*, p. 345.
15. *Ibid.* pp. 329–34.
16. Interview with IRA leader, November 2008.
17. *Ibid.*
18. Beresford, *Ten Men Dead*, pp. 333–4.
19. Interview with IRA leader, November 2008.

ELEVEN

1. Interview with Seán Flynn, 4 December 2008.
2. 'Documents still withheld', *Bobby Sands Trust,* 7 April 2009.
3. IRSP spokesperson Willie Gallagher, 2 April 2009.
4. O'Malley, *Biting at the Grave*, p. 97.
5. Bik McFarlane, RTÉ *Pat Kenny Show*, 31 October 2008.
6. O'Malley, *Biting at the Grave*, p. 97.
7. RTÉ documentary, *Hidden Lives*, May 2006.
8. Beresford, *Ten Men Dead*, p. 302.
9. O'Malley, *Biting at the Grave*, pp. 95–6.

TWELVE

1. O'Malley, *Biting at the Grave*, p. 94.
2. *Ibid.*, p. 120.
3. *Ibid.*, p. 121.
4. *Ibid.*, p. 121.
5. Beresford, *Ten Men Dead*, p. 335.
6. Interview with Hugh Logue, Dublin, 19 September 2008.
7. *Ibid.*
8. Liam Clarke interviews Hugh Logue, May 2008.
9. *Ibid.*
10. Padraig O'Malley, *Biting at the Grave*, p. 97.
11. Liam Clarke interviews Hugh Logue, May 2008.
12. *Ibid.*
13. 'Former comrades' war of words over hunger strike', *Irish News*, 11 March 2005.
14. *UTV News*, 28 February 2005.
15. 'British had no intention of resolving the hunger strikes', *Belfast Telegraph*, 4 June 2009.
16. 'Former comrades' war of words over hunger strike', *Irish News*, 11 March 2005.

THIRTEEN

1. 'O'Rawe's attack "untrue" ', *Daily Ireland*, 9 March 2005.
2. 'Hunger strike offer controversy rumbles on', *Daily Ireland*, 14 March 2005.
3. 'McFarlane denies hunger strike deal', *Andersonstown News,* 18 March 2005.
4. RTÉ documentary, *Hidden Lives*, 9 May 2006.
5. 'Out of the H-Blocks came determination', *Daily Ireland*, 10 May 2006.
6. *Daily Ireland*, 6 June 2006.
7. *Ibid.*
8. *Ibid.*
9. *Ibid.*

FOURTEEN

1. O'Malley, *Biting at the Grave*, p. 81.
2. *The Secret Peacemaker*, BBC documentary, 27 March 2008.
3. 'Will the IRA ever admit the truth over hunger strike?', *Belfast Telegraph*, 27 March 2008.
4. *Ibid.*
5. *Ibid.*
6. *Ibid.*
7. *Ibid.*
8. Eamonn McCann interview with Sandy Boyer, *WBAI Radio Free Ireland*, New York, 28 March 2008.
9. *Ibid.*
10. *Ibid.*

FIFTEEN

1. 'Hunger strike account "vindicated" ', *Irish News*, 2 April 2008.
2. *Ibid.*
3. *Ibid.*
4. *Ibid.*
5. *Ibid.*
6. '"There was no offer to end hunger strike" – ex-prisoner', *Derry Journal*, 8 April 2008.
7. 'Will the IRA ever admit the truth over hunger strike?', *Belfast Telegraph*, 27 March 2008.
8. 'There was no offer to end hunger strike' – ex-prisoner', *Derry Journal*, 8 April 2008.
9. 'Britain's offer to end hunger strike is still cloaked in mystery', *Irish News*, 17 April 2008.

SIXTEEN

1. Downing Street documents, 8 July 1981. See Appendix 1.
2. *Ibid.*
3. O'Rawe, *Blanketmen*, p. 184.
4. Brendan Duddy, Derry hunger strike conference, 23 May 2009.
5. Downing Street documents, 27 February 2009.
6. *Ibid.*

7. 'IRA said "No" to hunger strike deal', *Sunday Times*, 5 April 2009.
8. *Ibid.*
9. *Ibid.*
10. Richard O'Rawe interviewed by Anthony McIntyre for 'The Blanket' political website, June 2006.
11. 'O'Rawe never told me his views', *Irish News*, 19 May 2006.
12. 'Did Adams sign their death warrants?', *Sunday Times*, 5 April 2009.
13. *Ibid.*
14. *Ibid.*
15. *Ibid.*
16. *Irish Times*, 6 April 2009.
17. 'Morrison rubbishes renewed claims of hunger strike deal', *Irish News*, 7 April 2009.
18. *Ibid.*
19. 'Let's have the whole truth', *Bobby Sands Trust*, 9 April 2009.
20. 'Disputed events over hunger strike', *Irish Times*, 10 April 2009.
21. *Ibid.*

SEVENTEEN

1. George Bernard Shaw, *Annajanska*, 1919.
2. BBC Radio Foyle, *Sarah Brett Show*, 21 May 2009.
3. *Ibid.*
4. Conversation between John Cassidy and Richard O'Rawe, 21 May 2009.
5. O'Rawe, *Blanketmen*, pp. 176–8.

EIGHTEEN

1. Gerard Hodgkins, Derry hunger strike conference, 23 May 2009.
2. Brendan Duddy, Derry hunger strike conference, 23 May 2009.
3. *Ibid.*
4. Downing Street documents, 27 March 2009.
5. Brendan Duddy, Derry hunger strike conference, 23 May 2009.

1. Richard O'Rawe, Derry hunger strike conference, 23 May 2009.
2. *Ibid.*
3. Downing Street documents, 8 July 1981. See Appendix 1.
4. Brendan Duddy, Derry Hunger strike conference, 23 May 2009.
5. *Ibid.*
6. Downing Street documents, 8 July 1981. See Appendix 1.
7. Brendan Duddy, Derry hunger strike conference, 23 May 2009.
8. *Ibid.*
9. Tommy McCourt (former IRSP leader), Derry hunger strike conference, 23 May 2009.
10. Gerard 'Cleaky' Clarke, Derry hunger strike conference, 23 May 2009.
11. *Ibid.*
12. *Ibid.*
13. *Ibid.*
14. Carrie Twomey, Derry hunger strike conference, 23 May 2009.
15. Joshua Levine, *Beauty and Atrocity: People Politics, and Ireland's Fight for Freedom* (London, HarperCollins 2010), p. 221.
16. *Ibid* p. 217.
17. 'British had no intention of resolving hunger strikes', *Belfast Telegraph*, 4 June 2009.
18. *Ibid.*
19. *UTV News*, 28 February 2005.
20. 'Former comrades' war of words over hunger strike', *Irish News*, 11 March 2005.
21. 'British had no intention of resolving hunger strikes', *Belfast Telegraph*, 4 June 2009.
22. *Ibid.*
23. O'Rawe, *Blanketmen*, p. 176.
24. 'British had no intention of resolving hunger strikes', *Belfast Telegraph*, 4 June 2009.
25. O'Rawe, *Blanketmen*, p. 181.
26. 'British had no intention of resolving hunger strikes', *Belfast Telegraph*, 4 June 2009.
27. Beresford, *Ten Men Dead*, p. 337.

TWENTY

1. Downing Street documents, 27 March 2009.

TWENTY-ONE

1. 'Hunger strikers' families speak out', *Bobby Sands Trust*, 21 June 2009.
2. Interview with Tony O'Hara, Derry, 30 June 2009.
3. 'Families back inquiry into 1981 events', *Derry Journal*, 30 June 2009.
4. *Derry Journal*, 7 July 2009.

TWENTY-TWO

1. 'Deal with British government vetoed by IRA says FitzGerald', *Irish News*, 28 September 2009.
2. *Ibid.*
3. 'Stature of ten men unassailed', *Irish News*, 28 September 2009.
4. 'British had no intention of resolving hunger strikes', *Belfast Telegraph*, 4 June 2009.
5. 'Unionists in NIO scuppered deal', *Irish News*, 28 September 2009.
6. 'Deal allegations hurtful to family', *Irish News*, 28 September 2009.
7. *Ibid.*
8. 'Provos "kept rivals in the dark" ', *Irish News*, 28 September 2009.
9. *Ibid.*
10. 'Honour of those who died needs explanation', *Irish News*, 28 September 2009.
11. *Ibid.*
12. *Ibid.*
13. *Ibid.*
14. *Ibid.*

TWENTY-THREE

1. 'All evidence points to dark dealings', *Irish News*, 29 September 2009.
2. *Ibid.*
3. *Ibid.*
4. 'Deal claims "completely wrong": Ó Brádaigh', *Irish News*, 29 September 2009.
5. *Ibid.*

6. *Ibid.*
7. 'Independent inquiry may end "festering sore" ', *Irish News*, 29 September 2009.
8. *Ibid.*
9. 'O'Rawe warned of backlash from republicans – journalist', *Irish News*, 29 September 2009.
10. *Ibid.*
11. 'Hunger Strikers' children renew inquiry call', *Derry Journal*, 6 October 2009.
12. *Sunday Times*, 28 February 2005.
13. 'The *Irish News* and Garret FitzGerald's "new memory" about 1981 H-Block hunger strike deal', *An Phoblacht*, 8 October 2009.

TWENTY-FOUR

1. 'The *Irish News* and Garret FitzGerald's "new memory" about 1981 H-Block hunger strike deal', *An Phoblacht*, 8 October 2009.
2. *Ibid.*
3. *Ibid.*
4. 'You can't rewrite history, says leading republican', *Andersonstown News*, 21 August 2009.
5. 'The *Irish News* and Garret FitzGerald's "new memory" about 1981 H-Block hunger strike deal', An *Phoblacht*, 8 October 2009.
6. *Ibid.*
7. 'Léargas: ceart agus ceiliuradh', Gerry Adams blog, 9 October 2009.
8. '*An Phoblacht* and *The Irish News*', *Irish News*, 12 October 2009.
9. Brian Campbell, Laurence McKeown, Felim O'Hagan, *Nor Meekly Serve My Time* (Belfast: Beyond the Pale Publications 1994), p. 236.
10. 'There was an offer on the table – but the prisoners weren't told', *Irish News*, 22 October 2009.
11. 'Claims only add to pain says ex-hunger striker', *Irish News*, 22 October 2009.
12. 'The truth about the Hunger Strike', *Irish News*, 22 October 2009.
13. *Ibid.*
14. WBAI radio (New York) interview, Dublin, 15 November 2009.
15. 'All evidence points to dark dealings', *Irish News*, 29 September 2009.

1. O'Rawe, *Blanketmen*, pp. 258–9.
2. Author's interview with Eamonn McCann, Derry, 30 November 2008.
3. 'British had no intention of resolving hunger strikes', *Belfast Telegraph*, 4 June 2009.
4. John Adams, *Argument in Defense of the Soldiers in the Boston Massacre Trials*, 1770.
5. Beresford, *Ten Men Dead*, pp. 335–6.
6. Interviewed by Anthony McIntyre for 'The Blanket' political website, June 2006.
7. Adams, *Before the Dawn*, p. 305.
8. Interview with Eamonn McCann, Derry, 30 November 2008.
9. O'Rawe, *Blanketmen,* p. 126.

Bibliography

Adams, Gerry. *A Pathway to Peace.* Cork and Dublin: Mercier Press, 1988.

_____, *Cage Eleven.* Dingle, County Kerry: Brandon, 1990.

_____, *Before the Dawn: An Autobiography.* London: Heinemann, 1996.

_____, *An Irish Voice: The Quest for Peace.* Dingle, County Kerry: Mount Eagle, 1997.

_____, *Hope and History: Making Peace in Ireland.* Dingle, County Kerry: Brandon, 2003.

Alonso, Rogelio. *The IRA and the Armed Struggle.* London: Routledge, 2006.

Bell, J. Bowyer. *The Secret Army: The IRA, 1916–1979.* Dublin: Academy Press, 1979.

Beresford, David. *Ten Men Dead: The Story of the 1981 Irish Hunger Strike.* London: Grafton Press, 1987.

Bew, Paul (with Gordon Gillespie). *Northern Ireland: A Chronology of the Troubles, 1968–99.* Dublin: Gill and Macmillan, 1999.

Bishop, Patrick and Eamonn Mallie. *The Provisional IRA.* London: Heinemann, 1987.

Boyd, Andrew. *Orange and Green: Will They Ever Agree?* Belfast: Donaldson Archives, 2005.

Campbell, Brian, Laurence McKeown and Felim O'Hagan. *Nor Meekly Serve My Time: The H-Block Struggle, 1976–1981.* Belfast: Beyond the Pale Publications, 1994.

Clarke, Liam. *Broadening the Battlefield.* Dublin: Gill and Macmillan, 1987.

Collins, Tom. *The Irish Hunger Strike.* Dublin and Belfast: White Island, 1986.

Coogan, Tim Pat. *The IRA.* London, Fontana, 1980.

_____, *The Troubles: Ireland's Ordeal 1966–1996 and the Search for Peace.* London: Arrow, 1996.

De Baroid, Ciaran. *Ballymurphy and the Irish War.* London: Pluto Press, 1989.

English, Richard. *Ernie O'Malley: IRA Intellectual.* Oxford: Oxford University Press, 1998.

___, *Armed Struggle: The History of the IRA*. London: Pan, 2003.

___, *Irish Freedom: The History of Nationalism in Ireland*. London: Pan Macmillan, 2006.

Faul, Father Denis and Father Raymond Murray. *The British Army and Special Branch Brutality*: authors, 1976.

____, *The Castlereagh File: Allegations of RUC Brutality, 1976–1977*.

Feeney, Brian, David McKittrick, Seamus Kelters and Chris Thornton. *Lost Lives*. Edinburgh: Mainstream Publishing Company Ltd, 1999.

FitzGerald, Garret. *All in a Life: An Autobiography*. London and Dublin: Gill and Macmillan, 1992.

Holland, Jack, and Henry McDonald: *INLA: Deadly Divisions*. Dublin: Torc, 1994.

Ingram, Martin and Greg Harkin. *Stakeknife: Britain's Secret Agents in Ireland*. Dublin: O'Brien Press, 2004.

Levine, Joshua. *Beauty and Atrocity: People, Politics and Ireland's Fight for Peace*. London: Collins Press, 2009.

McCann, Eamonn. *War and an Irish Town*. London: Pluto Press, 1993; first edition, 1974.

McCartney, Catherine. *Walls of Silence*. Dublin: Gill and Macmillan, 2007.

McDonald, Henry. *Gunsmoke and Mirrors*. Belfast: Gill and Macmillan, 2008.

McIntyre, Anthony. 'Modern Irish republicanism: the product of british state strategies', *Irish Political Studies 10*, 1995.

____, *Good Friday: The Death of Irish Republicanism*. New York City: Ausubo Press, 2008.

McKittrick, David, and David McVey. *Making Sense of the Troubles*. Belfast: Blackstaff Press, 2000.

Moloney, Ed. *A Secret History of the IRA*. London: Allen Lane, The Penguin Press, 2003.

____, *Paisley: From Demagogue to Democrat?* Dublin: Poolbeg, 2008.

——, *Voices from the Grave: Two Men's War in Ireland*. London: Faber and Faber, 2010.

Morrison, Danny. *Then The Walls Came Down: A Prison Journal*. Cork: Mercier Press, 1999.

O'Brien, Brendan. *The Long War*. Dublin: O'Brien Press, 1995.

O'Hearn, Denis. *Bobby Sands: Nothing but an Unfinished Song*. London: Pluto Press, 2006.

O'Malley, Padraig. *Biting at the Grave: The Irish Hunger Strikes and the*

Politics of Despair. Boston, Massachusetts: Beacon Press, 1990.

O'Rawe, Richard. *Blanketmen: An Untold Story of the H-Block Hunger Strike.* Dublin: New Island, 2005.

Ryder, Chris. *Inside the Maze: The Untold Story of the Northern Ireland Prison Service.* London: Methuen Publishing Limited, 2000.

Sands, Bobby. *The Diary of Bobby Sands.* Dublin: Sinn Féin Publicity Department, 1981.

_____, *Prison Poems.* Dublin: Sinn Féin Publicity Department, 1981.

Sharrock, David and Mark Devenport. *Man of War, Man of Peace: The Unauthorised Biography of Gerry Adams.* London: Pan, 1998.

Taylor, Peter. *Provos.* London: Bloomsbury, 1997.

Index

THE STREETS OF
BRUM
PART TWO

Unless otherwise stated all photographs are from the archives of
Birmingham Lives at South Birmingham College.

Rear cover photo of Carl Chinn courtesey of Anthea Bevan.

THE STREETS OF
BRUM
PART TWO

Carl Chinn

BREWIN BOOKS

First published in 2004 by
Brewin Books, Studley, Warwickshire B80 7LG

British Library Cataloguing in Publication Data
A catalogue record for this book is available from
The British Library

ISBN: 1 85858 262 8

Typeset in Times and made and printed
in Great Britain by Warwick Printing Company Limited,
Caswell Road, Leamington Spa CV31 1QD

To
Those Brummies yet unborn to help them
to know who they are

Preface

This is the second volume of a work that I have been researching for as long as I have been studying the history of Birmingham. It is impossible to delve into the city's past without coming into contact with its street names. The city's landscape is shaped by its streets, roads, lanes, alleys and entries as much as it is by its natural physical features such as hills, valleys, streams and rivers; whilst the lives of its people are deeply affected by where they live, work, play and gather socially. Any person, family, group, business, or event that engages the attention of historians is inevitably attached to a street or streets. Without setting out intentionally to discover the origins and histories of Birmingham's streets, I found that I was learning about them through looking at other topics and soon I came to realise how much of our past is encapsulated in the names of our streets. My historical enquiries were enhanced by the fact that as a Brummie I had – like all Brummies – wondered about how streets connected to my family had gained their names.

Originally, I had intended to write one book that included the street and district names of Birmingham. However, I found that I had much too much information for a single work. Accordingly, the district names of Birmingham are covered in *1,000 Years of Brum* (Birmingham: Birmingham Evening Mail, 1999). *The Streets of Brum Part One* followed in 2003. That book and this one can be read separately or as part of a series. In the first volume I focused on a variety of street names beginning with the letters A to E, and in this volume I have attended to streets beginning with the letters F to H. Within each headlined street there is a discussion of closely linked streets that may not begin with these letters. For example, the entry under Gooch Street also includes explanations of **Benacre Street**, **Sherlock Street**, **Wrentham Street** and others – all of which can be understood only in relationship to Gooch Street. Such streets are made bold in the text and are included in the index. Where it is necessary, I have referred to other headline streets that are of relevance to a particular entry. Because of the style of the book there is no list of contents. In effect that is found in the index, whilst the headline streets are gathered in chapters according to the letter of the alphabet to which they pertain. Finally, in the light of my further research into the origins of street names I have revised and extended the introduction from Part One of this work. I have included it here for those who may wish to read Part Two in isolation and for the readers of Part One to take note of changes to the Introduction. I hope that you find reading this book as fascinating as I have found its research.

Foreword

Birmingham's streets, roads and lanes are an absorbing yet neglected aspect of our city's history. They call out to us about long dead landowners, notable figures from the history of Birmingham and England, Brummies long forgotten, farms that have been swept away by the outpouring of our city, remarkable physical features, distant battles, intriguing foreign places and mysterious happenings. Such names almost demand of us that we ask questions of them. Why is Conybere Street so called? Where is the Fashoda that is highlighted in a road on the borders of Selly Park and Ten Acres? How did AB Row gain its name? For what reason are the Adderleys brought to mind in Saltley? Did people wash themselves in Bath Row? And were cherries picked in Cherry Street?

The streets of Brum are a dynamic thing. Like Edgbaston Street, a select handful have been with us since our beginnings as a major town in the later Middle Ages, but hundreds upon hundreds of new streets have appeared with the expansion of the town – and many have disappeared with Birmingham's various redevelopments. Some of these lost streets are expressive and intriguing in their names and lead us to fanciful thoughts about their origins. Why was **Fish Lane**, off Harborne Road, so called and why was it changed to **Bullock Road**? And who decided that Bullock Road was not an attractive name and dropped it in favour of **Kingscote Road** in 1880? How did a **Fisherman's Hut Lane** come to be in Nechells, later becoming part of **Aston Church Road**? What were the origins of **Moses Lane**, Yardley and why did it become **Croft Road** in 1927? For what reason was the colourful **Noah's Ark Passage**, off Montague Street, Bordesley, abandoned in 1894 in favour of **Fawdry Street**? And who named the frightening **Devil's Tooth Hollow Yard** and the **Froggery**, redolent as it is with thoughts of frogs jumping?

Despite the fascination of street names, little has been written about them specifically. One of the first to do so was John Alfred Langford. A writer and journalist, he was a self-educated man who aspired for a better life for working-class people. Best known for compiling the indispensable *A Century of Birmingham Life from 1741–1841* (1868) and *Modern Birmingham and its Institutions from 1841 to 1871* (1873–7), he also published a paper on 'Birmingham Names' in 1870. He pointed out that a large number of street names came from owners of land, whilst churches, the army and conquerors in battle were also prominent. Suggestively he observed that 'whim and caprice have been busy in many cases of street nomenclature; while in others only the genius of misapplication and misappropriateness could have devised the names. At some of these almost everyone who passes them must be seized with an irresistible desire to hurl a stone.' Moreover, while streets with the most meaningless of titles are numerous, 'only a very few indeed are named after our great and memorable men'. Langford went on to declaim the 'barbarous' way in which streets were named in his time. As he stated, the old ones mostly had a meaning, a fitness, a history and vividly recalled past times. Now, unhappily, streets were named without method or system.

Forty-six years later, in 1916, Herbert New also presented a paper on 'Some Street Names'. He emphasised that 'a person of enquiring mind walking through the streets of an old town, can generally form some idea of its past history by reading the names of the streets'. New looked at about 250 street names, mostly in the city centre. He was followed in 1925 by A. H. Bevan, then deputy superintendent in Birmingham's Surveyor's Department. Bevan wrote two articles in *The Roadmaker* to bring to notice the importance of the City's Highway Register as a record of the meaning of local street names. It contained particulars of about 3,000 roads brought to notice since the Highway Register began 1893. Four years later, Bevan drew together 2,000 street names in a typescript aptly called *Birmingham Street Names* and divided them into five groups of origin: (1) landowners and prominent people; (2) places in Britain; (3) Christian names of families connected to owners of land; (4) buildings, institutions, business and physical features; and (5) foreign names. Bevan's task was brought up to date in 1946 by E. H. Sargent in his *Birmingham Street Names*. Both sources are valuable, but they rarely give more than one word about the source of a street's name. Thus the entry for Anderton Road (Sparkbrook) gives the date of its appearance as 1851 and notes its origin as 'landowner'; whilst Edmund Street in the city centre is given as coming to view in 1778 and was related to 'members of the Colmore family'.

Since then, the two most significant researchers into street names have been Vivian Bird and Joseph McKenna. For many years, Vivian Bird wrote a column for the *Evening Mail* called 'Streetwise', and he brought together many of the streets he covered in a book of that name in 1991. Like myself he was fascinated by names and stressed how they 'almost always have their story'. His book includes streets belonging to West Bromwich, Redditch, Tamworth and elsewhere, although the main focus was Birmingham; and it tended to concentrate on those streets connected to the great families of the City. Joseph McKenna's contribution came in 1986, in a book called *Birmingham Street Names*. It fastened upon streets in central Birmingham, giving their date, location and origin, and was compiled from material accessible to Joseph in his work as a librarian at Central Library. Both books are indispensible and have aided me. However, this work is broader. It seeks to look at streets across the whole of the modern city of Birmingham and to bring in a wider range of streets, so long as they are embedded in the history of the town and its people.

Unfortunately as Langford highlighted, many streets do not relate to the city, its history, its peoples or its landscape. Instead they have arisen from the fancy of builders and others who have imposed names from spots unconnected with Birmingham and its past. This trend became most noticeable in the massive growth of the city from the 1920s, when thousands of acres of farmland were overwhelmed by housing. In Kingstanding, the London builder of the district's corporation homes brought in places from the south east of England, for example in **Colindale Road** and **Charlton Road**. Nearby in Perry Common, another council estate was laid out with roads reaching out to Derbyshire as in **Dovedale Road**, and Sussex, as in **Hastings Road**. Similarly in Bournbrook a number of roads, such as **Tiverton Roa**d, call out to the south west; in Birchfield, the developers favoured names from Kent, of the ilk of **Canterbury Road**, and the west country, like **Tewkesbury Road**; whilst more Derbyshire place names occur in Hall Green, amongst them **Burnaston Road**, **Cubley Road**, **Etwall Road** and **Smirrels Road**.

Despite this marked tendency of names unassociated with Birmingham and its history in the twentieth century, there is a captivating array of indigenous names that we all should look at and learn from. How many of us have walked along a street and wondered whence it hailed? And how important is it for our children and our children's children that they gain a sense of place and stability, a feeling of belonging that surely leads on from an awareness of the place names and street names which embrace their lives? Perhaps one of the biggest problems we are faced with today is an alienated and apparently rootless youth. Hopefully through an understanding of local history, young people can be handed a consciousness of the past that leads them both to repect themselves and through such self respect to give respect to others who may be different to them.

Birmingham is not a rootless placet. Bronze Age man and woman passed this way, as the burnt mounds in Moseley Bog and Woodgate Valley show, and the pioneering local historian, John Morris Jones, believed that the ridgeway that is followed by Gravelly Hill, Gravelly Hill North, Erdington High Street and the Sutton Road 'may well be prehistoric'. He also felt that the Chester Road 'is perhaps equally as ancient' and went on to observe that a number of old roads in Erdington 'owe their routes to geology and/or relief; many are ridgeways, at least in part'. In his work *The Manors of North Birmingham*, Jones stresses that 'it is no accident that the five-way junction at Coton End (Six Ways since Wood End was made in the mid-19th c.) is on a well-drained ridge-end, nor that the meeting of lanes near the Navigation Inn is on drift, nor that very few old tracks crossed the clay.' Where tracks had to descend, then the surface was worn away into holloways as in Gully Lane, later **Gravelly Hill**.

Ridegways were apparent elsewhere in the Birmingham region. Ancient upland routes, they kept to drier and clearer land between rivers and avoided the boggy valleys of the Cole, Tame, Rea and smaller streams. Some major modern roads such as the Walsall Road, the Aldridge Road and the Kingstanding Road still follow the course of ridgeways. This latter road also follows the line of the Roman road, the Icknield Street, which came through the Birmingham area via Kings Norton, and Stirchley and after going up to Kingstanding went on through Sutton Park. Probably made in the middle years of the first century AD, it was, according to Roman style, a straight road. This meant that the Roman engineers had to negotiate low-lying ground and rivers, where they made ramps and cuttings. In particular, an artificial ford was brought into use across the River Tame at Perry Barr. After the Romans, their road was washed away at the crossing point.

From the time the Birmingham area was settled by the Angles from the sixth century onwards, there must have been routes connecting various places. Interestingly, the Anglo-Saxons used different terms to describe different types of route. Generally, the word path was restricted to unmade roads that went across open country; whilst the Old English word for road was 'weg', meaning way, as in **Holloway Head**. Victor Skipp, another fine and assiduous researcher of local history, has rescued for history two Anglo-Saxon ways in Yardley. The first was **Dagardingweg** on the Sheldon and Yardley border. It can be followed still as a path across Kent's Moat Park, before becoming **Pool Way** and then **Broadstone Road**. The second was **Leommannincgweg**, which Skipp feels may be what is now the **Stratford Road** in Hall Green. John Morris Jones noted that Leommannincgweg was named after Leomann, cited in the first documentary evidence for Yardley, the Charter of 972 whereby King Edgar confirmed the Abbey of Saint Mary of Pershore in its ownership of five households in 'gyrdleahe'.

The streets of Birmingham as a town, however, did not emerge until after 1166 when its lord, Peter of Bermingham, gained a charter entitling him to hold a market. Within a few years, a handful streets would have emerged and it is likely that **Edgbaston Street** was amongst them. Prior to the development of the new shopping centre in the Bull Ring and its opening in 2003, archaeological work revealed a substantial ditch in Edgbaston Street. This connected the moat around the Parsonage of Saint Martin's Church, close to the junction of Edgbaston Street and the later **Smallbrook Street** and **Pershore Street**, with the moat around the manor house of the lord of Birmingham, on the site of the old Smithfield Market, off Moat Lane. Pottery from the soil layers that filled this watercourse dated to the late thirteenth century, although elsewhere in the street and around the Bull Ring there was evidence for industrial activity, especially tanning, from the twelfth century. Across the way, remains found in **Moor Street** and **Park Street** indicate human activity from at least the late twelfth century onwards. Both these streets were cut out after Edgbaston Street and **Digbeth** and its continuation **High Town** (**High Street**).

Still, the earliest documentary evidence naming a street relates to a lane that was outside the borough, that is the built up part of the manor of Birmingham gathered around Saint Martin's, and in the foreign, the larger, rural part of the lordship. It is a release of property in 1289 from Ranulph son of Walter of Barre to Roger of Somerlone – **Summer Lane**. The first street recorded in the emerging town of Birmingham is Edgbastone Strete (**Edgbaston Street**) mentioned in a deed in 1347; and in 1449 Roger Cutte of Erdington granted to John and Juliane Knocks of Birmingham a burgage and butcher's shop in the same street. Another deed from 1437 concerns property in 'Mowlestrete' – **Moor Street**; whilst in 1454, Sir William Bermyngham, the lord of the manor granted to John of Birmingham one croft of land in **Dale End**. Later in the fifteenth century, in 1482-3, a deed stated that John Lench of **Deritend**, master of the Guild of Holy Cross, with the unanimous assent of the brothers and sisters of the guild, leased to William Wyot a tanner of Birmingham a parcel of land 'lying jux le cawsy' – next to the causeway (see Digbeth).

As well as the streets within the borough, there were a number routes connecting Birmingham with other places, especially nearby settlements such as Aston, Yardley, Castle Bromwich, Walsall and Halesowen. More important nationally was the road from Shrewsbury that went through Dudley and Birmingham to Coventry. Another was the north-south highway that came through the town from Worcester and Droitwich and which went on to Lichfield. The siting of Birmingham on this route led to the inclusion of the town on the Gough Map of about 1330. This road, said to be one of the four great royal roads of England, was a saltway and followed the fourteen-mile sandstone ridge above the valley of the Rea that goes from Northfield to Sutton, and upon which the medieval town of Birmingham was placed.

Unfortunately, there is no evidence that describes the look of Birmingham and its streets until 1538, when John Leland visited the town as part of his travels across Tudor England. He came by way of King's Norton, then an attractive country town in Worcestershire where there was a fine church and some good houses belonging to woolstaplers, which probably included the 'Saracen's Head' which is still there on The Green today. The wayfarer then passed through good areas of woodland and pasture before he came to Camp Hill and went down 'as pretty a street or ever I entrd'. This was Deritend High Street, or 'Dirtey' as Leland called it.

> In it dwell smithes and cutlers, and there is a brooke that divideth this street from Birmingham, and is an Hamlett, or member belonginge to the Parish t h e r e b y e (Aston).

> There is at the end of Dirtey a proper chappell (St John's) and mansion house of tymber (the 'Old Crown' pub), hard on the ripe (bank), as the brooke runneth downe; and as I went through the ford by the bridge, the water ran downe on the right hande (later Floodgate Street) and a few miles lower goeth into Tame, ripa dextra (by the right bank). This brooke riseth, as some say, four or five miles above Bermingham, towards Black Hilles.

> The beauty of Bermingham, a good market down in the extreame (border) parts of Warwickshire, is one street, going up alonge (Digbeth) almost from the left ripe (bank) of the brooke, up on the meane (modest) hill by the length of a quarter of a mile.

From Birmingham, Leland headed north and crossed the River Tame at Sharford Bridge, later to be known as **Salford Bridge** in Aston. He rode on to Sutton Coldfield across sandy ground upon which was grown rye, barley and oats.

The detailed researches of Toulmin Smith in the nineteenth century shed light on the origins of a number of streets from the period of Leland's journey. An indefatigable enquirer into the history of Birmingham, Toulmin' Smith's family were closely associated with the 'Old Crown' in Deritend. He examined a grant of properties dated 1532 to a John Pretty from Edward Bermingham, the last of his family to be lord of Birmingham. These holdings included a water mill to grind corn called Heth Mill, hence **Heath Mill Lane**; lands called the Conyngry, leading to **Congreve Street**; and the Dodwalls, which gave rise to **Dudley Street**. Toulmin Smith also scoured the Report of the King's Commissioners of 1547. Appointed in the first year of the reign of Edward VI, the commissioners gave an account of the Gild of the Holy Cross. Set up in 1392, this body had been broken up recently under Henry VIII's policy of dissolving monasteries and other religious bodies after he cut off the church in England from the the Roman Catholics.

The commissioners indicated that the Gild had operated with a variety of functions and was able to pay for its work by away of income from land given to it by leading people locally. As a religious association it maintained a chantry in Saint Martin's; and as a social gathering it brought together its members in various activities. It also undertook specific public duties for the benefit of the people of Birmingham. In particular, it relieved twelve poor persons and provided them with an almshouse in Digbeth, and it kept 'in good Raparaciouns, two greate stone bridges and diuers ffoule and daungerous high wayes; the charge whereof the towne of hitselfe ys not hable to mainteign; So that that the Lacke thereof wilbe a great noysaunce to the Kings ma^ties Subjectes passing to and ffrom the marches of wales, and an vtter Ruyne to the same towne – being one of the fairest and most profittuble towne to the Kinges highness in all the Shyre.' Another body that survives in modern Birmingham also repaired 'ruinous waies and bridges in and about the same towne of Birmingham'. This was Lench's Trust, founded in 1525.

Toulmin Smith's researches into the 1547 report highlighted the tenants and tenancies of the Gild of the Holy Cross and through them he was able to note a number of streets. These included the **Bull Ring**; Chappell Street (see **Bull Street**); Deryatend (see **Deritend High Street**); Dalend (see **Dale End**); Egebaston Street (see **Edgbaston Street**); Englishe Street (see **High Street**); Godes Cart Lane (see **Carrs Lane**); **High Street**; Mercer Street (see **Spiceal Street**); le Pinfolde (see **Pinfold Street**); Molle Strete Barres and Molle Strete End (see **Moor Street**); Newe Street (see **New Street**); Parke Strete (see **Park Street**); and **Well Street** (see **Digbeth**).

Six years later, the *Survey of the Borough and Manor or Demesne of Birmingham* (1553) gives a comprehensive number of Birmingham's streets. Carried out in the first year of Queen Mary's reign, it followed on from the attainder (forfeiture of land because of treason) of John Dudley, the Duke of Northumberland, who had come to be the lord of Birmingham. This survey brings to the fore a number of other streets: Bordesley (see **Bordesley High Street**); Dudwall Lane (see **Dudley Street**); Dygbeth (see **Digbeth**); Priors Conynge Lane (see **Congreve Street**); **The Shambles**; **Swan Alley**; and Welch Market (see **High Street**). From this list it can be seen clearly that Birmingham was based on one long street, running from

Bordesley High Street along Deritend High Street and Digbeth and into High Street Birmingham. All the other streets came off this main stretch, and an examination of deeds and tenancies would indicate that Edgbaston Street was the most important of these. This street pattern was shaped like a crescent, leading to some people to describe Birmingham as the town of the half moon.

By the time of Bradford's **Plan of Birmingham** of 1751, the earliest map to show street lines and mark the town's boundaries, this street pattern remained obvious – although development had now begun to spread up hill and across the ridge on which Saint Philip's is placed. Bradford lists 93 streets and the number of houses and people in each, giving a population of 23,688. The making of these streets was declaimed by Hutton:

The inhabitants of Birmingham may be styled masters of invention; the Arts are obedient to their will. But if Genius displays herself in the shops, she is seldom seen in the streets; though we have a long time practised the art of making streets, we have an art to learn; there is not a street in the whole town but might have been better constructed. When land is appropriated for a street, the builders are under no control; every lessee proceeds according to his interest or fancy; there is no man to preserve order, or prescribe bounds; hence arise evils without a cure; such as a narrowness which scarcely admits light, cleanliness, pleasure, health, or use; unneccesary hills, like that in Bull Street; sudden falls, owing to the floor of one house being laid three feet lower than the next, as in Coleshill Street; one side of a street, like the deck of a ship, 'gunnel to', several feet higher than the other, as in Snow Hill, New Street, Friday Street, Paradise Row, Lionel Street, Suffolk Street, Brick-kiln Lane, and Great Charles Street.

Hutton wrote his first edition of his *History of Birmingham* in 1781. By this time, the town had begun an extraodinary rise on to the world stage through the manufacturing prowess of its people. As its repuation waxed and its products increased, so too did the number of its people and the streets in which they lived. In 1808, *Bissett's Magnificent Guide of Birmingham* was published. Its author stated that the town had upwards of 300 streets and 600 courts and he included a curious verse about Birmingham that echoes the criticisms of Hutton.

The STREETS are spacious, BUILDINGS neat and clean,
As in a TRADING TOWN were ever seen;
And FIFTEEN THOUSAND HOUSES here you'll find,
With Ten Thousand Shops arrang'd behind.
Where *whirling* LATHES, and STAMPS' tremendous sound,
With tinkling HAMMERS are in concert found.
Whilst Shops in front assume a nobler grace,
Deck'd with the various wonders of the place.

> The STREETS are pav'd, 'tis true, but all the stones
> Are set the wrong end up, in shape of cones;
> And STRANGERS limp along the best-pav'd street,
> As if parch'd peas were trew'd beneath their feet,
> Whilst custom makes the NATIVES scarcely feel
> Sharp pointed pebbles press the toe or heel.

Birmingham was now entered upon a period of almost continual change, whereby new streets were cut out of farmland and old ones were swept away in redevelopments. Some of these changes were carried out by landowners, others by the Street Commissioners, a body established by legislation in 1769. Birmingham did not have a council until it was incorporated by Act of Partliament in 1838, and until then the Street Commissioners provided a limited form of local government for the town. As their title suggested, their powers related mostly to the condition of the town's streets. The Act that established the Commissioners stated that it was for 'laying open and widening certain ways and passages within the Town of Birmingham, and for cleansing and lighting the streets, ways, lanes, and passages there, and for removing and preventing nuisances and obstructions therein'. Strengthened by another Act in 1773, the Commissioners widened **Bull Lane**, **Moor Street**, **Mount Pleasant, New Street** and **Smallbrook Street**; and following a third Act in 1801, they solved the problem of the congestion of houses and small streets that hemmed in Saint Martin's.

In 1806 the houses on the east side of Spiceal Street and the west side of the Bull Ring were pulled down. This clearance led to the disappearance of a number of tiny streets: **Cock Street**, also called **Well Street** and **Well Yard**, indicating the plentiful water supply locally; **Corn Cheaping** was where corn had been sold; and **The Shambles** was where the butchers had put up their stalls. The action of the street commissioners allowed the forming of that great triangular space of land which had Saint Martin's as its base and the bottom of High Street as its top point and which is the old Bull Ring recalled so affectionately by many older Brummies. Such an opening up led to the injunction that no stalls should be set up above Philip Street. Market traders were to gather now in the Bull Ring which had been at the heart of the Medieval town and where there was ample room 'for every purpose of that kind'. Two more Acts further augmented the ability of the Street Commissioners to affect the look of Birmingham, and that of 1828, in particular, enabled them to fix the levels of new streets and of old ones when altered; to require property owners to pave the street in front of new buildings; and enjoined builders to set back by seven yards from the centre of the road new properties in streets that were not fully built up.

By the mid-1820s, the houses in Birmingham had been given numbers and each street had its name affixed in cast iron to a conspicuous situation. Importantly, as was pointed out in Drake's *Picture of Birmingham* in 1825, the most welcome development of all regarding the local streets was 'the gradual substitution of stone flagging for the causeways, instead of the sharp-pointed pebbles, so long the opprobrium of the place, and on which the stranger painfully worked his way, marvelling that streets so long should be made so execrably wearisome. This stigma is now in the course of removal …' This writer noted 280 streets for the 102,000 people of the town, and he bemoaned the 'multitude of mean houses and streets'. Though amazing, the growth of Birmingham had led to many streets 'composed of houses of inconsiderable description, abounding too in retired courts and yards, filled with multitudes of still smaller dwellings'.

The rapid ouward march of Birmingham and the transformation of the appearance of the older part of the town led James Dobbs to write the song 'I Can't Find Brummagem' in 1828.

I Can't Find Brummagem

Full twenty years and more are passed
Since I left Brummagem.
But I set out for home at last
To good old Brummagem.
But ev'ry place is altered so
Now there's hardly a place I know,
Which fills my heart with grief and woe
For I can't find Brummagem.

As I was walking down the street
As used to be in Brummagem,
I knowed nobody I did meet
For they've changed their face in Brummagem.
Poor old Spiceal Street's half gone,
And Old Church stands alone,
And poor old I stands here to groan
For I can't find Brummagem.

But amongst the changes we have got
In good old Brummagem,
They've made a market on the moat
To sell the pigs in Brummagem.
But that has brought us more ill luck
For they've filled up Pudding Brook,
Where in the brook jack-bannils took
Near Good old Brummagem.

But what's more melancholy still,
For poor old Brummagem,
They've taken away all Newhall-Hill
From poor old Brummagem,
At Easter time girls fair and brown,
Came roly-poly down,
And showed their legs to half the town,
Oh! the good old sights in Brummagem.

Down Peck Lane I walked along,
To find out Brummagem,
There was the dungil down and gone
What? no rogues in Brummagem,
They've ta'en it to a street called Moor,
A sign that rogues ain't fewer,
But rogues won't like it there I'm sure,
While Peck Lane's in Brummagem.

I remember one John Growse,
Who buckles made in Brummagem,
He built himself a country house,
To be out of the smoke of Brummagem
But though John's country house stands still,
The town has walked up hill,
Now he lives beside a smoky mill,
In the middle of Brummagem.

Among the changes that abound
In good old Brummagem,
May trade and happiness be found
In good old Brummagem.
And tho' no Newhall Hill we've got
Nor Pudding Brook nor Moat,
May we always have enough
To boil the pot in Brummagem.

Dobbs was a comedian and performed this song first at the Theatre Royal, New Street in 1828. Though written humorously, it has at its heart a lament at the loss of well-known streets. It is through this melding of wit and poignancy that Dobbs reaches out to each generation of Brummies. For in each generation, developers and planners seem to take our city, knock it down and replace it with new buildings and places. Brummies ourselves are too often excluded from the process of redevelopment, so that there is a sense of loss in each generation for the streets in which once we lived, shopped and worked and which have been chucked so carelessly into the miskin of history. The streets of Brum and their people deserve better.

Bradford's record of 93 streets in 1751 focused on the built-up part of Birmingham and does not mention Summer Lane or other streets and ways in the then farmland districts such as Hockley, Winson Green and Ladywood. And of course it excludes all those districts that were to join Birmingham from 1838 onwards. These included Duddeston, Nechells and Edgbaston (1838); Balsall Heath, Harborne and Saltley (1891); Quuinton (1909); Aston, Erdington, Handsworth, Kings Norton and Yardley (1911); and much of Perry Barr and Castle Bromwich (inter-war years). Bradford thus includes 50 streets, ten lanes, six alleys, four rows, two squares, one court and one green. These are supplemented by a variety of streets known by just a name – as with Corn Cheaping, Deritend, Digbeth, Froggary, High Town (High Street), **Lower Minories** See (The Minories), **Lower Priory** and others.

Within a generation the number of streets had risen markedly. The earliest Directory of Birmingham was published by Sketchley and Adams in 1770. It also covered Wolverhampton, Walsall, Dudley and a number of Black Country industrial villages. A most rare book, it was reprinted in 1886 under the auspices of Samuel Timmins, best known for the work he edited on *The Birmingham and Midland Hardware District* (1866). His friend, R. B. Prosser, re-arranged the Directory under an alphabet of streets. This was not a complete list of the streets of the time, for the Directory fastened upon the more prominent of Birmingham's inhabitants. Thus streets without such citizens may not have been included.

Allowing for this, the Directory does give an indication as to the expansion of the town and it names 128 streets, yards and rows. Amongst them were Little Lovely Street and Lovely Street, perhaps meaning **Loveday Street**; and **The Hill**, **Jennings Street** and **Saint Anthony Street** – none of which are named on any map or in any other document. Then there are a number of yards: **Bear Yard**, off Bull Street; **Boot Yard** in New Street; **Collins Court** behind Church Street; **Higgins's Yard**, near Russell Street; **Horse Shoe Yard**, off Saint Martin's Lane; **Hunt's Yard** in Digbeth; **New England**, a sign for which still exists in Deritend High Street; **Rann's Yard,** off High Street; and **Topham Row**.

Seven years after this first directory appeared the *Birmingham Directory* was brought out. It gave 148 thoroughfares with various endings – the most popular of which was still that of street. It continued to be so for several decades and it was customary to connect the word street to its name via a hyphen, as with High-street, Bull-street etc. The word street itself derives from the Latin 'strata via', meaning paved way, becoming 'straet' in Old English. The Anglo-Saxons used street in the names of settlements close to a Roman road, as with Stirchley (originally Strutley) and Streetly, both close to the **Icknield Street**. Later streets emerged within settlements. Usually they were associated with main thoroughfares and often indicated a route to somewhere, for example with **Edgbaston Street**.

In modern times, the word lane raises up visions of rural settings, but in earlier periods it was often used for a narrow street in a town, like with **Peck Lane**. As Birmingham expanded, these urban lanes were added to with lanes that had been in the country. These were longer and often wider. There are a number of examples, including **Sandy Lane**, **Summer Lane** and **Watery Lane** – each of which indicates the nature of the particular route through their expressive names. As for the term road, it is from the Old English word 'rad', from 'ridan', meaning to ride. This origin may explain the use of the term 'orse road' by working-class Brummies when warning their children 'to mind the 'orse road'. The word road occurs only once in Shakespeare and it remained unusual until the eighteenth century when it was used in association with the building of military routes in Scotland and turnpikes in England. Administered by trusts authorised by private acts of Parliament, turnpikes took their name from a pike that formed a barrier to traffic and that was turned to allow access. These turnpike trusts were empowered to levy tolls on travellers. The money raised was spent on the upkeep and maintenance of the route. This involved the digging of drainage ditches and the laying down of a surface of stones and cinders.

For many years the word road was restricted to these turnpikes that led to other places, such as the **Alcester Road**, **Bristol Road**, **Coventry Road** and **Dudley Road**. Road was also applied to routes that were not turnpiked but which went to a nearby village or town, as with the **Aston Road** and **Saltley Road**. But as late as 1834, *Guest's Plan of Birmingham* included little more than a handful of roads, only four which were not linked with a route to a place outside Birmingham. These were **Asylum Road**, Summer Lane; **Tookey's Road**, Hockley, about which there is a no information; and **Lee Bank Road** and **Wellington Road**, Edgbaston. Over the next thirty-odd years, a few more roads appeared, but from the 1870s there was a massive increase in the number of roads. This extraordinary rise is tied up with the issue of class.

The development of the locality of The Square (Old Square) in the early eighteenth century allowed manufacturers, merchants and professionals to move up the hill and away from Digbeth to a drier and healthier spot that afforded good views. As Birmingham developed, this area became surrounded by manufactories and was enveloped in pollution and so the middle class moved again, this time to Handsworth in the north west and to the Calthorpe Estate in Edgbaston in the south west. Edgbaston was fortuitously placed in the direction of the prevailing winds in England, and so was upwind of the smoke and smells of Birmingham. With the flight of the more prosperous of the citizenry, the gardens and open spaces in central Birmingham were filled in with workshops and back-to-back houses. This infilling increased the overcrowding and fumes and led to the connection of streets with the older parts of Birmingham in which the poor lived in badly-built and decrepit housing. Regarded as short, narrow and unpleasant, streets were not places that were attractive to the wealthier folk of Birmingham.

Leading figures associated with the Calthorpe Estate recognised quickly the negative connotations of streets. In 1870 the word street was mostly expunged from

Edgbaston when Calthorpe Street, Frederick Street and George Street were renamed **Calthorpe Road**, **Frederick Road** and **George Road**. Only **Parker Street** and **Bellis Street** have remained as streets in the whole of this populous and extensive district. Builders of new houses for the lower middle class and better off of the working class soon followed the example set in Edgbaston. In 1870, the Balsall Heath Local Board of Health (an independent authority until it joined Birmingham in 1891) gave permission for the cutting of **Henry Street** through the small estate of Henry Ludlow off the Ladypool Road. This was the last street to be named in Sparkbrook. Twenty years later when the Watkins Estate was developed, the forming of **Brunswick Road**, **Colville Road, Fulham Road** (later **Leamington Road),** **Kingsley Road**, **Oldfield Road** (into which Henry Street was absorbed) and **Ombersley Road** indicated the dominance of roads. The same pattern was apparent elsewhere. Bordesley Green was urbanised from the late nineteenth century and it has only one street, **Denbigh Street**. There are no streets in Alum Rock, Bournbrook, Ward End, and Washwood Heath, all of which were suburbanised from the 1880s onwards. In Erdington and Kings Heath, the only streets are in the old village parts of the districts; whilst in Handsworth the few streets in the area are clustered in the vicinity of **Booth Street**. As for Aston, Saltley, Small Heath and Stirchley, streets dominate the localities developed before the 1880s and roads those built up from that decade.

In his book *The Birmingham I Remember* Leslie Mayell emphasised the higher social status of roads. He stated that Sparkhill was superior to Sparkbrook as 'For one thing it had no streets. They were all called roads.' This was a slight exaggeration as there were six streets around **Shakespeare Street**, developed in the 1850s and well before the roads of Sparkhill. Still, there can be no dispute with Mayell's overall impression that the address of a road gave a better impression than that of a street. The use of lane also suffered from the prejudice of the prosperous of Birmingham. In 1883 Ladypool Lane, Sparkbrook became known as **Ladypool Road**, and four years later 'a resident' wrote to the *Balsall Heath Times* asserting that, 'The postal address of **Highgate Lane** is bad, and has a tendency to drive away some householders to the more congenial and pleasant sounding road'.

Ten years later Highgate Lane and **Thomas Street**, which was the continuation of Highgate Lane between the Ladypool Road and the Stoney Lane, were renamed **Highgate Road**. Lanes disappeared in other parts of Birmingham. In 1875 **Bear Lane** was changed to **Sandon Road**; in 1878, Monument Lane, Ladywood was made **Monument Road**; in 1888, **Love Lane**, Sparkbrook became known as **Medlicott Road**; in 1897 **Brick Kiln Lane**, Erdington was renamed **Summer Road** and **Barrel Lane**, Handsworth was turned into **Louise Road;** and in 1898, **Workhouse Lane**, Yardley was transformed into **Holder Road**.

The rise in prominence of the word road and the prevalence of streets and lanes in older, working-class Birmingham may well have led to the humorous Birmingham monologue called 'The Lord Mayor Had a Coachman'. The author is unknown, although it must have been written after 1895 when James Smith became the first lord mayor of the city. Interestingly a Leslie Waller of Sparkbrook wrote to the *Evening Mail* and stated this monologue was a party piece of his father, whose own father was coachman to Sir James Smith when he held office.

The Lord Mayor Had a Coachman

The Lord Mayor had a coachman and the coachman's name was John,
Said his lordship to the coachman, take your wages and begone.
I want a better coachman, for I'm going to take a drive.
Said John, I'm the finest coachman you will find alive.
And if you'll let me drive today I'll show I can't be beat.
I'll drive you all around Birmingham and I won't go through a street.
Said his lordship, John you must be mad but still I'll humour you,
But remember that you lose your place the first street you go through.

The mayor jumped in his carriage and the coachman on his seat,
He then drove down Victoria Road which we know is not a street,
Lozells Road, Villa Road – said his lordship, 'What's his game'?
And John drove into Soho Road and turned down Queens Head Lane,
Foundry Road and Slough Lane and Foundry Road he drives
And thus he keeps out of a street he artfully contrives.

Winson Green and Icknield Port, said his lordship, 'Well that's good',
And John wheeled round the corner into Ladywood.
Islington Row he next drives through said his lordship. 'Now he's beat.
For if you go straight on', my man, you must go through Sun Street.
But John said, 'No that will not do, for I have another mode',
He then turned round from Lea Bank and into Ryland Road.

Charlotte Road and Wellington Road, the coachman next drives through,
Bristol Road and Belgrave Road away he quickly flew.
Now we're into Moseley Road – said his lordship in a pet –
'Dash my wig and barnacles, I think he'll do it yet.'
Highgate Place and Kyrwicks Lane and Auckland Road the same,
Stratford Road up to the Ship and then down Sandy Lane.
Coventry and Bordesley Green are the roads that next they pass.
Park Road, Mill Lane, Saltley Road through the yard they make the gas,
Then the Recreation Ground and on through Nechells Park,
Holborn Road and Lichfield Road, said his lordship, 'What a lark.'
Said John, 'It's now Victoria Road and I think your lordship's had a treat,
For I've driven all round the city and I've not been through a street.'

The move away from the use of street and lane was accompanied by a changing of names that were thought to be unappealing. In this way **Grindstone Lane**, Edgbaston was made more acceptable as **Westfield Road** and **Hermitage Road** in 1866; **Jawbone Lane**, Handsworth was turned into **Laurel Road** in 1879 whilst **Tonk Street** was erased for **Hill Street** in the city centre; **Sheep Street**, Erdington made way for **Station Road** in 1897; **Donkey Lane**, Acocks Green was dropped for **Harvey Road** in 1906; **Tanyard Lane**, Yardley was transformed into **Amington Road** in 1907; and **Madcap Lane**, Yardley became **Graham Road** and **Bedlam Lane**, Northfield gave way to **Tessall Lane** in 1927.

Many other names have disappeared, and hundreds upon hundreds of more have arisen. An understanding of the origins and location of such streets enhances not only our appreciation of Birmingham's past but also an awareness of our city's place in the wider contexts of time and place. The past is not a foreign land. It is part of a continuous line running into the present and the future, informing and affecting both. If we ignore our past we cannot face the present with confidence nor can we look forward positively to the future. In a period when the cult of individuality threatens our social fabric, the street names of Birmingham call to us to understand them and understand our collective self.

F

Fallows Road, Sparkbrook

Running south east between Anderton Road and Walford Road, this road would seem to recall Thomas Stratton Fallows. The grandson of a Birmingham solicitor and the son of a local auctioneer with offices in Needless Alley, Fallows was born at Griffin's Hill, Northfield in October 1836. Educated at a private school in Handsworth, he joined his father's business in 1852 and stepped into public life in 1867 when he was elected to the Board of Guardians. The same year he was appointed as an Overseer of the Poor. An active citizen, Fallows was also a member of the Edgbaston Select Vestry, on the Committee of the Blue Coat School, a guardian for the parish of Edgbaston, and Council Governor of the Birmingham and Midland Institute. In 1881, he stood for Birmingham Council and won a seat for the Market Hall Ward. Praised as 'one of the most industrious and useful members of the Council', Fallows was most associated with the Free Libraries Committee. Elected on to the Birmingham Tame and Rea District Drainage Board and a JP sitting at West Bromwich and Stafford, he was 'a thorough Conservative' and was a leading member of the party locally.

Farm Street

In 1825, in Drake's *Portrait of Birmingham*, William Hawkes Smith explained that Saint George's was a new church 'lately erected in the open fields, but already surrounded by a new town'. The place of worship had been consecrated just three years before, and was sited on the corner of Tower Street and Great Hampton Street. This latter was the main thoroughfare locally and so quickly did the neighbourhood grow that when Birmingham was incorporated as a municipal borough in 1838, it was split into two wards: Hampton and Saint George's. Leading on from the bottom of Snow Hill, **Great Hampton Street** was, according to Hawkes Smith, 'a wide, untidy-looking, irregular range of middling houses; but at the farthest end, an interesting prospect presents itself, over a well-varied country'. Standing on Hockley Hill, he could pick out both Barr Beacon and Aston Parish Church. To the east, of Great Hampton Street, urbanisation had reached out to Hospital Street – although Tower Street did strike out further to Great Hampton Row. The other streets on this side of Hockley were Bond Street, Little Hampton Street, Barford Street and part of Hockley Street. They boasted few buildings and most of the land was small gardens – although there were a number of large fields between the future New John Street and the Hockley Brook.

Apart from a small section of land owned by Colonel Vyse and through which would be cut Mott Street, the whole of Hockley east of Hockley Brook was owned by Caroline Colmore. Her rural property was transformed within a decade of

The 'White Swan', Farm Street, on the corner of Villa Street, in the 1950s. Thanks to Dr Hans Reichenfield.

Hawkes Smith's observations. By the mid-1830s, Hockley Hill had been reached by New John Street, from which a host of smaller streets had been cut on the town side. Within another ten years, roads had also begun to strike out northwards and by the 1850s the only reminder of the countryside was the name of Farm Street, extending from Hockley Brook to Summer Lane and running parallel with Bridge Street West and New John Street. Just north of Farm Street, west of Guildford Street, lay the border with Lozells, then part of Aston, and outside Birmingham until 1911.

Farm Street was the birthplace of Will Thorne, who went on to found the Gas Workers' Union in the 1880s and become Labour MP for West Ham. Born in 1857, Thorne wrote in his autobiography, *My Life's Battles* (1925), that he had 'no memories of the free air of a farm during those early far-off days; just the ugly houses and cobbly, neglected streets that were my only playground for a few short, very short years'. The son of Thomas Thorn (the 'e' on the surname was added later) and his second wife, Emma Everiss, Thorne knew what it was to rough it. His mother and father worked in the brickyards, whilst his dad also worked as a gas-stoker at Saltley gasworks during the winter months. A heavy drinker, Thomas was a fighter and died after he was struck a blow from a horse dealer who was sent to prison for nine months for manslaughter. Will, his widowed mother, older sister and two younger sisters then knew even harder times. His mom did whatever she could to earn money, sewing hooks and eyes on to cards, twelve of each to a card for three ha'pence (less than 1p) per gross (144). Out of that meagre sum she had to find her own needles and cotton. The family was so poor that Thorne's mother applied for Poor Law relief from the Birmingham Board of Guardians. She was granted four loaves and four shillings (20p) a week, but 'the bread was about as bad as it could possibly be, and it was my job to collect the relief every Wednesday from the Poor Law office about two miles from our home'. They were hungry days, especially on Tuesdays when bread and money ran out. So clammed were the Thornes that Will even resorted to pulling down the shutters of the publican who was responsible indirectly for his father's death. His pay was a few coppers and sometimes a swede turnip, out of which Will made a breakfast. He recalled that 'I did not like the publican, but the hunger pain in my stomach drove likes and dislikes away'.

Just before the manslaughter of his father and aged a little over six, Thorne himself had started work, turning a wheel at a rope spinner's in Vauxhall. It was mighty work, twelve hours a day Monday to Friday. Even on Saturday, when he finished early Thorne had no chance of dashing about outside his house in Farm Street, Hockley. He couldn't play tipcat, glarneys or acky-one-two-three. He had to go to a barber's and lather the faces of the chaps who wanted a shave – as he did again on Sunday morning.

Childhood was something for the children of the rich. Will Thorne and his kind had neither childish things nor childish thoughts. Little grown-ups they were with responsibilities way beyond their years. No wonder that as he toiled, Will railed against the hardships of his people. As he grew older, he went from job to job, always seeking to improve not only his pay but also his position. From the rope mill, he moved on to the Small Heath brick works, and after that he had spells as a plumber's mate, a lath splitter, a cow and pig-hair dresser, a brass roller, a nut and bolt tapper, a builder's labourer and a navvy.

But it was when he was employed at the Saltley Gas Works that Will Thorne started to think about what he could do to change things for himself and his fellow workers. The thing which pushed him into action was the back-breaking shift system. A fortnight of day work ended at 6 o'clock on a Sunday evening and straightaway the same set of lads began two weeks of nights. That change-over meant that they grafted for a full 24 hours. Thorne called a meeting of the stokers to press for the abolition of Sunday work. He strove to get them to back him and when they did, he went off to see the chief engineer. The gaffer was enraged, telling them to sling their hook if they did not like things. Will did not back down and a couple of weeks later he heard that the men had won their battle.

By now Thorne was married to Harriet Hallam, the daughter of John Hallam, a fellow worker at Saltley and an active radical. Following the success of his action he remained dissatisfied with the conditions at the works and in November 1881 he tramped to London with two friends to seek work at the Old Kent Road gasworks of the South Metropolitan Gas Company. Thorne's family joined him in south London, but soon after he was dismissed because work was slack, and he returned with his family to Birmingham, going back to work at Saltley. Once again he left because of a dispute about conditions and tramping back to London he found a job at the Beckton Gasworks. London was to be his home thereafter. About 1884 Thorne joined

Dad's Lane, Moseley in 1932. It takes its name from Dod's Farm.

the Social Democratic Federation of H. M. Hyndman, and through his friendship with socialists such as Ben Tillett, Edward Aveling, and Eleanor Marx Aveling he gained the education he had been denied as a youngster.

Five years later Thorne established the National Union of Gasworkers and General Labourers. Soon after, the union achieved for its members a reduction in their working hours to eight a day – and without the need for a strike. The Union spread rapidly and in June 1889 Thorne was elected general secretary, a position he held until he retired in 1934. A leading figure in the Trades Union Congress for many years, he was elected to West Ham town council in 1891 and later became an alderman and mayor of the borough, for which services he was made a freeman. In 1906 Thorne won the local Parliamentary seat for the Labour Party and kept it until he retired in 1945. He died a year later.

Farm Road, Sparkbrook, **Farm Lane** until 1872, refers to The Farm, the house in which the Lloyds lived for many years (see Sampson Road); whilst there are a number of other streets in Birmingham that hark back to farms that have disappeared under the outpouring of the City. They include: **Barton Lodge Road**, Hall Green; **Broadyates Road** off Stockfield Road, Acocks Green; **Broomfield Road**, Erdington, which tells us that once broom grew in the fields hereabouts; **Brook Lane**, Billesley; **Bushmore Road**, Hall Green, and once on the road from Robin Hood to Shirley; **Crick Lane**, Handsworth; **Dads Lane**, Moseley, and formerly **Dod's Lane**; **Faulkeners Farm Drive**, Erdington; **Frogmill Road,** Frankley; **Gayhill Lane**, Walkers Heath; **Grove Lane**, Handsworth, originally called **Cape Lane** until 1894; **Holly Bank Road**, Kings Heath; **Hyron Hall Road**, Acocks Green; **Lindsworth Road**, Kings Norton; **Manor House Road,** Tyseley; **Outmoor Road**, Garretts Green; **Scribers Lane**, Hall Green; **Warwards Lane**, Stirchley; and **Woodthorpe Road**, Kings Heath.

Farmer Street

Later renamed **Sand Street**, Farmer Street was a short street linking Whittall Street and Weaman Street in the Gun Quarter. The lower part of the modern **Printing House Street**, as it turns on a right angle and enters Whittall Street, is close to the line of the former Sand Street. Printing House Street was cut out in the 1960s and refers to the Post and Mail Building and its printing machines in Weaman Street. Farmer Street itself recalled a Joseph and James Farmer. Joseph was mentioned in 1701 in the local records of The Society of Friends (Quakers) and a year later he was based at a shop on the corner of Bull Street and the Minories. An ironworker, he became a gunsmith and from his marriage in 1711 to Sarah Abrahams of Bromsgrove until 1735 he lived in The Square (see Old Square). Newly-laid out, this was the most fashionable address in the town and it drew a number of wealthy Quakers because of the proximity of their Meeting House in Bull Street.

After leaving The Square, Joseph moved to a part of Steelhouse Lane then called Whitehall's Lane, where he lived in what was known as Farmer and Galton's House and which became Galton's Bank. Dying in 1741, he was succeeded by a son, James, and a daughter, Mary. James went to London in the late 1740s but was beset with major financial problems in 1755. In the ensuing years, he recovered his position and regained his prosperity. He returned to Birmingham a decade later to live in a mansion on the country lane to Halesowen, later to become Broad Street. This was called Bingley House, its name harking back to the **Binges** – fields mentioned in The Letters Patent of the Free Grammar School of Edward VI in 1552. A mansion had stood on this site since at least the sixteenth century and it had been home to some of the leading families of Birmingham such as the Shiltons and Fenthams (see Fentham Road). Farmer's Bridge over the nearby canal brings to mind James Farmer who died in 1773. The next year his only child, Mary, married Charles Lloyd, one of the Quaker Lloyds who had come to Birmingham from Wales (see Sampson Road). Then involved as ironmasters in Edgbaston Street, the Lloyds went on to co-found Taylor and Lloyd's Bank. Mary and Charles lived at Bingley House after the death of her mother in 1796. Their eldest child, Charles, became known as 'poet Lloyd' and was a friend of Coleridge, Wordsworth, Southey and Lamb.

Joseph Farmer's other child, Mary, married Samuel Galton from Somerset in 1748. The betrothal caused problems, for Mary had been courting another Quaker, Joseph White, who was reluctant to give her up. After an investigation by a respected

'The Green Man' on the corner of Sand Street and Weaman Street (on the left) in the 1950s. Saint Chad's Cathedral is in the background. Thanks to the Birmingham Evening Mail.

Friend, Henry Bradford (see Bradford Street), it was revealed that White had kept Mary's letters at the same time as he had contrived to get back those that he had written to her. This 'bad behaviour' enabled the marriage of Mary Farmer and Samuel Galton. It seems that Galton had been associated with the Farmer's gunmaking business for a number of years and that he became a partner of James, later taking over the concern. In 1777, after living in Farmer's old home in Steelhouse Lane, the Galtons moved to Duddeston, where Joseph and later James Farmer had rented land from Sir Lister Holte.

Samuel took out a 99-year lease from Sir Charles Holte, Sir Lister's younger brother, so enlarging the old Farmer estate and upon which he had built a mansion. Years later his great-great granddaughter, Mary Anne Galton (Mrs Schimmelpenninck) described the setting of the house. It had a pond 'or rather the lake, since the stream on which Birmingham stands runs through it. This lake occupied four or five acres and was of considerable length. It was truly beautiful, its borders indented, and clothed with the finest willows and poplars I have ever saw. The stillness was delightful, interrupted only by some sparkling leaping fish, or the swallow skimming in circles over the water, the hissing of the swans from their two woody islets, or the cries of the wild fowl from the far off sedges and bulrushes.

Samuel the elder died at Duddeston in 1799 and left a fortune of £200,000. He and Mary had eight children but only one, another Samuel, survived. Educated at the Warrington Academy, where Joseph Priestley was a professor (see Priestley Road) Samuel inherited the gunmaking firm of Farmer and Galton. This led to difficulties with the Society of Friends. Staunchly pacifist, the Friends were against the production of weapons and in 1796, after several years of agitation, Samuel was disowned as a member by the Society. He ignored this action and continued to attend meetings until his death in 1832. Samuel was married to Lucy Barclay of the great London banking family and it may be that this connection encouraged him to join Paul Moon James, who was married to a daughter of Charles and Mary Lloyd, in founding the successful bank of Galton and James. This venture ended in 1831 when James joined the newly-formed Birmingham Banking Company.

Later living at Great Barr Hall (to become Saint Margaret's Hospital) which was leased from Sir Joseph Scott, Samuel Galton the younger was an influential person. Deeply interested in science, he was a Fellow of the Royal Society and a member of the Lunar Society. In particular, he was friends with Dr Joseph Priestley and Erasmus Darwin. Samuel and Lucy had seven children. The oldest was Samuel Tertius Galton. He married Frances Violetta, a daughter of Erasmus Darwin, and was the father of Francis Galton, who was born in Birmingham. Later knighted, Francis was a scientist and explorer who travelled widely in Africa and who is best remembered for his studies examining the connection between heredity and intelligence, which led to the field of study of eugenics.

Another son, Hubert, inherited the Warley Hall Estate which Samuel had bought in 1792. This passed to Hubert's only child, Mary Galton, who left much of it to her cousins, Leonard and Major Hubert Galton. They sold most of the land for development, and **Galton Road** and **Barclay Road** still recall the family. Closer to Smethwick town centre and by the Birmingham Canal, **Galton Valley**, **Galton Bridge** and **Galton Street** emphasise the involvement of the Galtons with the Birmingham Canal Navigation Company. In Birmingham, the Galtons were remembered in the short **Galton Street** in Vauxhall, not far from their mansion at Duddeston, and in **Scott Street**, probably relating to the Scotts from whom the Galtons leased Great Barr Hall. Both roads disappeared in the post-war redevelopment of Birmingham. Confusingly known as Duddeston Hall and Dodson House, the Galtons home passed through a number of hands in the mid-nineteenth century, before becoming Saint Anne's School in 1868. It was knocked down in 1972.

Farnol Road, Yardley

Close to the old Yardley Village, Farnol Road brings to mind Jeffery Farnol, the author of romantic adventure stories set in the Georgian period whose books were popular in the early twentieth century. Born in 1878 in Edgbaston, when he was ten his family moved to Kent. Known as Jack to his family because his first name was John, when he was a small child his father used to read him tales of derring do. Becoming an avid reader himself, he was drawn to the deeds of Sir Francis Drake, Sir Walter Raleigh, the Black Prince and other heroes. After leaving school Farnol was determined to follow a career as a writer. He had his first short stories published in 1895 and worked on a pirate novel called *The Skull of the Inca* that was never published.

Farnol Road, Yardley. Thanks to the late Carl Thomas.

Something of a fighter, Farnol took up painting at night school. In 1896 he had a fierce row with his father who was angered by his son's lack of income other than small sums from his writing. Ordered by his father to take up a job with an engineering firm in Birmingham, Farnol went to live with his favourite Aunt Kezehia in Kings Heath. The post lasted six months, for Farnol was sent packing after a stunt. His workmates were not impressed by his story telling and sketches and challenged him to prove his manhood by climbing the high and unused chimney at the works and to hang from it a hanky. On the way back down he fell into a deep bed of soot and was almost 'drowned' by more soot falling down on him. Managing to free himself, he was spotted by the night watchman who thought the soot-covered Farnol was the devil.

Returning to Kent and his writing, Farnol met Blanche Hawley, the youngest daughter of an American painter, and married her without telling his family. Moving to the United States, he rowed with his father-in-law and went to New York where he worked as a scene painter at the Astor Theatre. During this time he wrote *The Broad Highway* which was published in 1910 and which made his name as a novelist. Returning with his wife to England, Farnol gained a reputation for Regency stories set on the open road, such as *The Amateur Gentleman* (1913). **Vibart Road**, off which Farnol Road runs, refers to a character in his novels. Farnol died in 1952.

Fashoda Road, Selly Park and Ten Acres

In the late nineteenth century, major European powers were desperately trying to take over as much territory as possible to add to their empires, so much so that their efforts to grab land in Africa became known as 'The Scramble for Africa'. This led to confrontations, especially between Britain and France in northern and western Africa. Determined to protect the Suez Canal and its route to Indian, the jewel in the Imperial Crown, the British occupied Egypt in 1882 – much to the annoyance of the French. In 1898, still smarting from this takeover, the French sent a force from their possessions to the west to Fashoda. This was on the White Nile, to the south of Egypt, and in the Sudan, which the British saw as in their sphere of control. Led by Colonel Marchand, the French arrived on 10 July. The British reacted swiftly and on 18 September an Army led by Kitchener reached Fashoda. It seemed that war would follow, but instead the two leaders sat down, drank champagne and swapped stories until the diplomats sorted out the wrangle, and on 3 November the French backed down.

Kitchener himself is remembered in **Kitchener Road**, close to Fashoda Road, and **Kitchener Street** in Winson Green, near to the Black Patch Park on the borders with Smethwick. Born in County Kerry, Ireland and partly educated in Switzerland, Horatio Herbert Kitchener joined the British Army in 1871. After serving in Palestine and Egypt and learning Arabic, he was an aide-de-camp for the unsuccessful relief column sent out to save General Gordon and his Egyptian forces that were besieged by the Mahdi in Khartoum in 1884. He came to national prominence during his second spell of service in Egypt, during which time he achieved the re-conquest of the Sudan and the re-capture of Khartoum by leading Anglo-Egyptian forces to victory at the Battle of Omdurman on 2 September 1898.

A reforming governor of the Sudan who respected the Muslim religion, Kitchener went on to become commander-in-chief of the British forces in the Boer War from November 1900. He was a ruthless military opponent and brought in blockhouses and gathered the Boer families in concentration camps. With the outbreak of the First World War, Kitchener became War Minister and is recalled famously as the face on the recruiting posters calling out 'Your Country Needs YOU'. He had great success in raising the biggest volunteer army in history and he recognised that the war would be one of attrition in which Britain would need a huge army. Made an earl in 1914 he was drowned two years later on a mission to Russia when the cruiser he was on was sunk by a mine.

Cecil Road (see Aberdeen Street), parallel to Fashoda Road, highlights Robert Cecil, Marquess of Salisbury, a noted Conservative who was prime minister for the greater part of the period between 1886 and 1902. **Manilla Road** lies on the other side of Fashoda Road. It may be named after the Battle of Manila, at which the Americans destroyed a Spanish Fleet in 1898 and as a result of which the Philipines and its capital Manila were lost to the Spanish Empire.

Fast Pits Road, Yardley

Named in a deed from 1649 that mentions 'Fast, alias **Hurst Lane'** leading from the Coventry Road to the Birmingham Road, Fast Pits Road now runs from Holder Road to the Haybarn Farm Recreation Ground. Pits near to the junction of nearby Hob Moor Road and Wash Lane are shown on C. H. Blood's Map of Birmingham in 1857; whilst the 1899 Kings Norton Map indicates an old gravel pit nearby. Confusingly, until 1926 Fast Pits Road was called **Hob Moor Road**.

Fawdry Street, Bordesley

A very short street off Montague Street and near to Lawley Street, Fawdry Street was the wonderfully-named **Noah's Ark Passage** until 1894. Its origins are shrouded in mystery, but in an old newspaper description of Old Square there is a suggestive hint. For it described a central garden 'with trim grass plots and Noah's-Ark-like trees'. Did Noah's Ark Passage once have similar trees? Be that as it may, a James Fawdry of Birmingham was given as owning five acres of land in the 1873 Return of Owner's Land. A Fawdry was also a partner of Benjamin Stone (see Grange Road).

Fentham Road, Erdington and Handsworth

Both these roads relate to George Fentham, who owned about 100 acres of land in Erdington and Handsworth. In 1712 he left this property to a trust after his death. Originally receiving an income of £20 a year, the trust paid for the teaching to write of poor children of Birmingham and for the clothing of ten poor widows from the town. All of the recipients had to live within 100 yards of the Old Cross in the Bull Ring. From 1741 at least, Fentham's bequest was used to send such children in green clothes instead of blue to the Blue Coat School in Birmingham. It is believed that Fentham had grown up poor in Hampton in Arden, but that he made his wealth as a tanner in Birmingham. He lived for a time at Bingley House and it was he who devised to Samuel Bradford the Warner Fields Estate (see Bradford Street).

Fisher Street, Gosta Green

A short street linking Gosta Green and Corporation Street and now cleared, Fisher Street would seem to connect with a family embedded in eighteenth and early nineteenth-century Birmingham. In 1678, a bond from George Field of Birmingham, inn holder, to Anne Fisher, widow of Birmingham, was given for performance of covenants; and in the same year, a Thomas Fisher of the town and a knife forger, entered into a bond for performance of covenants with Anne Field, inn holder. Andrew Johnson, the uncle of the famed man of letters Dr Johnson, was married to one of the Fishers; however, the most prominent of the Fishers in Birmingham was Clement.

In 1702 there was recorded a settlement upon marriage between Clement Fisher, a gentleman, and Ann Jarvis, of lands and premises in Moor Street and Hobmore Lane and Stanschmore Lane, Bordesley. It seems Fisher was also an attorney and that he was the father of Thomas Fisher, another legal man and who was employed regularly by the local Friends (Quakers). In 1802 a Miss Fisher let out for building several quantities of land fronting to the newly-laid out Fisher Street, Legge Street (see Digby Walk and Heneage Street) and Moland Street.

Five Ways, Ladywood

A lease from King Edward's School to John Shilton of Birmingham in 1565 mentioned 'the lane leadinge from the horestone towards the five ways', indicating the antiquity of the name Five Ways. As its suggests, the place was the meeting place of five old roads: to the north and coming from Brum was Islington, now part of Broad Street; to the east ran Islington Row, going down the hill towards Bristol Street; to the south Long Lane was the route to Harborne; to the south-west Hagley Row took you to Halesowen; and to the west was Ladywood Lane, going towards Rotton Park and Smethwick. In the 1820s these five ways were joined by a sixth – Calthorpe Road. Yet although there are really six ways, the ancient name of Five Ways has remained in use.

Flavells Lane Yardley

Victor Skipp's painstaking investigations into Yardley's history have shown that the Flavell family was first mentioned in Yardley's records in 1465. It appears that they were newcomers to the parish, and along with other incomers such as the Acocks,

Five Ways in the early twentieth century. The Sturge Statue is now in front of the Marriott Hotel.

Estes, Greswolds and others they made a mark. In 1531 the will of Wyllyam Flawell bequested his soul 'unto all mighty gode, to hys blessyd Mother of mcy oure Lady seynte Mari, & to all the holly company of heavyne', and committed his body to the churche yeard of Seynt adborre (Saint Edburgha's, Yardley). William also left 40 shillings to the poor of the parish. The Flavells remained prominent locally until the twentieth century. They lived in Yardley House for many years before letting it out. In 1919 they sold the building and grounds to Mitchell's and Butler's who put up the 'Yew Tree' pub six years later (itself knocked down only recently and replaced with a new development). The house itself was demolished after the Flavells sold their estate in 1930. The site of the house was in front of the present Hobmoor Primary School on Hobmoor Road, and it backed on to Heathmere Avenue.

Flaxley Road, Stechford

Stretching from the old Manor pub, near the Stechford Bridge over the River Cole, and up to Kitts Green, Flaxley Road was given as The Flaxleys in 1916. It means the clearing where flax is grown and by the fourteenth century it is apparent that there were three fields hereabouts on a sand patch which gave lighter soil suitable for growing flax. A William Flaxleye is mentioned in the 1327 subsidy roll and it is likely that he took his name from the three fields collectively called The Flaxleys. The route from the village of Yardley to Stechford and thence Aston and Lichfield ran by Flaxley.

Flaxley Lane, Stechford at the turn of the twentieth century.

Fletcher's Walk

A walkway going under the Inner Ring Road from what is left of Easy Row (by Alpha Tower) and up to the steps that lead to the Birmingham Conservatoire, Fletcher's Walk is named after Eli Fletcher, the noted owner of the 'Hope and Anchor' in Easy Row, close to Edmund Street. Sam Smith recalls Eli well for he was 'my father's half-brother and in 1914 wanted me to go and live in to be trained to look after the Builliard Room. But both parents said "No".' Eli's pub was a popular port of call for many couples who had just married at the Registry Office in Broad Street.

Flint Green Road, Acocks Green

Harking back to a green that was on the junction of the present-day Warwick Road and Flint Green Road, this is one of the high points of the old parish of Yardley at 433 feet. It takes its name from the Flint family, mentioned in the Middle Ages and in a deed from 1661.

Foden Road, Perry Barr

Roger Henney has carried out much research into the history of Perry Barr and Great Barr and he informs me that Foden Road, off Beeches Road, 'was named after the Foden family who were very big in Perry Barr, running most of the farms in the area at one time or another and also drinking houses such as the 'Royal Oak' (now the 'Parson and Clerk'.

Fordhouse Lane, Stirchley

Leading into the Pershore Road, this lane takes its name from Fordhouse Farm, itself meaning the house by the nearby ford over the River Rea.

The Fordrough, West Heath

Indicating a rough way – one difficult to pass through – the name fordrough was given to a farm of nineteen acres in West Heath that was sold for development in 1946. It is now remembered by a road going from West Heath Road to the West Heath Recreation Ground. There is also **The Fordrough** in Hay Mills. Aptly enough it leads from the Bridge over the River Cole on the Coventry Road to the Church of Saint Cyprian and Webster and Horsfall's wire works. **The Fordrough** in Four Oaks, Sutton Coldfield is a short and narrow link between Irnham Road and Four Oaks Road; whilst **Fordrough Lane and Fordrough Avenue,** Bordesley Green are amongst the few roads locally that recall the area's rural past. There was once a **Foredrove Street** in Birmingham City Centre, between Wharf Street and Cross Street (later Severn Street).

The Fordrough, West Heath in the 1950s. Thanks to the Birmingham Evening Mail.

Fore Street

Originally called **Little Cannon Street**, this is a short street leading from Cannon Street to Corporation Street. Its name was changed in 1887 when the nearby part of the new Corporation Street emerged. As Joseph McKenna suggests it is in front or leading to Corporation Street.

Formans Road, Sparkhill/Springfield

The valley of the River Cole tends to be narrow and flanked by sharply rising banks so that when it rains heavily the water flows down fast to the river and quickly leads to floods – as still happens at the ford in Green Road, Hall Green. Before the development of drains and culverts, this flooding could be dangerous and the Assize Rolls of 1275 recorded a death at what was called Greet Mill Ford (see Greenbank Avenue). Today the ford is crossed by the bridge on the Stratford Road just below the 'College Arms'. The person who lost his life was Roger Fullard, who 'wishing to cross the water with his cart at the mill of Greet, by the flooding of the water, he and his horses were drowned'. Fullard's surname may have been derived from Fullford meaning foul ford. This was the name given to the ford over the Cole that is now crossed by Formans Road, itself derived from the Foulemoreslone noted in a deed from 1359/60 and the later Folmur Lane, as mentioned in 1562.

Formans Road – the top photo shows it before most of the road was built up in the late nineteenth and early twentieth centuries and before a road bridge went over the River Cole.

Four Oaks Road, Sutton Coldfield

As the name suggests, once there were four oaks in this locality, which is mentioned on Henry Beighton's Map of Warwickshire for 1725.

Fowler Street, Nechells

Called **Green Street** until 1872, there were still corn fields and elm trees in this vicinity in the 1850s. Like many streets affected by the post-Second World War redevelopment of Birmingham, Fowler Street is shorter than it was and is no longer straight but curved. At least it has survived, in contrast to so many old streets. Not far from the superb Bloomsbury Library, it is probable that it is named after William Fowler who died at Wood End, Erdington in 1887, owning 202 acres of land in that district. A surveyor and land agent, Fowler was an important historian and an expert on the utilisation of sewage.

The old and the new in Fowler Street in 1966.

Fox Street, City

In his pioneering book on street names, fittingly called *Streetwise*, the late Vivian Bird declared that 'a minor menagerie disappeared under the College of Technology, later Aston University (1966) – Buck, Doe, Fox, Sheep and Bullock Streets'. As it is, Fox Street is still there. Short and narrow, it connects Curzon Street with Jennens

Row, but Bird was right about the clearance of **Buck Street**, into which Fox Street ran, and **Doe Street**, which came off Buck Street; and both do seem to have been a play upon the female and male names of deer. However, **Bullock Street** is still there in Ashted and would appear to be too far away from the other three to have been connected with them. As for **Sheep Street**, it has also gone. Further up in Gosta Green and stretching between Aston Street and the now-cleared Lawrence Street, Sheep Street again would seem to be unconnected with Buck Street and Doe Street. Known as **Jenning Street** until 1778, Fox Street itself may not have been named after the animal but instead may refer either to the name of an inn or to the Fox family. In 1613 a conveyance of land in Bordesley was made from Edmund Wharton and his wife to Richard Fox; and Birmingham Archives hold the will dated 1797 of a John Fox, a refiner. Interestingly, an assignment of a leasehold messuage in Woodcock Street was made in 1834 from a John Fox of Uttoxeter to William Duke of Birmingham. Woodcock Street runs south east from Gosta Green as if it is a spoke off a wheel, as does **Duke Street** – perhaps called after William Duke.

Fox Hollies Road, Acocks Green and Hall Green

In the two and half centuries following the Norman Conquest, the population of England increased greatly from about 1.5 million in 1066 to about 6 million by 1300. In these circumstances there was a need to develop uncultivated land that had been

Fox Hollies Road, in 1932 after it was widened.

avoided before because it was wooded or its soil was difficult to farm. In the Arden area of north Warwickshire and the adjacent parts of Worcestershire such as Yardley, this expansion led to a number of pioneers striking out from established villages and setting up isolated farms that belonged solely to them. Victor Skipp has brought to the fore this process in Yardley, to which the Fox Hollies locality belonged until 1911. One of these adventurous families was the atte Hollies, meaning at Holly and presumably signifying that they lived where holly trees were abundant.

This farm was purchased by the Fox family who are mentioned in a document from 1465 and by 1624 so bonded were they with the place that it was called Foxholleys, as it was written in a deed. An important route from Yardley Village passed along the ridgeway that is now Fox Hollies Road and Highfield Road and went to Kings Norton and Bromsgrove. By the mid-nineteenth century the Fox Hollies Estate was owned by the Walkers. The family originated in the Lake District, and the Reverend Robert Walker was mentioned in one of Wordsworth's poems. His son, Zaccheus Walker I, married a sister of Matthew Boulton, and their son, Zaccheus Walker II , was nearly killed in the French Revolution but was saved by his friendship with the Revolutionary leader, Robespierre, whom he had met in the United States of America.

Zaccheus Walker III was another merchant and he bought the Fox Hollies Estate and had built Fox Hollies Hall, where he was living by the late 1860s. One remaining entrance pillar to the hall stands still on the green space at the end of the parade of shops just before Fox Hollies Road crosses Olton Boulevard. The other was accidentally knocked down but thanks to the efforts of Alderman Matt Redmond it has been replaced (2004).

Zaccheus IV was another colourful character. A lieutenant colonel in the Volunteers, he was known locally as Colonel Walker and was vice-chairman of Yardley District Council. Active in public life, older folk recall him as something like a squire who bred horses and prize-winning mastiffs. In the 1890s he used to open his grounds to poor children from Birmingham on outings. His sister, Mary, was also well known. A leading figure in the Girl Guides, she used to go about in an open carriage with her parasol up. Eventually in 1925 Colonel Walker sold 262 acres of his estate to the city for £334,000, and 2,500 council houses were built there. He continued to live at Fox Hollies Hall amidst the grounds he still owned until he died in 1930. The next year the Fox Hollies Road was widened in front of the hall, which was knocked down in 1937. The tower blocks built in **Curtis Gardens** in the 1960s are named after fields on the estate: Holly Piece, Home Meadow and Coppice.

Franchise Street, Perry Barr

Although it is now regarded as in Perry Barr and is mostly under the car park of the University of Central England, Franchise Street was actually south of the River Tame and thus in one the furthermost corners of Handsworth. It takes its name from the fact that the men who built houses in the street were able to get the franchise – the vote.

When the 1832 Great Reform Act was passed, the qualification for voting was based upon property and the level was set high so that it excluded the working class. However, two different types of franchise were introduced. In the boroughs, such as Birmingham, you gained the vote if you rented property valued at £10 for local rates. That was out of reach for working people, but in the shires you could gain the vote if you were a 40 shilling freeholder, that is, if you owned property worth £40 a year based on an annual return of 5%. During that period you could build a decent house for £70.

This shire qualification held out some hope for the best paid of the skilled working class. In order to gain property and thus the vote, they joined freehold land societies and building societies – both of which movements began in Birmingham. The freehold land society purchased a large estate in a shire at a wholesale price, divided it into plots and sold it on to building society members. Franchise Street itself was on the first freehold land society estate in Birmingham. It was an area of eight acres near the railway station at Perry Barr and was laid out by William Benjamin Smith, secretary of the Manchester Order of Odd Fellows, in 100 lots auctioned at Hawley's Temperance Hotel 10 January 1848. Four months later, members of the Birmingham Freehold Land Society marched in a grand and triumphant procession to take possession of the site. Each lot carried the right to vote and the purchasers mostly were members of the Investment and Permanent Benefit Building Society, started in 1847 in conjunction with Oddfellows.

Frankley Lane, Northfield

The continuation of Merritt's Hill, Frankley Lane lies between the Bartley Reservoir and Frankley Reservoir and heads towards Frankley Green. Written as Franchlei in the Domesday Book of 1086, Frankley means the woodland clearing made by a man called Franca. However, some folk believe that it is derived from the Old French word frank, meaning free. In the later Middle Ages a franklin was a landowner who was of free birth but was not of noble descent. Accordingly, it is proposed that Frankley means a free or privileged place and that in Anglo-Saxon times it was granted by a lord to tenants who did not have to perform base services.

Frankley Beeches Road, Northfield

Going in a semi circle from the Bristol Road to Tessall Lane, Frankley Beeches Road highlights the beech trees prominent on a hill above Egghill Lane. Cadbury's bought Frankley Beeches in 1930 in memory of the founders of the business, Richard and George, both of whom cherished the environment. The firm made over the land to the National Trust, stating that 'One of the best known landmarks in the country which immediately adjoins the City of Birmingham on the south west is Frankley Beeches, a clump of fine beeches which stands at the summit of a hill about 800 feet high. From this eminence fine views are obtained over the surrounding country.'

Frederick Road, Aston

Extending between Witton Road and Whitehead Road, Frederick Road is supposedly named after an Irishman, John Frederick Feeney, who arrived in the city in 1835 to work as a journalist on a radical newspaper called the *Reformer*. Later he bought the weekly *Birmingham Journal* and through its columns in 1850 he appealed for tolerance when the Pope's decision to set up a hierarchy in England was accompanied by anti-Catholic outbursts. Seven years later Feeney started the *Birmingham Daily Post*, which continues to carry his name on its editorial page. For a man whose business was public affairs his own life was deeply private. Indeed, very little is known about him and no business or family papers relating to the Feeneys have survived.

There are no glimpses of Feeney's childhood, no hints as to his upbringing and no tantalising leads about his teenage and early adulthood – other than a tradition that he had begun work as a compositor in a printing room. In fact, there is little hard information about him at all until he came to Birmingham, although it may be that he had been a journalist elsewhere and a significant number of Irishmen did write on newspapers in England. Whatever the case, Feeney took to Birmingham and stayed here for the rest of his life. In 1837 he switched to the staff of the *Midland Counties Herald*, where he worked for seven years until he bought the *Birmingham Journal*. This had been started in 1825 as a weekly and within a few years it had gained a reputation as an important radical publication that backed reform, but now it was in decline. The Irishman transformed its position and soon he had increased weekly sales to 12,000 copies.

According to the 1851 Census, Feeney was living at 145, Highgate – the Moseley Road neighbourhood. Aged 42, he was given as a newspaper proprietor who was born in Ireland. His wife, Barbara, was fifteen years younger than he and was local, having been born in Edgbaston. Living with them were his sister, Margaret White and her son who had been born in New South Wales, Australia; his sister-in-law; two servants and three children. These were Peregrine (thirteen), Mary (eight) and William (six). All were born in Birmingham. Ten years later, Feeney had moved to the more affluent Church Road, Edgbaston where another son, John is noted. Barbara was Feeney's second wife. We do not know the surname of his first wife, Rebecca Sophia, who was the mother of all the children mentioned above and all of who were baptised in Anglican churches. Feeney's marriage to Barbara in 1850 was also consecrated according to the rites of the established Church of England in Saint Peter's and Saint Paul's, the parish church of Aston, and both of them are interred in a vault beneath the Erdington chapel of the church. Feeney was a great benefactor to the church and this may have led to the naming of Frederick Road after him.

On his marriage certificate to Barbara, Feeney's father was named as John Feeney, book seller, but what little else we know about the newspaper publisher comes from information gleaned from an obituary to his nephew Alfred Feeny – whose name did not include the final 'e' as with John Frederick Feeney. Alfred came to Birmingham in 1857 to work in the commercial department on his uncle's new venture, a daily newspaper. He stayed with the paper until his retirement in 1904. Alfred's father was Patrick Malvogue Feeny of Sligo, who was John Frederick Feeney's brother.

Patrick was also involved in the newspaper business, having worked on the *Connaught Telegraph*, had a share in the *Mayo Constitution* and then taken a leading position on the *Morning News* of London, in which city Alfred was born. A major influence on the *Post* through the quality of his writing, his versatility and his journalistic flair, Alfred was also the Birmingham correspondent for *The Times* and was involved in *The Ironmonger*, which focused upon the hardware trades of Birmingham and elsewhere. A Liberal in politics, he was a staunch Catholic and was one of the best-known and most highly regarded members of the Edgbaston Oratory, attending mass daily at 8.30 in the morning.

It may be speculated that John Frederick Feeney had also been a Catholic but had converted to Anglicanism – perhaps, as did others to avoid difficulties at a time when there was marked anti-Catholic prejudice and when there were very few Irish Catholics in positions of authority. Whatever the case, it seems likely that he was from Sligo or Mayo, where the family had relatives in the early twentieth century, and he is an Irishman who has had a lasting effect upon Birmingham. Known as the 'Governor', for all he was self-effacing Feeney was a dogged and determined man who had successfully come through severe difficulties in the newspaper business and who was resolute in his belief in toleration. He died aged 61 on 11 May 1862 and John Jaffray, his partner in the *Birmingham Daily Post,* used the columns of the publication to praise his colleague. He stated clearly that 'the history of Mr Feeney's career in Birmingham is indeed the history of the later developments of newspaper energy amongst us'. He was tactful, courteous, hard working and thorough in his business habits. Living a peaceful and uneventful life, he was 'one of the purest minds that God ever created, and as kind a heart as ever beat in human breast'.

After Feeney's death, his newspapers were run by his son, John Feeney, in partnership with Jaffray. The oldest son, Peregrine, had started work as a newspaperman but soon went to London to become an artist. One of his paintings, that of Lyn Idwal, Wales, hangs in Birmingham's Art Gallery. John also had artistic leanings, especially towards industrial art, and profoundly affected the provision of art in Birmingham through his extraordinary generosity. It was John Feeney and Jaffray who established the *Birmingham Daily Mail* in 1870. Nineteen years later they set up the Birmingham Mail Christmas Tree to raise funds for 'toys and cash to brighten the lives of poor children in hospital'. In 1906, the fund began giving out Christmas dinners to poor families and boots to unshod children. Tens of thousands of English Brummies, my own Nan and aunts and uncles amongst them, owed the shoes on their feet to a charity set up by a second generation Irish Brummie.

John Feeney had other positive and long-lasting effects on Birmingham. When the Art Gallery was opened in 1885 he gave the first instalment of an outstanding collection of works from abroad, in this case of Japanese enamel, porcelain, lacquer, silver, armour and swords, and also of Chinese bronze, silver and lacquer. This was later supplemented by work from Persia, Turkey, Scandinavia, Germany, France, Spain, Austria and Russia. By 1899 the liberality of John Feeney had led to a collection of 1,693 pieces. Seven years later when he died, his generosity to the Art Gallery staggered the citizens of Birmingham by his bequest of the magnificent legacy of £50,000'. This huge sum was crucial for the building of a new Picture Gallery as an extension of the Council House in both Edmund Street and Great Charles Street. These Feeney Galleries were opened in 1912. Nobody who enters them should be unaware that they were paid for by a man whose father came from the west of Ireland.

Feeney's will also left £20,000 to The University of Birmingham, adding to the £5,000 he had given whilst alive; £10,000 to the General Hospital, which swelled the £1,000 handed over previously; and £1,000 each to nine other hospitals and charities. His obituarist exclaimed with no exaggeration that 'it is hardly possible to exaggerate the importance of this final and signal recognition on Mr Feeney's part of the true duties of citizenship'. Other philanthropic acts whilst he lived included donating £1,000 each to the Women's Hospital, the Coventry and Warwickshire Hospital and the Birmingham Bishopric Fund; and paying for the restoration of the Erdington Chapel and its monuments and the carrying out of the entire chancel end of Aston Parish Church.

Freeman Street, City

Hutton believed that this short street off Moor Street, which emerged before 1731, was named after a landowner.

Freer Road, Handsworth

Striking eastwards from Hampton Road and Fentham Road and on the borders of Handsworth with Aston, Freer Road keeps alive George Freer who in 1813 was elected one of the governors of the King Edward VI Grammar School, then at the bottom of New Street. Seventy years later, King Edward's Grammar School, Aston was opened in nearby Frederick Road, leading to the remembrance of Freer. His family was a prominent one. In 1769 a John Freer was one of the first of the Street Commissioners; and in 1902 Canon Freer offered £10,000 in the campaign towards the establishment of a Bishop of Birmingham.

Freeth Street, Ladywood

John Freeth is one of the most remarkable of all Brummies. His family was mentioned first in 1690 in a conveyance from Joseph Rann (see Rann Street) and Mary his wife to Jonathan Freeth of Harborne, a yeoman. In the early 1700s, Charles Freeth was running a coffee house and public house in Bell Street, at which the trustees of the Jackson Charity met – which had been set up to help two or males

Freeth Street in the late 1960s

from the poorest backgrounds in Birmingham to become apprentices each year. However, it was his son, John, who was to ensure that the Freeth name would reach out to modern Birmingham.

Dubbed Freeth the poet, he was born in 1731 on the corner of Lease Lane and Bell Street in the Bull Ring and came to notice at a dinner to celebrate the release of John Wilkes from prison on 17 April 1770. Wilkes was a radical who advocated religious tolerance and who became associated with the cause of liberty at a time when Parliament was dominated by the aristocracy and the landed gentry. Elected MP several times, he was imprisoned for obscene libel and was a target for the establishment. In the ensuing years, Freeth became noted for his support for radical causes and he and his friends were regarded as Jacobins by their opponents. The Jacobins were a political group in the aftermath of the French Revolution of 1789 and were associated with Robespierre and The Terror, during which Royalists and Girondists (moderates) were guillotined. Freeth and his associates met at the 'Leicester Arms', a coffee house he ran in Bell Street and which he had taken over from his father. Meanwhile the Anti-Jacobins gathered at Joe Lindon's 'Minerva Tavern' in Peck Lane.

Freeth and his pals numbered twelve and were also nicknamed 'The Twelve Apostles'. One of them was James Bissett who brought out the *Magnificent Directory* of Birmingham in 1808. A staunch believer in reform, Freeth wrote many verses on topics as varied as the 'Birmingham Ale-Tasters' and the 'Bowling-Green Festival'. He said that his 'hobby horse and practice for 30 years past have been to write songs upon the occurrence of remarkable events, and nature having supplied me with a voice somewhat suitable to my stile of composition, to sing them also, while their subjects were fresh upon every man's mind; and being a Publican, this faculty, or rather knack of singing my own songs, has been profitable to me; it has in an evening crowded my house with customers, and led me to friendships which I might not otherwise have had.' Amongst his poems was 'Inland Navigation. An Ode', which celebrated the arrival on 7 November 1769 of the first boat load of coal brought in from the Black Country on the Birmingham Canal Navigation. This and other verses were collected in Freeth's *Political Songster* (1790).

Freeth died in 1808 aged 77. His passing was recorded in *Aris's Birmingham Gazette* which stated that 'his morals were unsullied, and his manners unaffected. Formed to enliven the social circle, possessing wit without acrimony, and independence and mind without pride, he was beloved by his friends and courted by strangers and respected by all'. Buried at Old Meeting House, on his gravestone was inscribed this verse:

> Free and easy through life 'twas his wish to proceed
> Good men he revered, whatever their creed.
> His pride was a sociable evening to spend,
> For no man loved better his pipe and his friend.

The Froggery, City

Also spelled as The Froggary, this once lay between New Street on the east and Dudley Street and Pinfold Street on the west. The Froggery was a short and narrow street that emerged in the mid-eighteenth century and which fell beneath the building of New Street Station in the 1850s – along with Colmore Street and Old Meeting Street. Decried as 'an unsavoury portion' in *Showell's Dictionary* (1885), it was believed that 'as there was a Duck Lane close by, the place most likely was originally so christened from its low-lying and watery position, the connection between ducks and frogs being self apparent'.

G

Garbett Street, Ladywood

Samuel Garbett was amongst the most prominent and influential citizens of Birmingham in the eighteenth century and is commemorated in a street that ran from Summer Hill Street to Shakespeare Road. Although little known today, he played a powerful role in thrusting Birmingham on to the world stage as a town renowned for its manufacturing. The eighteenth century was an exciting and dynamic time for Birmingham, when men like Matthew Boulton (see Boulton Road) and James Watt (see James Watt Street) gained attention for the town through their industrial and scientific achievements and through their involvement in social advancement.

Although he was not a member of the famed Lunar Society, Garbett stood alongside Boulton as a key figure in Birmingham's rapid expansion into one of Britain's leading towns. About 1760, Dr Alexander Carlyle, a noted Scottish cleric and shrewd observer, visited Birmingham with some friends and was impressed by Garbett's welcome. In his *Autobiography*, the Scot praised Garbett as 'truly a very extraordinary man', who had been 'an ordinary worker in brass at Birmingham'. Garbett had no education 'further than writing and accounts; but he was a man of great acuteness of genius and extent of Understanding'. As a workman he had invented a stamp for shortening labour and was noticed by Mr. Hollis, a great merchant in London, who employed Garbett as his agent for purchasing Birmingham goods, whereby he was brought 'into notice and rank among his townsmen; and the more he was known, the more he was esteemed'.

Carlyle went on to declare that 'I have known no person but one more of such strong and lively feelings, of such a fair candid, and honourable heart, and of such quick and ardent conceptions, who still retained the power of cost and deliberate judgment before execution. He received us with open hospitality, and we were soon convinced we were welcome by the cordiality of his wife and daughter, who lodged the whole company but me, who, being their oldest acquaintance, they took the liberty to send to a friend's Homely Mode house.' The Garbetts lived simply and although they provided Carlyle and his party with very good claret, and an excellent table they had 'only one maid (his wife's cousin) and a blind lad as servants. This last was a wonder, for he did all the work of a man, and even brewed the ale, but that of serving at table . . .'

After his time with Hollis, Garbett had struck out as a merchant in his own right and made his fortune, and then he became the partner of Dr John Roebuck. Having studied medicine at the University of Edinburgh, Roebuck had settled in Birmingham as a physician. However, he was deeply drawn to chemistry and its application to industry, becoming the first ever consulting chemist for manufacturing in the

Midlands. In particular, Roebuck improved the method of refining the gold and silver that was used in a number of trades in Birmingham, and in 1746 he and Garbett established a laboratory in Steelhouse Lane for the assay and refining of precious metals. Roebuck had also improved the making of sulphuric acid, so that the cost of production was reduced by 75%. This development encouraged the use of sulphuric acid instead of sour milk for bleaching in the linen trade. Consequently, the laboratory also became a testing place for linen manufacturers and a manufacturing centre for the acid.

Three years later Garbett and Roebuck set up a plant for the production of the acid in Prestonpans and in 1760 and with other partners they started the famous Carron Iron Works, also in Scotland. This venture and others placed Garbett under great financial strain, worsened by the economic crisis of 1772. Ten years later he became bankrupt, having been forced into insolvency by 'external monetary influences' apparently brought about by the incompetence of his son-in-law, who was his partner in certain enterprises. Despite this marked downturn in his financial affairs, he remained a close friend of Boulton, who encouraged Garbett to re-establish his business in Birmingham. He did and was eventually able to leave more than £12,000 on his death, though with his creditors not fully discharged.

Despite his money problems, Garbett continued to be deeply involved in the commercial and life of Birmingham. He was influential in the emergence of the town's first Assay Office in 1773 and ten years later he became the first chairman of the Commercial Committee, the forerunner of the Birmingham Chamber of Commerce. In this capacity he was involved in a scheme to ensure a constant supply of copper to Birmingham. He was also vigorous in promoting the interest of sword blade makers locally; whilst he spoke with the Prime Minister, William Pitt, about the fears of local manufacturers concerning the emigration of skilled workers and of the detrimental impact of taxation. In fact, Garbett was a pioneering political lobbyist.

Garbett was also an active public figure. He was a member of the committee that was formed in 1765 to provide Birmingham with a general hospital; four years later he was one of the first of the town's Street Commissioners; and in January 1788 he was made chairman of a local committee formed to campaign against the slave trade. This meeting passed the following resolutions

First, That the practice of going to Africa to purchase Men to sell for Slaves should be publicly execrated.

Second, That, as Englishmen and Christians, it behoves us to exert our best Endeavours to abolish Slavery.

Third, That it is the Duty of this Meeting to petition Parliament to take into Consideration the inhuman Practice of purchasing harmless Men, Women, and Children, to sell in British Dominions for Slaves, and to restrain the Cruelties that are inflicted upon them, and earnestly to solicit Relief for our Fellow-creatures.

Later that year, Gustavus Vasa the African visited Birmingham. Raised as Olaudah Equiano in what is now Nigeria, he had been kidnapped as a child and sold into slavery in America. As a slave to a captain in the Royal Navy, and later to a Quaker merchant, he eventually earned the price of his own freedom by careful trading and saving. He travelled the world as a seaman and settling in London he became involved in the movement to abolish the slave trade. This led him to write *The Interesting Narrative of the Life of Olaudah Equiano, or Gustavus Vassa the African* (1789) a strongly abolitionist autobiography. On visiting Birmingham, Vassa remarked upon the 'great marks of kindness' he had received from Charles and Sampson Lloyd. Matthew Boulton and number of others – amongst whom was Garbett. The Birmingham man died in 1803 and was buried in the church yard of Saint Philip's, of which he was a church warden. Boulton write of his old friend that 'I have always found his principles unfailingly just, honourable and liberal'

Garretts Green Lane, Garretts Green

Garrets Green Lane takes its name from a part of Sheldon which was called Garrett's Green by the early 1600s and which recalls a family of local landowners.

Garrison Lane, Bordesley and Small Heath

A farm shown on Henry Beighton's map of 1725 is named on Tomlinson's Map of 1760 as Garrison Farm. There are stories that soldiers were garrisoned there during the English Civil War, but these are unsubstantiated. Located by Tilton Road, the farm disappeared about 1880 when it became a brick works. Nearby **Arsenal Street**, **Artillery Street** and **Camp Street**, were so named because of the military connotation of Garrison Lane, as were **Gordon Street** and **Wolseley Street**. These latter two streets relate to General Gordon and Sir Garnet Wolseley, who led British troops to victory at the battle of Tel-el-Kabir in 1882, which led to the occupation of Egypt. Sir Garnet was the older brother of Frederick York Wolseley who invented the mechanical sheep shearer. Wolseley's company later employed Herbert Austin and from the end of the nineteenth century its base was the Sydney Works in Alma Street, Aston.

In late 1884, after a massive campaign by the national newspapers, the British Government sent Lord Wolseley, as he now was, to lead an army to relieve General Gordon who was besieged in Khartoum, the capital of the Sudan. This country was mostly in the hands of rebels against Egyptian rule headed by a religious leader, the Mahdi. Wolseley quickly formed a Camel Corps to strike out across the desert towards Khartoum and give moral support to Gordon. A picked force, it was led by Colonel Stewart, and after his death by Sir Charles Wilson. Defeating attacks by the Mahdi's followers, the Camel Corps pressed through its opponents towards the Nile. They came upon four of Gordon's steamers and were handed a letter from the beleaguered general. It was dated 14 December and

Garrison Lane in the 1920s by the flats that are still there.

declared, 'I think the game is up'. Sadly it was. On 26 January Wilson set off on a steamer down the Nile with a small bodyguard to find out what was happening in Khartoum. It was too late. They reached the outskirts of the town and realised it had fallen. On 24 January, the Mahdi's men had breached the defences. Gordon and all his troops were killed, as were thousands of the town's folk who had not previously surrendered into slavery.

Gate Street, Saltley

For generations the Gate, Saltley was famous for the pub called the 'Gate' and also because it was a major stopping point on the Inner Circle Number 8 route. However, it does not take is name from the pub but rather from the gate that used to be here on the turnpike road and which was called Saltley Gate or Halfpenny Gate in *Aris's Gazette* on 23 November 1829. This was an old-established way. In the Middle Ages, folk from Saltley and district passed over the Rea just below Gate Street to go to worship at Aston Parish Church. This crossing was also part of the road that went from Birmingham, through Saltley and on to Ward End, Castle Bromwich and then Coleshill. It was mentioned in a deed as early as 1250, but it was not a good one. In the late eighteenth century Hutton stated that at Saltley 'every flood annoys the traveller'. The section to Castle Bromwich was turnpiked in 1759. It was later transferred to another turnpike trust that expired in 1877. Coming of High Street, Saltley, Gate Street itself emerged in 1886.

The old 'Gate Inn', Saltley about 1850 in a photograph taken by a G. Squires.

Geach Street, Summer Lane Neighbourhood (Newtown)

Leading off Summer Lane and heading towards Guildford Street, Geach Street lies just south of the Hockley Brook and the old border between Aston and Birmingham. It is named after Charles Geach, a Cornishman who made a big impact upon the town. Born in 1808, he became a clerk with a draper in St Austell and through the influence of relatives, when he was eighteen he gained a position as clerk with the Bank of England. He must have made a positive impression because in 1828 he was sent to Birmingham with Sir George Nicholls to establish a branch of the bank, and within three years he had become second inspector there. However, Geach felt it was difficult for him to make further progress and he looked to move on. With a detailed knowledge both of banking and the commercial life of Birmingham he was instrumental in forming two local banks, becoming manager of the one – the Birmingham and Midland Bank. He was only twenty-eight and had never held such a position before but he had the confidence of the bank's promoters.

Cleverly overseeing the financial affairs of the Bank and working closely with the Bank of England, Geach avoided too many bad debts and succeeded in keeping the Birmingham and Midland afloat when other banks were failing. He also showed personal courage in protecting the bank's interests. In 1839 during the Bull Ring riots many business premises were attacked by Chartists, a movement campaigning for the vote for working-class men. To protect the bank in Union Street, Geach placed his staff on the roof and armed them with missiles. He himself rode through the mob to fetch support from the barracks.

Shrewd and ambitious, in 1838 Geach led a group of Birmingham businessmen in purchasing the patents and works of an iron-axle manufacturer in Wednesbury. The company was reconstructed and six years later Geach bought out his partners. In the railway boom that followed, the Patent Shaft and Axle Tree Company was transformed into a massive concern by the increase in demand for its products that were essential to trains. In 1842 Geach also bought the Parkgate Company, a failing iron manufacturing business in Rotherham. It was a fortuitous move just before the mania for railway building triggered a boom in the demand for iron. On one occasion Geach supposedly took an order for 30,000 tons of iron at £12 per ton when it cost him not half that amount. Geach was also a promoter and director of the Manchester, Sheffield and Lincolnshire Railway, and of the Shrewsbury and Birmingham Railway.

Like so many successful businessmen in this period, Geach entered public life. A Liberal in politics, according to his obituary 'his love of liberal legislation arose from a dislike to class privileges or restrictions, rather than from any theoretical notions of abstract right, and in this sense he advocated the widest extension and the freest exercise of the franchise'. Geach was deeply involved in the campaign to repeal the Corn Laws. This protectionist measure prevented the entry of cheap foreign corn into Britain and thus safeguarded the incomes of landowners. The Corn Laws were loathed by manufacturers and businessmen in the industrial districts because they kept the price of bread artificially high, which meant that working people needed higher wages than that which their gaffers were often prepared to pay. A staunch advocate of free trade, Geach was made an alderman of Birmingham in 1844 and three years later was chosen as the town's mayor. During his office he overhauled the corporation's accounts and bookkeeping procedures.

Having to resign as manager of the Birmingham and Midland because of his civic duties, Geach joined the board as managing director. In 1851, following his nomination by the National Parliamentary and Financial Reform Association, he was elected MP for Coventry. Three years later he died after a short illness. At the time of his death he was a director and one of the chief promoters of the Crystal Palace Company.

Gem Street, Gosta Green

Once going from Coleshill Street to Aston Street, Gem Street replaced the older **New Thomas Street**, probably at the time of the Corporation Street Improvement Scheme in the later nineteenth century (see Corporation Street). This was a time when the Council was seeking to create a civic and shopping centre in this locality. It cleared many old streets in which the poor had lived and changed the names of others in an attempt to push forward a new up-market image. Ironically, Gem Street itself disappeared in the post-Second World War redevelopments of the City. It recalls the Gem family, members of which were of some consequence in Birmingham. William Henry Gem was a notable Birmingham solicitor and one of the clerks to the

Birmingham magistrates, whilst his son, Thomas Henry, was also a lawyer and is credited with inventing lawn tennis.

Born in 1819, Thomas 'Harry' Gem built up an extensive private practice in Birmingham and succeeded to the office of clerk to the Birmingham magistrates when his father died in 1856. Additionally he was magistrate's clerk to the Kings Heath and Balsall Heath petty sessions and clerk to the commissioners of taxes for the hundred of Hemlingford. Despite his activity as a lawyer, Harry Gem was best known for his sporting and literary interests. A keen sportsman who was involved in cricket, horse-riding, athletics, and 'pedestrianism', and he played a crucial role in the development of lawn tennis – a role underestimated outside the Midlands.

In the 1850s, Gem played the game called racket but he was put off by the need for expensively constructed courts. With his friend J. B. A. Perera, a Birmingham merchant with premises in Great Charles Street, Gem drew up rules for a game named 'pelota' and later 'lawn rackets'. Their emphasis was on simplicity and athleticism. The first game was played about 1865 in the garden of Perera's home in Ampton Road, Edgbaston. Seven years later both Gem and Perera moved to Leamington Spa where they established a club and changed the name of their game to 'lawn tennis'. A staunch Conservative, Harry Gem was enthusiastic about the volunteers and held the rank of major in the 1st Warwickshire (Birmingham) Rifles. He also wrote on a sporting matters and a variety of other topics such as politics; composed songs; wrote verses; and performed light comedy. He died in 1881.

Genners Lane, Bartley Green

There are a number of intriguing names in Bartley Green, amongst them Genner's Lane. In his history of King's Norton and Northfield, Arthur B. Lock explained that the Middle English word 'engynour' meant someone who managed engines of war and he mentions a John de Jenners living locally in 1603. Investigations by youngsters at Shenley Fields School suggested a possible ancestor of de Jenners. He was Adam le Gynur, an engineer and possibly a retired soldier. Interestingly the lane was also spelt as Gynor's.

Gibbins Road, Selly Oak

Going from Harborne Lane and up to Weoley Park Road, Gibbins Road relates to the family that founded the Birmingham Battery Company. During the later eighteenth century, Joseph Gibbins was a gilt and plated button maker in Prospect Row and it seems he was also involved in banking. In 1793 he joined his friend Matthew Boulton and other Birmingham manufacturers in forming the Rose Copper Company. Copper was vital for Boulton in the minting of coins, a major part of his business, and he needed a regular and dependable supply of the metal. Within four years, the Rose had bought a smelting works in Swansea. Then in 1809 Gibbins was approached by Boulton to become the general manager of the company. Gibbins accepted, but died within two years.

Two of his sons, Brueton and another Joseph, similarly were involved with banking and were amongst the thirteen owners of the Birmingham Banking Company, set up in 1820. Brueton and another brother, William, also owned a glass works in Aston; whilst Joseph had other interests in chemical and copper works. Seven years later, Brueton, Joseph and eleven others began the Birmingham Battery and Metal Company. Four of the partners were also proprietors of the Birmingham Banking Company, whilst three more were other Gibbins brothers: William; George; and Thomas, who had a colourful life. Aged 22 in 1818, Thomas sailed to South America in connection with the glass business of Brueton and William. Visiting Brazil, he wrote about the country's economic conditions. He returned home and went back to Brazil in 1823. Two years later he and another brother, Bevington, took over a chemical works in Neath, but he left that to become managing partner of the Birmingham Battery and Metal Company. In 1837 Thomas married Emma Joel Cadbury, the youngest daughter of Richard Tipper and Elizabeth Cadbury.

The new company took over the brassfounding concern of William Jenkins in Digbeth, and Thomas and Emma lived in an old house next to the works, which boasted a rolling mill that supplied narrow brass strips to the wire mill. Here the brass strips were rounded and drawn into wire for pin making, although brass and copper rods were made from the thicker wire. The rolling mill also sent metal strips to the tube mill, where a tube was made by drawing a die through the metal on a draw bench; and it made up large brass sheets for working up into battery. Before the appearance of rolling mills, wrought metal sheets were produced by hammering a cast ingot of metal. Four or more light and heavy hammers could be used, and these were known as a battery of hammers. A flat service was ensured by the use of a flat hammer, whilst hollow ware came about through a shaped hammer. By the early nineteenth century, rolling mills had made the use of hammers redundant in the making of flat plate, but hammers continued to be important for a raising a pan from a flat sheet, so that the products kept the name battery. These included kettles, basins, pans, bowls and other hollow ware raised by power hammering.

In the early years, much of the Battery's products were sold to merchants trading in West Africa; whilst the coming of the railways led to a demand for tubes. By the 1860s, the Gibbins family had bought out the other shareholders and the running of the company was in the hands of two sons of Thomas: William and Thomas junior. In 1870 they were joined by their brother, John, who became general manager of the new works at Selly Oak. These opened in 1873, despite opposition from some local people who did not want a factory spoiling a country district and destroying the amenities. Erected by the canal, these premises soon grew. By now, the company had abandoned the making of battery and had extended its making of brass condenser tubes. In 1877 a refinery for copper was opened at Selly Oak and fifteen years later it became the Battery's headquarters with the closing of the offices in Digbeth. In 1895 a new rolling mill was erected in Selly Oak and all work ceased in Digbeth.

Shortly afterwards, the Gibbins family decided to do something for Selly Oak and so they gave over eleven acres of the Weoley Park Estate as a park. Named Selly Oak Park, it was enlarged by two more gifts of land from the family in 1913 and 1919. Gibbins Road runs alongside the park. Thomas Gibbins junior was a local and county councillor and presented the land for the building of Selly Oak Library, the building of which was paid for by the Carnegie Foundation. Sadly, the Birmingham Battery Company is no longer a presence in Selly Oak.

Gibb Street, Deritend

Another very short street, now running towards the Custard Factory arts centre, Gibb Street is thought to recall a landowner. Its smallness emphasises that not all landowners should be regarded as having extensive estates. Some had small plots upon which short streets or yards of back-to-back houses were built.

Gilbertstone Avenue, South Yardley

Coming of the Coventry Road, Gilbertstone Avenue takes its name from Gilbertstone House, itself recalling the hamlet of Gilbertstone in the parish of Yardley, which was mentioned in 1275. The house was the home of Richard Tangye – one of the two Cornish brothers who began the famed hydraulics firm based in Cornwall Road, Smethwick. In 1880, it was described as a modern residence where 'the atmosphere of the country is breathed, and in the summer days it would be difficult to select a place at once so picturesque and so charming to the view'. Tangye's home replaced a mansion that had been on the site, so that it had 'delightful old gardens in which there is a fine collection of plants and flowers. At one spot in the grounds, which, with the long adjoining stretch of fields, cover many acres, there is a huge stone which marks the boundary lines between Warwickshire and Worcestershire.'

Legend has it that this stone was placed there by a giant called Golbert, but it is likely that it recalls the Gilberts or Gilbards who lived hereabouts in the later Middle Ages. The stone was left over from the Ice Age and it marked the boundary not only between two counties but also between Sheldon, Bickenhill (Lyndon) and Yardley. The Tangyes were great benefactors to Birmingham and were associated deeply with gifts towards the city's Art Gallery. Gilbertstone House was later lived in by Thomas Rowbotham, a builder who developed an estate on his land.

Gillott Road, Rotton Park and Edgbaston

Joseph Gillott was the son of a workman in the Sheffield cutlery trade who became one of Birmingham's greatest manufacturers and a noted patron of the arts. Born in south Yorkshire on 11 October 1799, he grew up to be a working cutler, acquiring a reputation as a 'noted hand' at forging and grinding knife blades. About 1822 he was out of work and he walked to Birmingham. When he arrived he spent his last penny on refreshments in pub where the Mucker music hall later stood on the corner of Park

Street, across from the markets. Luckily he found a job straightaway and soon after he rented a little house in Bread Street, which became Cornwall Street. Here he set up as a small gaffer in the light steel toy trade, the making of steel buckles, chains, and other works and ornaments. A merchant who bought his buckles and steel toys from Gillott said the new arrival 'made very excellent goods and came for his money every week'.

With a fine reputation for his products, Gillott began to prosper but he may have remained just another successful small manufacturer if he had not met a young woman called Maria Mitchell. Her brothers, John and William, made steel pens but the process was laborious and quite expensive. Using shears they cut out the shape of nibs from sheets of metal and then trimmed and filed them. Their products could be bought only by the wealthy, and most other folk used goose quills – themselves quite costly and out of the reach of working men and women. In this way, the art of writing remained the preserve of the better off.

Sharp, clever and persevering, Joseph Gillott put his mind to the task of devising a quick, efficient and cheap way of producing steel pens. Quietly and carefully he tried first one approach and then another and at last he hit upon an idea. He knew that in the pearl button trade craftsmen used a hand press to force out a blank from the shells which were the raw material of the industry. So why not contrive a press that could push out the shape of a steel pen from a sheet of metal and which he could then finish off so that it was ready for sale? Working in his garret, Gillott made the tool he desired and with it he turned out steel pens which were 'blued' and varnished in a frying pan over the kitchen fire. His wares were superior in quality to any on the market. More than that, on his own he was able to make as many steel pens as could twenty people labouring without a press.

Another problem overcome by Gillott was the extreme hardness of the pens. This he obviated by cutting side slits in addition to the centre slit, which had been solely in use up to that period. Afterwards he added the cross grinding of the points; and these two processes imparted an elasticity to the pen, making it in this respect nearly equal to a quill. In 1831 Gillott registered his first patent for the manufacture of pens. Demand for his goods was great and he was joined in his endeavours by Maria Mitchell. Even on the morning of their wedding, Joseph made a gross (144) of pens and sold them at a shilling a piece before he went to the ceremony at the church.

At first Gillott made these pens for others, selling them to a firm of stationers called Beilby and Knott. But the orders poured in because of the quality of his goods, their increasing cheapness, and the demand for them from a growing population that was becoming more literate. The young couple were hard pressed to keep up – but they did. As their business waxed so did their fortunes and it was reckoned that Joseph had several bank accounts as well as a stash of money buried in his cellar. Soon it became obvious that he needed to take on workers to help them and to have bigger premises, so the Gillotts moved to Church Street and then again to a yard off Newhall Street. Finally Joseph decided to pay for purpose-built premises in Graham Street.

Birmingham was a town where most gaffers operated in small workshops, attics or narrow and low buildings known as 'shopping' and Gillott was the first to erect a modern and planned factory.

The output from these Victoria Works was enormous and in 1836 alone it reached 250,000 gross of pens – 36 million individual pens. In the following years production grew spectacularly so that a workforce of 450 was needed. Crucially, the price of pens was reduced from 5*s* per gross (144) in the late 1830s to as low as 1¹/₂*d*. per gross in the mid-1860s. By now there were twelve penmaking concerns in Birmingham making 98,000 gross of goods each week – ranging from three ha'pence to twelve shillings a gross. This expansion was stimulated by the introduction of Penny Post, which boosted letter writing and by sharp reductions in prices. Such cost effectiveness was achieved by mechanisation and the sub-division of labour.

In the Victoria Works itself large sheets off Sheffield steel were cut into strips four inches wide. These were dipped and rolled thinly so that blanks could be pressed from them – each of which was pierced with a hole to form the nib itself. After they were slitted on each side, the blanks were toughened by annealing, embossed with a pattern and marked with Gillott's name. These processes were followed by tempering, smoothing, polishing, varnishing, grinding, cleaning and colouring before the finished pens were checked and boxed. Perry's pens, Mitchell's Pens and others from Brum were well known but it was Gillott who was the most acclaimed penmaker internationally. Indeed it was said to be doubtful if any article of such wide and universal use was ever so identified with the name of one man.

Almost every pen used in the classrooms of the United States was made at the Victoria Works, Hockley. According to Elihu Burritt, the American Consul in our city, the factory had become 'a king or central celebrity in Birmingham to visitors from America and other countries'. He went on to praise the quiet order, neatness, comfort and elegance of the works and then described the products exhibited in the show-room, a place which really was 'a museum of art, filled and embellished by an infinite variety of specimens of the utmost perfection. There are pens so large that they seem to be made for giants … then there are others so minute, that it requires a magnifying glass to see the split and point. Between the two extreme range gradations in size and varieties in form, stars, slowers and various pictures are exquisitely formed out of these varieties, in which nearly all the tints of the rainbow have their place and play.'

An enlightened and paternalistic employer, Gillott ensured that his works afforded much convenience and comfort to his employees, most of whom were women. He established a benevolent society among the workpeople, to which he subscribed liberally; he seldom changed his managers; and apparently he never had a dispute with his workforce. A lover of art, Gillott began to buy paintings from an early age, and his collection, housed in his homes in Westbourne Road, Edgbaston, and at Great Stanmore, near London, contained many gems of English art. Its great strength lay in paintings by J. M. W. Turner and William Etty, the latter being a special friend of the collector. Gillott appreciated Turner's talents before they had been generally recognized, and purchased his paintings when others doubted their worth. The collection was also very rich in the work of John Linnell, David Roberts, and others. After the owner's death the paintings were sold for £170,000. His collection of violins, on which he much prided himself, was also sold, fetching £4000.

Yet for all Gillott's wealth and fame he was not a show off. Short, sturdy and broad set, for many years he was a familiar figure at the Birmingham Theatre Royal, after which he would adjourn to the Hen and Chickens Hotel to smoke a 'churchwarden' and converse with friends. Until about ten days before his death, the only sign he gave of old age was failing eyesight. On Boxing Day 1871 Gillott entertained as usual some of his children and their friends; the next morning he was attacked by a complication of pleurisy and bronchitis, and he died at home at Westbourne Road, Edgbaston, Birmingham, on 5 January 1872.

Twenty years previously Gillott had bought most of Rotton Park, 242 acres, the last part of the Perrott estate (see Monument Road). It cost him £90,000 and was laid out gradually in imitation of the adjoining middle-class district of Edgbaston. **Gillott Road** runs through the heart of this estate, stretching all the way from the Hagley Road to Icknield Port Road; whilst **Stanmore Road**, brings to mind his house in Middlesex. **Bernard Road** is named after his son and **Algernon Road** after one of his grandsons. Joseph Gillott was a man of many parts. He was craftsman, grafter, designer, inventor, innovator, salesman, publicist, patron of the arts and supporter of good causes. But there can be no doubt about Joseph Gillott's foremost contribution to history. He was penmaker to the world. With his workers and his Brummagem competitors he sent out a multitude of affordable pens. Together these Brummie men and women democratised writing.

Glebe Farm Road, Glebe Farm

Glebe land was that which belonged to the parish church, and it had become such through bequests of small portions of land made by parishioners over hundreds of years. As such glebe was part of the living of the vicar and provided him with income. All Church of England parishes had such properties, although in not all parishes was the glebe large enough to make a farm. When it was, the glebe could be farmed directly or leased out. In the case of Glebe Farm Road it recalls the land that belonged to the parish church of Yardley, Saint Edburga.

From the later Middle Ages, what became Glebe Farm was in the occupation of the Walters family. As Victor Skipp has shown, it was like so many farms in Yardley in that it was cut out of the trees of the Forest of Arden. This is shown by the existence as late as 1847 of fields called Stocking, which was the Middle English word for 'a clearing of stumps, a piece of ground cleared of stumps'. Again in common with other isolated farms in Yardley, the Walters put a moat around their house just above the junction to what would become Church Lane and Kitts Green Road. The name of the farm changed in the later eighteenth century after it was bought by Matthew Boulton who then sold it to Yardley Parish Church.

Glebe Farm Road is an extension of Church Lane, which starts at the Yew Tree and goes past Yardley Old Village and the church to the junction of Audley Road and Kitts Green Road. From there Glebe Farm Road itself heads off towards Glebe Farm Recreation Ground, well known from the 1950s to 1970s for the playing of Gaelic Football matches.

Until its clearance in the 1930s, there was a **Glebe Street** in Ladywood, Birmingham. This had been cut on land that belonged to the parish church of the town, Saint Martin's in the Bull Ring, and which was bounded by the estate owned by the Grammar School (see King Edward's Road) and Sheepcote Lane. Across what would become Broad Street lay more glebe land. This was marked out to the south by what are now Islington Row and Bath Row and to the north west by Islington – now the Five Ways end of Broad Street. It was developed after an act of Parliament passed in 1773. Known as the Six Closes, or 'by ancient description called the Five Ways Closes', it consisted of upwards of 22 acres of land. Within fifteen years of the legislation, building leases were advertised for the area and according to Pye's map of 1795 a number of streets were laid out.

Two of them ran downhill from Islington to Bath Row. These were the unsurprisingly-named **Saint Martin's Street** and the equally religious-sounding **Bishopsgate Street**. Going across them at a diagonal from Islington Row were **William Street** and **Tennant Street**. These recalled a William Tennant who had

A view of the Glebe Farm area in 1937 before it was developed. The photo was taken from Yardley Old Church.

Glebe Street before its clearance in the 1930s.

the advowson of Saint Martin's – that is, he had the right to appoint the vicar. For hundreds of years, this privilege had belonged to the lords of the manor, but it passed out of their hands in 1720 and it seems that William Tennant was patron of Saint Martin's for at least 50 years from 1771. Referred to originally as the Islington Estate, hence **Islington Row – New Bridge Street** until 1885 – and later **Islington Row Middleway**, the district became a vital working-class neighbourhood.

A wonderful source of material about rural Birmingham is provided by the Glebe Terrier of Saint Martin's from the 1820s. This gives an account of the parsonage and its lands and brings to life two long forgotten field names. One was a close called the **Parson's Meadow** or **Shoulder of Mutton** along Sherlock Street; whilst another was the **Horsepool Croft** at the top of Smallbrook Street. It is a pity, that more street names are not based on the old field names of the city.

Glover Street, Bordesley

Coming off Great Barr Street and going on to Adderley Street, Glover Street may be named after a Joseph Glover of Camp Hill who was mentioned in an assignment of property in Rea Street from William Bradnock of Yardley in 1811.

Glover Street, Bordesley in the 1930s.

Golden Hillock Road, Small Heath, Sparkbrook and Sparkhill

Glover's Farm used to cover much of this area, hence **Glovers Road** (**Glovers Lane** until 1872), Small Heath which comes off Golden Hillock Road and heads to Jenkins Street. Mentioned as Sylvester's Farm in an advertisement of 1763 and as near Golden Hillock, its farmhouse stood on the corner of the modern Glovers Road and Golden Hillock Road, believed by many to be the 'most romantically-named thoroughfare in the city'. Its origins were the stuff of legends. Glover's Farm had a tump, hillock, under which according to a legend there was buried a medieval robber and his treasure. Other tales say that the hillock was the place where an ancient chieftain had been buried with gold and that if anyone opened the hillock he or she would be smitten blind. Thus the hillock was golden, leading to the name Golden Hillock Road, which had been called **Danford's Lane**. Interestingly a Hillock Leasow was indicated hereabouts on Tomlinson's Map of 1760. Similar stories are connected to the pimple in Kingstanding (see Kingstanding Road).

Another story attributes the name Golden Hillock to the buttercups that covered the fields locally. Golden Hillock Road was the home of artist Thomas Wood Downing. Born in 1849 on **Kingston Hill**, then called **Dark Lane**, in 1881 Downing married Emilie Harris and moved to 42 Golden Hillock. Working at first as started as a draughtsman engraver he became a painter of street scenes.

Golden Hillock Road in the 1910s, by what is now Poets Corner.

Gooch Street, Highgate

Once one the busiest shopping roads in working-class Birmingham, Gooch Street brings to the fore a landowning family that still benefits from its ownership of parts of Birmingham. In his pioneering history of Birmingham, William Hutton stated that:

> About the year 1730, Thomas Sherlock, late Bishop of London, purchased the private estate of the ladies of the manor, chiefly land, about four hundred per annum. In 1758, the steward told me it had increased to twice the original value. The pious old bishop was frequently solicited to grant building leases, but answered? 'His land was valuable, and if built upon, his successor, at the expiration of the term, would have the rubbish to carry off:' he therefore not only refused, but prohibited his successor from granting such leases. But Sir Thomas Gooch, who succeeded him, seeing the great improvement of the neighbouring estates, and wisely judging fifty pounds per acre preferable to five, procured an act in about 1766, to set aside the prohibiting clause in the bishop's will. Since which, a considerable town may be said to have been erected upon his property, now about £2400 per annum.

The sisters referred to by Hutton were of the Marrow family, which had held the lordship of the manor of Birmingham since 1555. With no male heir to their lands, the four sisters sold the private estate in the manor to Bishop Sherlock, hence **Sherlock Street** and **Bishop Street**. Sherlock's sister, Mary, was his heir. She was married to Sir Thomas Gooch, who lived at Benacre Hill in Wrentham, Suffolk –

A view along Sherlock Street in 1955 towards the Pearks Stores on the corner of Wrentham Street. Across the way is the famous 'canine depository' of Carleton Hinks, which stood between Macdonald Street and Hurst Street.

Suffolk Street with its tram lines in the 1930s.

Hope Street in 1960, with attic high back-to-back houses fronting to the street. It looks as if the shot is taken from Vere Street, with Hope Street School in the background and across Sherlock Street.

giving rise to **Gooch Street**, **Gooch Street North**, **Benacre Street**, **Wrentham Street** and **Suffolk Street**. The East Anglian connection was made even plainer by the cutting of **Norfolk Street**, off Suffolk Street, which was demolished in 1886 as part of a major redevelopment of Birmingham City Centre. Sir Thomas was aware of the growth of Birmingham and realised the potential in the development of the land he had inherited. As Hutton noted, he set aside Sherlock's wishes in his will by an act of Parliament that allowed him and his sons Thomas, William and John and their guardians to grant building leases of certain land.

This move led to the slow urbanization of the Gooch land between Bristol Street and Gooch Street, where **Hope Street** and **Vere Street** perpetuate the name of Harriet Hope Vere, the second wife of Sir Edward Sherlock Gooch, the sixth baronet. The Gooch family also owned land in Brookfields; along Broad Street, where they leased six acres to the Birmingham Canal Navigations for their wharves; and in Bordesley, leading to **Benacre Drive** off Fazeley Street. A lease from Sir Thomas Gooch of land in Bordesley Street and dated 1788 indicates the beginnings of urbanisation in the latter area. Since the mid-nineteenth century, the Gooch Estate in Birmingham has been administered locally by James and Lister Lea. Some land has been sold off, but much remains in the possession of the Gooch family. Its members have played little part in the life of Birmingham, although the present National Trust Museum of back-to-back houses in Inge Street was property donated by the Gooch Estate.

Goode Street, Hockley

Now called **Goode Avenue**, Goode Street would seem to be connected with a family about whom little is known. In 1803 the shares in the Ellesmere Canal of a Benjamin Salisbury Goode were transferred after his death to Joseph Johnson. Two years later, a W. Goode sold by auction 'an excellent garden planted with fruit trees and vegetables in a high state of cultivation with brick summer house' in the cottage field. This was the central field leading from the Cottage of Content to the Sand Pits. W. Goode was an auctioneer based in New Street and in 1786 he had been alluded to in a poetical advertisement in *Aris's Birmingham Gazette*.

> Fine Teas, China-ware, and Glass of the best,
> Coffee, Chocolate, and Cocoa that will stand the Test,
> Stone Blue, Poland Starch, and Rice Caroline,
> New Mustard Flour, best, second, and fine,
> All kinds of Spices, neat as imported,
> Moist, Powder, and Lump Sugars, properly sorted
> Turkey Figs, new Currants, and Raisins o'th'Sun,
> Also Malagas, Prunes, and curious French Plumb :
> Blacking Balls, the best of any in Town,
> W. P. for to play at, Laugh and Lie Down;
> With many more Articles, I wish you to know,
> May be bought of T. Farror on Terms very Low.
> His Warehouse in Bull Ring is No. Thirty-eight,
> And Shop to sell Retail is in Temple Street,
> Auctioneering performed, we take Leave for to mention:
> To insure your Property I beg your Attention.

Goodrick Street, Nechells

Now called Goodrick Way, this may refer to a C. Goodrick who was a committee member Birmingham School Association formed in 1850 to campaign for the introduction of a free, secular and compulsory system of national education supported through the rates. In **Wrightson's Directory** of 1818 a John Goodrick was given as a rope maker in Smallbrook Street. Carol Cresser has conducted much research into the Goodrick-Cresser family and has a copy of the will of John Goodrick, who owned land in Edgbaston, Bristol Road, Ladywood, Smallbrook Street, Saint Lukes Road and elsewhere. She believes that Goodrick Street was named after him.

Goodrick Street in 1966. It looks like this has been taken from the bottom of Fowler Street looking down Goodrick Street on the right and Lingard Street with its school on the left.

Gospel Lane, Acocks Green

A Gospel Oak was a place on a parish boundary where a passage from the Gospels in the Bible was read at the annual Rogationtide perambulation. This took place on the Monday, Tuesday or Wednesday before Whitsun and entailed groups of parishioners walking the parish bounds and marking stones and trees to make plain the dividing line. They were usually accompanied by the rector or vicar who read the passage and led prayers. Gospel Lane was originally called **Longley Lane** and was part of the boundary between the parishes of Yardley and Solihull. It still provides part of the division, running from close to Pollard Road and into **Redstone Farm Road** and thence Streetsbrook Road. Redstone Farm itself had been on the Warwick Road end of Gospel Lane, opposite to where it is now, and was farmed by the Beech family, so that Gospel Lane was also known as **Beech Lane** or **Beeches Lane**.

Gospel Oak Farm, hence **Gospel Farm Road**, recalled the Gospel Oak itself, which was felled in the 1840s. This farm was owned by the Severne family, thus **Severne Road**, and it was compulsory purchased by the Council in 1929 for £12,900. The Severnes had inherited Hall Green Hall, a fine building that had been the home of Job Marston in the late eighteenth century. They sold their Hall Green Estate in 1912.

King's Farm, Gospel Lane, in 1920.

Gosta Green

Squashed between Aston Street and the Aston Road, Gosta Green was both a street and an area, and its name is an old one. The Assize Roll of 1306 mentions a William de Gorsty, and as late as 1758, Tomlinson's Plan of Duddeston and Nechells indicates both an Upper Gorsty Green and a Lower Gorsty Green. By this date the two places were also called Gostie Green. This was indicated in 1750 by an assignment of lease from Benjamin Pinley to Josiah Jefferys and Joseph Stephens of tenements at Gostie Green in Coleshill Street.

John Alfred Langford explained this spelling change. In a number of old deeds he found reference to Gosty Green, Upper Gosty Green, Gosty Piece and Gosty Field in different parts of Birmingham, and he explained that gorse was still pronounced as goss by local country folk. Tomlinson in his map also noted fields with names such as Upper Gorsty Close and it is apparent that once the spiny, yellow flowered shrub called gorse had been common locally. By 1795 when Pye's Map was surveyed, Gosta Green was the hub of streets reaching west to Lancaster Street and Stafford Street, south to Coleshill Street and Prospect Row, and east and north to the Digbeth Branch of the Birmingham to Fazeley Canal. In this manner, the Gosta Green neighbourhood included parts of Birmingham and Duddeston. In the late eighteenth century, William Hutton stated that Gosta Green derived from goose stead and its use was in decline. He was wrong on both counts, and the name survived strongly into the later twentieth century. **Goosemoor Lane**, Erdington was originally spelled Gosmore and has the same derivation as Gosta Green

Goodby Road, Moseley

In the mid-1930s, the Ideal Benefit Society began work on the Pitmaston Estate, which had belonged to Sir John Holder (see Holder Road). The first sod of a new road linking Russell Road with a proposed arterial road was cut by the Lord Mayor of Birmingham, Alderman H. E. Goodby JP – hence Goodby Road.

Gough Road, Edgbaston

A short road connecting Carpenter Road and Charlotte Road, Gough Road calls out to us of the ownership by the Gough family of the manor of Edgbaston. Of Welsh descent, the Goughs had emerged in Wolverhampton by the late sixteenth century and were involved in that town's important wool trade. A John Gough, who died in 1597, was given as a draper – as was his son, Henry Gough. He was mentioned in 1602 and it appears that he was one of the wealthiest men in the locality. During the English Civil war, King Charles arrived in Wolverhampton on 15 March, before he went on to Aston Hall. The monarch stayed with a relative of Henry, whilst he put up Prince Charles and his brother, James the Duke of York. Over 80 years old and with hardening arteries, Henry went secretly at night to the King and gave him the huge sum of £1,200. In return, Gough was offered a knighthood, which he declined. His son, John, took up arms for the Royalists, but is best remembered for setting up 'an everlasting monument of his love of the town, almost at his own cost, a building fit for a council house, market hall and court of law, and would have done more had not death alas, intervened'. This building was knocked down in 1780 to make more room in Wolverhampton's Market Place.

John's son, Henry, became 'one of the finest gentlemen of his time' and was knighted in 1678 after he was introduced to the court of Charles II. He was so wealthy that when he was in the street he was followed by children who called out: 'Here's old justice Gough, who has money enough'. Sir Henry had bought half of the manor of Perry, also known as Perry Barr, in 1671. In 1715, he wrote to his son that he was snowed up in Perry Hall, declaring, 'This weather almost kills me, and impoverishes the country to that degree, that, if it continue, it will ruin many families, and destroy abundance of creatures'. Two years later he also purchased Mansell's Farm from the Middlemores. Lying off Suffolk Street and on Holloway Head, **Gough Street** was cut through this land. It became the steepest street in Birmingham with a gradient of 1 in 7.5.

The Perry Estate remained in the hands of Sir Harry's descendants until 1844, when the direct line died out and it passed to the Honourable Frederick Gough, later the 4th Baron Calthorpe, who was a great-grandson of a brother of Sir Henry. Within a few years the other half of the manor of Perry had passed from Wyrley Birch (see Wyrley Road) to the Goughs. Perry Hall itself was a moated site on the left-bank of the River Tame and was set in a small park. Bearing the date 1576, it was added to in the later 1840s and in 1871 it was described as a three-storied gable house which enclosed a courtyard and which had massive projecting chimneys on its east side. In the early twentieth century it was the seat of General S. J. Gough-Calthorpe, hence **Calthorpe Road** off Westminster Road. The house was sold about 1928 and was pulled down, whilst the park became Perry Hall Playing Fields and the moat survived as a boating pond.

Sir Henry's brother, Sir Richard Gough, bought the manor of Edgbaston in 1717, also from descendants of the Middlemores and for the vast amount of £20,400. A London merchant who traded in the eastern Mediterranean, he made four highly profitable voyages to the East Indies, becoming a director of the East India Company and an MP. His purchase of Edgbaston allowed him to move from trade and into retirement as one of the landed gentry. He was succeeded by his son, another Henry who was created a baronet in 1728. His second wife, Barbara, was the only daughter of Reginald Calthorpe, who owned 2,000 acres of land in Norfolk, a mansion in Ampton, Suffolk and another in Elvetham, Hampshire, hence **Norfolk Road**, **Ampton Road** and **Elvetham Road**. Sir Henry died in 1774 and his wife eight years later. Their son inherited his paternal and maternal estates and added his mother's family name to his own, becoming Sir Henry Gough-Calthorpe, leading to **Calthorpe Road**. In 1796 he was made a peer under the title of Baron Calthorpe of Calthorpe, Norfolk. This Sir Henry and his father are brought to mind in **Sir Harry's Road**, whilst his wife, Frances Carpenter, is remembered in **Carpenter Road**.

Sir Richard Gough had built a new house for himself in Edgbaston and surrounded it with a park. His son and grandson lived there until 1786, when Sir Henry the younger moved to Elvetham Hall. His descendants never returned to live in Birmingham and their old home is now Edgbaston Golf Club. It was Sir Henry's younger son, George the 3rd Baron Calthorpe, who began the development of Edgbaston soon after the Napoleonic Wars. By this time, the 3rd Baron had bought all the land in Edgbaston south of the Hagley Road that had not been part of the purchase by Sir Richard. Amongst the first roads to be cut was **George Road**, aptly named after George Gough-Calthorpe himself. The urbanisation of Edgbaston led one commentator to state:

A few years since the only buildings which Edgbaston contained were the church (St Bartholomew's), the hall, the parsonage and a few farm houses. The present proprietor is Lord Calthorpe who lets out portions of land on long building leases; and the number of its inhabitants is yearly increasing, and the businessman of Birmingham carries with him into his retirement a correct taste not only for the useful, but also for the beautiful and picturesque.

Many other roads in Edgbaston relate to members of the Gough-Calthorpe family. **Duchess Road** and **Beaufort Road** are named after Charlotte Sophia, Duchess of Beaufort and mother-in-law of the 3rd Baron Calthorpe; whilst Frederick, the 4th Baron Calthorpe, is brought to notice in **Frederick Road**, and his wife, Charlotte Somerset, is recalled in **Charlotte Road** and **Somerset Road**. Augustus, the 6th Baron Calthorpe, hence **Augustus Road**, died in 1910. His estates passed to his daughter, Rachel, who was married to Sir Hamilton Anstruther, thus **Anstruther Road** and **Hamilton Avenue**, who took the name Anstruther-Gough-Calthorpe. Their descendants continue to own Edgbaston and belong to one of the wealthiest landowning families in England.

Gowan Road, Alum Rock

Called **Dingley Road** until 1909, it is thought that Gowan Road is called after a landowning family.

Gower Street, Lozells

Another street named after a landowner about whom there is no information.

Graham Road, South Yardley

Lying between Stockfield Road and the Coventry Road, Graham Road refers to George Graham who moved to the Oaklands on Coventry Road in the 1870s and whose family was involved in the Yardley Stud Farm. It was called **Madcap Lane** or **Madcat Lane** until 1927.

Graham Street, Hockley and Lozells

Formerly a country lane called **Harper's Hill**, Graham Street is the extension of Legge Lane and is named after Thomas Graham, Lord Lynedoch, a gallant soldier and hero of the French Wars. Raised in Perthshire, he married Mary, a remarkable beauty, who died of consumption off the coast of France. At Toulouse her coffin was broken open by drunken officials in search of contraband and this disrespectful treatment made Graham a bitter opponent of the French Revolutionary Government. A staunch supporter of the war against France, he joined Lord Hood's fleet as a volunteer and served during the siege of Toulon (1793). On returning to Scotland he raised the Perthshire Volunteers and gained the reputation as Britain's leading trainer of light infantry. Elected an MP in 1794, the military dominated his life and he served with distinction in Italy, in the taking of Menorca and in the siege of Malta.

Admired for his courage and training capabilities, Graham joined Sir John Moore in the Spanish campaign and witnessed Moore's heroic death at Corunna, to which port the leader had retreated with the British forces so that they could be saved by the Royal Navy. Made a major general, Graham returned to Spain and joined the Duke

Graham Street, Lozells in the 1970s. Thanks to Birmingham Evening Mail.

Looking down Legge Lane, across Newhall Hill and Frederick Street into Graham Street, Hockley and down to Newhall Street in the 1950s. This was a time when back-to-back houses still remained locally, as can be seen on the right. Thanks to the Birmingham Evening Mail.

of Wellington's Army in 1811. In ill health and with his eye sight failing, still Graham was a formidable opponent. Highly regarded by his men, he was one of the Duke's most able subordinates. In June 1813 he commanded Wellington's (see Wellington Street) left flank in the victory of Vitoria, hence **Vittoria Street** in the Jewellery Quarter. Wounded soon after at the Battle of Tolosa, Graham went on to lead the capture of San Sebastian. Unwell, he returned to Britain and then took charge of the forces helping the Dutch in their revolt against the French. After Napoleon's first abdication in 1814, Graham was acclaimed and awarded honours by the Spanish, Portuguese and Dutch. A distinguished figure, he resumed his political career and died in 1843.

Grange Road, Erdington

In the Medieval period, a grange was an outlying farm belonging to a monastery. However, in the Victorian period the name grange was given to many grand houses which had no monastic connections. On such house was in Grange Road. Formerly **Pike Hayes Lane** or **Pype Hayes Lane** and before that **Blakehale Way**, this used to lead to the home of the Bagot family at Pype Hayes. It became Grange Road because Grange Farm gave its name to Grange House, the home of Sir Benjamin Stone, photographer and politician. Stone was born on 9 February 1838 at Birmingham, the son of Benjamin Stone, a glass manufacturer, and his wife, Rebecca, the daughter of Richard Matthews of Cookley, Worcestershire. Little is known about his parents, although his father's company was in Aston Manor—a district that did not become part of Birmingham until 1911. After being educated at King Edward's School, New Street, Birmingham, Benjamin Stone moved into his father's business, to which he later succeeded, the firm then being known as Stone, Fawdry, and Stone. He was well respected in his trade and was a juror at a number of important exhibitions in London, Edinburgh, and Paris. On 5 June 1867 he married Jane Parker of Yorkshire. They had four sons and two daughters. Stone was made master of the court of the Glass Sellers' Company in 1882, and he also became a partner in the paper firm of Smith, Stone, and Knight, which had large paper mills in Birmingham.

Stone's success in business ventures at a comparatively early age allowed him to become active in political and municipal affairs and to follow his deep interests in history, literary study, and, particularly, photography. An ardent Conservative at a time when Birmingham was a Liberal stronghold, he was elected to the town council for the working-class ward of Duddeston in 1869. For a time he was one of only two Conservative councillors in Birmingham. An assiduous member of various committees, he left the council in 1878, but returned to public life four years later, when he was elected to the Aston Board of Guardians. He also served on Sutton Coldfield council, and in 1886 he was chosen unanimously as the first mayor of that borough. Stone held this office for five years and was then presented with the freedom of the town. In addition he was a justice of the peace for Sutton Coldfield, Warwickshire, and Birmingham.

For ten years from 1874 Stone was president of the Birmingham Conservative Association, and it was thanks largely to him that the party's local organization was kept up. Indeed, he remodelled it on the lines of the successful Liberal Party organization, with a system of ward committees overseen by a central executive. When Lord Randolph Churchill stood for election in Birmingham in 1884, Stone presided at the Conservative meeting which led to a notorious riot in Aston Park, following clashes between the supporters of rival candidates. Along with Lord Randolph, Sir Drummond Wolff, and Colonel Burnaby, Stone was prominent in founding the Primrose League. He was an active philanthropist in Birmingham and was a member of the Bean Club, reputedly the oldest political society in England.

Following Joseph Chamberlain's acrimonious split with the Liberal Party over Home Rule for Ireland, the Chamberlainites allied themselves with the Conservatives. In Birmingham this alliance came to dominate municipal and parliamentary elections, and in 1895 Stone (who had been knighted in 1892 on the recommendation of the Marquess of Salisbury) was returned unopposed as MP for East Birmingham. He retired on account of ill health in 1910. While in the House of Commons, Sir Benjamin played little part in debate, but he was prominent in the social side of Parliament. His camera came to be an introduction to men of all parties, and it was as a photographer that he was best known to the public. Dubbed the 'Knight of the Camera' by *The Spectator*, he had begun collecting photographs in a systematic way from the late 1860s. In the early 1880s he found he could no longer buy the photographs he wanted, and after making a study of the medium he started to take his own. In an interview he later explained:

> my photographic work has been done with the intention of securing records for my scientific investigation, and not merely for the pleasure of a photograph in itself. I look upon photography as being a most valuable aid to education because pictorial illustration is by far the easiest mode and pleasant manner of obtaining instruction. (*Tit-Bits*, 16 April 1898)

In 1897 Stone's plan for a national photographic record, occasioned by Queen Victoria's jubilee, was taken up, and between then and 1910, 4478 prints were deposited in the British Museum. The founder of the Photographic Record Association, an organization of photographers, Stone was also the first president of the Birmingham Photographic Society. He had a deep concern for British heritage, and among his photographs were recorded many British customs and festivals, Parliament and parliamentarians, Westminster Abbey, and royal palaces. His photographs of the coronations of Edward VII and George V caused him to become known as the royal photographer. Seven years after his death the trustees of his estate presented to Birmingham Reference Library his collection of 22,000 photographs, 600 stereographs, 2500 lantern slides, 17,000 glass negatives, 50 albums of collected prints, and 50 volumes of press cuttings relating to his work. These remain in the care of the city's library and archive departments. This massive collection includes

Great Hampton Street, in 1901. This photo shows premises close to Harford Street. Numbers 19 and 20 are occupied by E. Webb and Sons, advertised in Kelly's Directory in 1901 as pencil case makers. Downstairs at number 20 is Charles Taverner's Dairy, and number 21 is a saddlery business. Above the entry is a sign for a die sinker, obviously working in 'shopping' – the name given to small workshops that might be found above a brewhouse or elsewhere in the yard behind.

Great Russell Street on the corner of Brearley Street, 1960.

topographical and other photographs relating to Europe, North and South America, India, and Australasia.

Stone was widely travelled; a fellow of both the Royal Geographical Society and the Royal Historical Society and a member of the Geological Society, the Linnean Society, and the Society of Arts, he was never without his camera and notebook on his journeys. His notes led him to write a number of books, such as *A Summer Holiday in Spain* (1873) and *Children in Norway* (1882). Among other works were a description of his tour of Japan, a fairy tale for children, and a history of Lichfield Cathedral. In 1890 he went as photographer with the Royal Astronomical Society to Brazil; while on this trip he persuaded rebels to postpone their shelling of government positions so that he could photograph them. Sir Benjamin also visited the West Indies, South Africa, Syria, Egypt, and Palestine. He died at his home, The Grange, in Erdington, Birmingham, on 2 July 1914. His wife was seriously ill and did not know of his death; she died four days later and was buried with him in Sutton Coldfield graveyard on 7 July 1914.

Grange Road, Kings Heath relates to the Grange Estate developed by the Birmingham Freehold Land Society in the late nineteenth century. The estate had been owned by Isaac Bates, who also kept the 'Cross Guns' pub on the High Street, and it took its name from his house – The Grange. Built in the mid-nineteenth century, it had grounds of about 55 acres. Bates died in 1895 and the land society paid £40,000 for his estate, upon which it laid out seven roads.

Gravelly Hill, Erdington

First mentioned by this name in 1817, this was the old road to Lichfield and takes its name from the fact that it is literally a gravelly hill. According to the assiduous researcher John Morris Jones it used to be called **Gully Lane** because the way was worn hollow into a gully. (See also Holloway Head).

Great Barr Street, Deritend/Bordesley

The extension of Heath Mill Lane, this street is named after the area of Great Barr.

Great Hampton Row, Hockley

The 1553 Survey of Birmingham is a fascinating document, bringing to life long-forgotten names of Birmingham families and places. One such is **Heybarnes**, pastureland which Joseph Bickley thought became **Heybarnes Lane**, then **Hangman's Lane** and finally Great Hampton Row. Nearby were the **Great Rosells** and **Little Rosells**, hence **Great Russell Street**, Hockley, and perhaps named after a family called Russell. Abstract of titles for Great Hampton Street indicate building activity between 1713 and 1823. In 1825 it was described it as a 'wide, untidy-looking, irregular range of middling houses'. Nearby Hampton Street was once known as **Little Hampton Street**.

The Green at Kings Norton in the late 1890s, with the old Bull's Head.

Great Stone Road, Northfield

A glacial boulder from the Ice Age, the great stone lay on the narrow pavement outside the 'Great Stone' inn. Because it was dangererous through its blocking of the footpath, after the Second World War the stone was lifted and moved to the ancient pound of Northfield. It was always believed that the stone was massive and that much of it lay beneath the earth. However, when it was lifted it was found to lie only eight inches into the ground. Close to the pub, the pound was the place where stray animals were kept. It is the only surviving manorial pound in Birmingham. Because of the pound and the stone, the motto of the 'Great Stone' inn was that customers could buy beer 'By the Stone and By the Pound'.

The Green, Kings Norton

In the Middle Ages, many villages had a green in a central position, which was used for recreation and rough grazing. Kings Norton was one of them. At the heart of Kings Norton and in the shadow of the historic church of Saint Nicolas, The Green is a prime example of an English village green now in the midst of a major city. When John Leland came to Birmingham in 1538, he approached the place by way of Kings Norton, which he described as 'a pretty uplandish town in Worcestershire' that contained some good houses belonging to woolstaplers and a fine church with a good stone spire over the bell frame. It is likely that one of those houses included the 'Saracen's Head', one of the key historical buildings on The Green.

For generations on the first Monday in October, The Green was the site of a statute fair, known as a statty or a mop. Domestic servants and agricultural labourers were hired at this fair, which also included festivities and ox roasting. Today The Green itself is part of a conservation area that also encompasses the church, the Saracen's Head and the Old Grammar School – the latter two of which featured in the BBC One 'Restoration' programme in 2004. It is approached from the back by the aptly-named **Back Lane** that leads into the Pershore Road.

Green Lane, Small Heath

Green Lane was a popular name for an unmetalled country track. Such lanes were often used for moving livestock. Heading out from the Coventry Road and running in to Yardley Green Road at Blake Lane and Hobmoor Lane, Green Lane, Small Heath once was a country lane of 'charming sylvan scenery', overhung with the branches of elm, oak and chestnut. Its name reflects its former green outlook, as does **Green Road, Hall Green** and **Moseley**. **Green Lane, Quinton** is named not after the landscape but after the Green family. In 1522 the Abbott of Hales Owen leased land for 60 years to 'William Grene and Jane his wife of Ruggacre'. The Greens remained prominent locally until the late nineteenth century.

Greenbank Avenue, Hall Green

My great-uncle Wal Chinn, was born in 1897 and I interviewed him about his life when he was in his eighties. He told me that when they were young, my Granddad and his middle brother, Bill, used to go to Greet Mill Hill on Sundays. Here the horse brakes that took out the well off for a drive out towards Henley had to slow down, and Granddad and Uncle Bill joined other poor kids in doing cartwheels and gambols to try and get the rich to throw them some coppers. This Greet Mill Hill puzzled me and not till years later did I learn that it was the slope that rises from the River Cole and goes up the Stratford Road, past the 'College Arm's to Hall Green Parade.

Greet Mill itself was on the Rover Cole close to the modern bridge below the 'College Arms'. It was mentioned in 1275 and was the manorial mill for Greet, then a bigger area than it is now. In 1775 it was advertised as a 'complete new erected water corn mill', although later it became a blade mill. Its last use seems to have been as a needle mill, for it was mentioned as such in 1873. It had disappeared by the end of the 1880s. Its name lived on in Greet Mill Hill, although this also died out and the slope became known as Green Bank. Of course, bank or bonk was used widely in the West Midlands as a term for a slope.

Greenhill Road, Moseley

Coming off the Wake Green Road, Greenhill Road is named after the Greenhill Estate.

Greenwood Road, Acocks Green

This road commemorates Arthur Greenwood, a leading Labour politician who was Minister of Health in the Labour Government of 1929-31. As such he introduced a Housing Act in 1930 that was far-reaching and momentous, laying down as it did the foundations of modern 'slum' clearance schemes. For the first time a government subsidy was provided for getting rid of bad housing, and this was related to the numbers of people displaced and rehoused. This was intended to prevent clearance without rehousing, which had been so common before 1914 and which had been so obvious in the Corporation Street Improvement Scheme of 1875 (see Corporation Street).

Crucially, the Act brought in a subsidy on people rather than houses and it made it easier for councils to rehouse large and poor families, because the amount of the subsidy increased with the size of the family concerned. Local authorities also had to make a contribution to any scheme under Greenwood's Act, and they were allowed discretion at the setting of rental levels. This enabled rent rebates and differential renting schemes, provided that the rents were at a figure that tenants could be reasonably expected to pay. The new law also ensured that local authorities had to submit 'slum-clearance' plans with the aim of solving the problem within five years if it were possible.

Bill James pushing his pram along Green Lane, Small Heath in 1975, with Eversley Street on his left. Thanks to the Birmingham Evening Mail.

Green Lane, now Green Road, Hall Green, in the late nineteenth century. The house on the left is still there, although the road now bends to the right just below the tree on the right and heads down to the ford.

Birmingham's Conservative led Council adopted enthusiastically this important piece of social legislation and planned to build 7,000 homes as part of a 'slum-clearance' programme. The Ashcroft Estate was the first to be built in the city that was related to the scheme. One hundred and seventy, two-storey maisonettes were built in Great Brook Street, Ashted on the site of an old cavalry barracks. Each had a large living room, scullery, bathroom and two or three bedrooms. A second estate was developed on a five acre site in Highgate, bounded by Angelina, Dymoke, Leopold and Vaughton Streets and through which ran Emily Street. The buildings here were an experimental block of concrete flats, 276 in total. Finally, 98 maisonettes were built on cleared land in Kingston Road, Bordesley. These schemes, though important, did not provide the 7,000 homes anticipated. Keen as it was, the Council was unable to build more homes because of the financial crisis that followed the Wall Street Crash of 1931 and the ensuing Depression.

Greethurst Drive, Moseley

Meaning the gravelly (greet) wooded slope or hill (hurst), Greethurst was a severalty, an individual farm, in Yardley, and was associated with a family that took the name of their property. The Greethursts disappeared in the fourteenth century and by the early fifteenth century their land was owned by the Holts (see Holte Road), a family first mentioned in Yardley in 1361 when they bought two fields called Malte Feldes from Joan, daughter of Henry of the Heth. Greethurst boasted its own mill and in 1437 Aymer Holt granted it to the Mountfort family. Called Holt Mill or Greethurst Mill, this came into the possession of the Greswolds in 1519. It may be that this mill was the same as the Coldbath Mill, which stood below the Yardley Wood Road close to Coldbath Road. It was pulled down in the late 1830s. The manor of Greethurst was later disputed between the Holts and the Greswolds (see Greswolde Road). Greethurst Drive off Hayfield Road, is near to the old Greethurst which occupied the area to the east of Billesley Lane and where Moseley Golf Club now is.

Grevis Close Moseley

The Grevis family, also known as Greves, rose from humble origins to become the lords of Yardley and the wealthiest landowners in Moseley – and fell back again. Living at a large, half-timbered farmhouse close to the modern Chantry Road and Salisbury Road, they appear prominently from the fifteenth century. In 1468, a Thomas Grevis joined the Guild of Saint Anne at Knowle and in 1520 another Thomas was elected as Master of that body. Three years later, the family obtained a grant of arms and by the time Richard Grevis made his will in 1600 he was able to describe himself as a gentleman.

His social status had been assured by his wealth, made plain by his bequests for he left to his son, Richard, 'my beste nest of goblets duble gylte with the cover, and my best Salte double gylt, with the cover thereof, and my three cruses, with the footes, stopper and cover thereof of double guilte, and my twelve spoones of the Apostles and one little white sylver cope'. Eight pounds was left to each of his two daughters, £100 to his son Thomas, 40 shillings to his servant John Howles, and six shillings and eight pence to each of his other servants. Thirty shillings was left to the poor of Kings Norton and one shilling to each poor household in Moseley. There must have been some family disputes, because Richard gave his Berkswell property to his son Thomas 'without interference from Anne his wife', and she was made a residuary legatee and executrix only if she left Thomas in peace.

Richard Grevis the younger seems to have gained the favour of royalty, for in his will of 1632 it is mentioned that he had free warranty of Yardley and Solihull 'lately graunted to me and my heires by the King's Majesty'. A man of consequence, Richard also owned land in Bickenhill, Lyndon, Castle Bromwich, Little Bromwich, Bordesley, Sutton Coldfield and Sheldon. Knighted in 1604, he became Deputy Lieutenant to the King in Wales, and High Sheriff of Worcestershire in 1616. Sir Richard died in 1632 and was buried in the church of Saint Nicolas, Kings Norton. His tomb has an effigy of him in armour beside his wife, Ann. The vicar of Saint Nicolas was Thomas Hall, a

The monument to Sir Richard Grevis in Kings Norton Parish Church.

noted puritan, who like others who shared his beliefs, was persecuted under Charles I. Hall stated that Sir Richard was a 'valiant and religious knight' who 'by his wisdom and courage' sheltered non-conformist ministers.

Sir Richard was succeeded by his oldest son, Thomas. His younger son, another Richard, fought in the English Civil War on both sides. A growing market town and manufacturing centre, Birmingham's citizens were keen supporters of the Parliamentarian cause. After King Charles I had stayed at Aston Hall in October 1642 (see Kingstanding Road), he then passed through Birmingham. The next day the people seized his carriages with royal plate and other valuables and sent them to Warwick Castle. In the ensuing months, the townsfolk attacked small parties of Royalists and took their prisoners to Coventry, hence the term sending someone to Coventry. Additionally, Birmingham manufacturers supplied the Parliamentarians with large numbers of swords. After Charles II was restored to the throne, this staunch devotion to Parliament ensured the hatred of Royalist writers like Clarendon who declared that Bromwicham was 'a town so generally wicked', whilst the poet Dryden called the devil the Brummagem uniter of mankind. I believe that the anti-Birmingham bias so obvious amongst the establishment in London dates to this period.

In the spring of 1643, Prince Rupert was ordered to take a Royalist force to Lichfield, which meant that he had to march through Birmingham a town 'of great fame for hearty, willful, affected disloyalty to the king as any place in England', as Clarendon thundered. Supported by a force of Parliamentarian troops, the people of Birmingham put up barriers and refused entry to Prince Rupert and his men. Attacked by the Royalists, the Brummies fought bravely, but outnumbered they were overwhelmed. Captain Grevis, or Greaves as he spelled his name, was commanding a troop of horse at the northern end of the town that was put to flight by Royalists led by the Earl of Denbigh. Chased into Bearwood, 'Captaine Greaves observing his time, betwixt two woods, faced about and charged the pursuers most valiantly … and drove them backe againe; in which charge Denby was slaine immediately, and the rest fled, and so we escaped safely; onely Captaine Greaves received one shot in the face, and a cut in the arme, but not mortal'.

After the defeat of Charles I and his capture, Colonel Grevis, as he then was, guarded the king. It seems that he then shifted sides and went to The Netherlands where he joined Charles II. Returning to England with the monarch, Grevis fought at the Battle of Worcester in 1652 where the Royalists were soundly beaten and he was captured. He was released on condition that he lived within five miles of his mother's home in Worcestershire. His son, yet another Richard, inherited the Grevis lands from his uncle, Thomas, and passed them on to his brother, Benjamin. It would appear that financial problems were having an adverse effect on the family, for Richard's will required the selling of land and timber to pay his debts. Benjamin himself married twice and strained relations with his second wife, Elizabeth, are apparent in his will. Although calling her his dear and loving wife, he left her only the furniture that was in the nursery of Moseley Hall, which 'was hers before her inter-marriage with me' and £20. As for Benjamin's son, Richard, by his first wife, he was left just one shilling.

After Benjamin's death, his daughter Jane was sole executrix and she renounced this obligation to her brother. Four years later, his money worries led Richard to mortgage land and then in the 1750s to sell property. Praised as 'a gentleman of polite understanding, humane and courteous deportment', he was unwise with finances. His will directed that his wife, Ann, and friends should be trustees and sell or mortgage the manor of Yardley and estates in Yardley, Kings Norton and Harborne 'to raise sufficient money to pay his debts'; and for the sum of £2,000 to be left to Ann and £1,500 each to their second son, Charles, and their daughter, Eleanor. The oldest son, Henshaw, was given a poisoned chalice. He was to have what was left over.

Bedevilled by disputes with his mother over the terms of the will, Henshaw had to sell his Moseley estates in 1767 just to clear the debts and raise the funds for the bequests to his brother and sister. The sale was carried out by two trustees, Thomas Russell and John Healey. When they had completed their task, the sum of £195 11s 3d was due to Russell. Unable to pay, the unfortunate Henshaw remortgaged his last piece of land and then sold it. Almost penniless, by 1782 he and his family were living in a back house in Edgbaston Street. Four years later he appeared before William Hutton as a defendant at the Birmingham Court of Requests. Almost 60 years old, Henshaw was wearing clothes not worth 'eighteenpence'. Hutton wrote:

> I well remember to have seen him thirty years before, completely mounted, and dressed in green velvet, with a hunter's cap and girdle, at the head of his pack … At other times the arms he carried were a gun and ornamented pouch, his companions were his dogs, and the regions he commanded, the earth and the air. But now his gun was metamorphosed into a spade, his companions were labourers upon the turnpike road, and the principal scene of action was the gravel pit. I could not forebear drawing a slight comparison between the devoted outcast of fortune and myself; he could prove a long line of wealthy and honourable ancestors, but mine had never been off the dunghill for two hundred years; his had been fixed upon one rich domain for many centuries, mine had been desolate wanderers, and had tried many parts of the kingdom, but found every spot barren. He, in the morning of his days, decorated as above, with the trappings of affluence; I, in humble poverty and dirty apron should have been disdained even a look.

The sorry Henshaw Grevis died in 1788 and was buried a pauper. His death was announced in *Aris's Birmingham Gazette*: 'though he was heir to one of the oldest and most opulent families in this neighbourhood, (through the dissipation and extravagance of his parents) died in the humble capacity of distributor of this paper to and in Leicestershire'. His fortunate brother, Charles, forged a successful military career and married an heiress. The names of Grevis Close off Trafalgar Road and **Grevis Road, Yardley** could never convey the anguish of the fallen Henshaw Grevis.

Greswolde Road, Springfield

The Greswolds were a family of some note in the Arden district of north Warwickshire. Based in Kenilworth and Solihull, where they are brought to mind by the 'Greswolde Arms' in Knowle, they moved into Yardley in the early fifteenth century, buying a farm of 38 acres in 1420/1. Then in 1447/8 a deed of release of the manor of Gretehurst in Yardley and land and tenements in Lichfield was entered into between Aymer Holt, esquire, and Thomas Greswold. However, the ownership of Greethurst was later disputed by the Holts and was regained by them in the early sixteenth century. By now the Greswolds owned at least four other properties in Yardley. Their holdings grew in the following years.

When Henry VIII dissolved the monasteries and other religious bodies, he took over their land and then sold it. The Greswolds profited from this process by purchasing Grove Farm, which had been owned by Maxstoke Priory and which is now remembered in **Grove Road**, **Springfield**. The farmhouse stood close to the Stratford Road, between Grove Road and Greswolde Road. Lords of Greet Manor, the Greswoldes were also lay rectors of Yardley, hence **Greswolde Road**, Yardley, off Station Road and almost opposite Vicarage Road; and also **Greswolde Park Road,** Acocks Green, off the Warwick Road. The Greswolds owned Grove Farm until it was sold for building in 1896 by an heir who added an 'e' to the end of his name.

Griffins Brook Lane, Northfield

Close to Northfield Village, this lane is called after the brook which probably takes its name from a local family called Griffin.

The old Griffin Hill, Northfield.

H

Haden Street, Balsall Heath

In 1791, Thomas Haden, a Birmingham button maker, bought from Elizabeth Townsend, a spinster of Sutton Coldfield property on the borders of Balsall Heath and Highgate. He died soon after and because he was unmarried his property went to his brother, Henry, who lived in a 'beautifully situated' house on Highgate Hill. Substantially built, it had a staircase of stone and a flagged entrance hall, 'beneath which were excellent cellars', and it boasted a water closet – rare in those days – and eight lodging rooms. The gardens were 'productive', and there were also plantations, a lawn, and several pieces of old pasture ground. Henry died in 1837 and by his will, his estates were to be sold, and within a year, **Belgrave Street**, later **Belgrave Road**, had been cut out. Both Haden Street and the newer **Haden Way** recall the Haden brothers.

Hagley Road, Edgbaston

On Sparry's Map of 1718 this was shown as **Grindle's Stone Lane**. The route to Halesowen and thence Kidderminster, it was turnpiked in 1753. Just eighteen years later, its condition was described by Hutton as 'chequered with good and evil, chiefly

The Hagley Road in the early 1900s. Albert Newton's shop on the right was a draper who had three premises locally at numbers 169, 175 and 189. The shop in view is 189. Going along are Owen's bakery, the West End Library, and Hadley's house decorator's. The church in the background is the Baptist Chapel.

in the latter'. Mentioned as **Hagley Row** in an advertisement from 1787, by 1840 the road was reported as not in very good repair. Little changed in its condition until after 1877 when the turnpike, the Birmingham and Blakedownpool Trust, expired. The section of Hagley Road between what is now Balden Road and Lordswood Road. was called **Beech Lanes** (see Beech Lanes).

Hallam Street, Balsall Heath

Known as **Heath Street** until 1897 and coming off Edward Road, this was named after Alderman Hallam, who was president of the Balsall Heath Ward Conservative Association. A prominent freemason in the Masefield Lodge that met at the Moseley and Balsall Heath Institute, he was also an overseer of the poor for Balsall Heath on the Kings Norton Union and had been a leading member of the Balsall Heath Local Board of Health. This was a separate local authority until 1891 when Balsall Heath became part of Birmingham. Hallam was first elected to the Board as a Conservative in February 1886 and the next April gained the largest number of votes in an election in the Board's history. Chairman of the authority's Fire Brigade, Public Lighting and General Purposes committees, Hallam opposed the annexation of Balsall Heath to Birmingham, but after it happened he entered public life in the enlarged city of Birmingham.

Hallewell Road, Rotton Park

Hallewell Rogers was Lord Mayor of Birmingham in 1902, and again in 1903 as Sir Hallewell Rogers. The road named after him emerged in 1907 and comes off Rotton Park Road.

Hamstead Road, Handsworth

A main road leading from Handsworth Wood Road to Hamstead Hill, Hamstead Road keeps alive an estate called Hamstead that lay just south of the River Tame in the manor of Handsworth. This was focused on Hamstead Hall, hence **Hamstead Hall Road**, and by the Tudor period it was owned by the Wyrley family – members of which had been landowners in Handsworth and Perry since at least the thirteenth century. From 1546 the Wyrleys owned half of the manor of Perry, and from 1679 they were the lords of the manor of Handsworth. In the later eighteenth century the Wyrley Birch family, as it had become, also bought the manor of Witton (see Wyrley Road).

Hampson Grove, Sparkbrook

Nick Deeley informs me that Hampson Grove, off Grantham Road, was named after a friend who was a Financial Advisor with the Birmingham Friendship Housing Association that built the Grove.

Hanley Street, Summer Lane

Emma Bygrave, nee Hanley, tells me that 'when I was a child my father used to say that Hanley St and Cecil St belonged to a relative of his (an uncle I think), also a pub in that area. This relative cleared off to America and as there were 12 in my father's family what little they would have shared was not worth fighting over so these two streets became unadopted'. Emma wondered if this story was true or if her Dad was romanticising. I firmly believe that family stories have a kernel of truth, greater or smaller depending on the case, and I would not dismiss the explanation of Emma's father.

Hanley Street, showing a fancy draper's shop at number 21 in the 1930s.

The magnificent 'Marquis of Lorne' pub in Cecil Street and on the corner of Newtown Row (with the bus stop) in 1961.

Hannon Road, Kings Heath

Coming off Brandwood Road, Hannon Road highlights the significance of Sir Patrick Hannon, who represented Moseley as MP between 1921-45. Born in 1874 at Taverane, Cloonloo, County Sligo, Patrick Hannon was educated at university in Ireland. Deeply concerned about improving conditions for Irish workers, he became involved in schemes for the agricultural and economic regeneration of Ireland. After a time in South Africa, he came to England in 1910 where he gained influence in the British Commonwealth Union and the Comrades of the Great War. In 1921 he became the Unionist member of Parliament for Moseley. He held his seat until he retired in 1950, even doing so in 1945 when Labour swept the board in Birmingham bar for Moseley. A deputy chairman of the BSA, Sir Patrick Hannon was involved in a wide-range of business and social activities in Birmingham. A devout Catholic, he was president of Aston Villa and was knighted in 1936.

Harborne Lane, Selly Oak

Harborne Lane goes from Selly Oak into Harborne Park Road and thence Harborne; whilst **Harborne Road, Edgbaston** heads into High Street, Harborne. Joe McKenna believes that Harborne is made up of the Old English words 'har' or 'hor' meaning boundary, and 'borne' signifying brook. The stream in question is the Bourn Brook – after which the district of Bournbrook is named – and which formed part of the old dividing line between Harborne, Staffordshire and Weoley, Worcestershire. By contrast A. D. Mills feels that the name is derived from the word 'horu' meaning dirty; an interpretation favoured also by leading place-name expert Margaret Gelling. The Bourn Brook does cut Harborne off along its whole southern length, whilst the Chad Brook provides the dividing line with Edgbaston in the north east; however, it would seem that it does not mean boundary brook but dirty brook.

Harding Street, Winson Green

Cut out in 1883, again this is a street named after an owner of land.

Hart Road, Erdington

The Harts was a prominent family in Erdington, represented on Erdington Urban District Council. In 1866 Alderman W. H. Hart gave land on Gravelly Hill for a Methodist Chapel. It opened in 1890 and became abandoned in the twentieth century.

Hart Street, Winson Green

Shown on the Ordnance Survey Map of 1857, this was absorbed into the Black Patch Park. For many years this was an inhospitable and desolate spot on the borders of Birmingham, Handsworth and Smethwick – and upon which the waste from nearby furnaces was dumped. For many years the locality was the chosen winter encampment of Romanies, and from at least the 1870s they fastened upon the Black Patch itself as their own. The main families were the Smiths, Badgers, Davises,

A Romany encampment in Bullock Street, Duddeston in about 1908. Thanks to Birmingham Library Services.

Claytons and Loveridges. Getting by through horse-trading, labouring, the hawking of pegs and durkerin, fortune telling, the Romanies had their own king, Esau Smith. He died aged 92 in 1901 and a great crowd gathered to pay their respects when he was laid to rest at Handsworth Old Church.

With his passing, so came trials and tribulations for his people. The owners of the Black Patch wanted to build upon it and tried to push out the Romanies. At first they failed, but then on 27 July 1905 the Romanies were evicted by a large force of sheriff's officers and policemen. Esau's wife, Queen Henty, was allowed to stay with a few of the Smiths. They themselves were forced out when Henty died on 7 January 1907. A week later a funeral pyre was made of her vardo, caravan, and possessions, and soon after what was left of the Black Patch was laid out as a park. The evicted Romanies tended to move into Winson Green Road and many of their descendants remain in Birmingham. The origin of **Gypsy Lane**, Witton is not known, although it is an ancient way and was called **Witton Slade Road.**.

Harts Green Road, Harborne

In 1733, a green spot of Harborne – much of which was heathland – was in the possession of John Hart; and supposedly the last nightingale heard in Harborne sang in Harts Green in 1872. Another family called Hart also made their mark upon Harborne. Charles Hart had an ecclesiastical metal work business that he transferred from London to Birmingham. The gates, brasses and railings of Saint Martin's Church were made by his company, as was other brass work in civic and public buildings such as the Council House and Victoria Law Courts. In 1868 Hart took over Harborne Hall. This had been built for Thomas Green, who made a fortune from the iron trade and bought the manor of Harborne from George Birch in the late eighteenth century. Hart was a benefactor to Saint Peter's Church, the parish church of Harborne. Its brass eagle lectern was given in memory of his son, Frank, and he also donated the lych gate nearest to the hall. Charles engaged John Henry Chamberlain, the architect of many splendid buildings in Birmingham, to add Gothic extensions to Harborne Hall. It later became a school and then a convent.

Charles Hart died in 1880. His son, Captain Charles Joseph Hart, took over the business, founded the Harborne Voluntary Fire Brigade in 1879, and was active as an office in the First Volunteer Battalion of the Royal Warwickshire Regiment. He was prominent in the recruitment campaign for volunteers for the Army in the First World War, a great supporter of the Birmingham School of Art, and his firm made the column for the Chamberlain Clock in the Jewellery Quarter in 1903

Harrison Road, Erdington

Coming off High Street, Erdington, Harrison Road is named after Reverend J.H. Harrison, who was one of the chief landowners in the district in the early nineteenth century.

Hatchett Street, Summer Lane

Leading from Summer Lane to Pritchett Street, Hatchett Street emerged before 1851 and recalls a landowner.

Harvey Road, Yardley

Running between Church Road and Moat Lane, until 1906 this was called the more expressive **Donkey Lane**.

Haunch Lane

In 1495, 'the true boundes of the parish' were viewed by 'the xii men of Yardley'. After coming up the Spark Brook from what is now Walford Road to Highgate Road, they came to Sparke Green, the area probably around Alfred Road, Sparkhill, and went along Low Lane, now the Stoney lane and part of Yardley Wood Road. At **Gylden Corner**, by the junction of the modern Belle Walk and the Yardley Wood Road the route headed up Bulley Lane, today's Belle Walk and Billesley Lane. From there, they went over the heath that gave its name to Kings Heath 'to the corner of the ground of Thomas Byssell called the Haunche … and soe downe the Haunche ditch after the Launde to the Water of Chynne' (Chinn Brook). The Haunch Ditch ran alongside the western edge of Billesley Common, probably parallel with Hollybank Road, across the bottom of which runs Haunch Lane. This haunch of land also gave its name to a farm.

Havelock Road, Saltley

As with **Havelock Road** in **Greet** and **Havelock Road** in **Handsworth**, this Saltley Road commemorates Sir Henry Marshman Havelock Allan an army officer and politician. Born in India, he joined the Army in 1846 and nine years later he served in the Anglo-Persian War under his father, a major-general. Havelock was mentioned in dispatches and from Persia, he went with his father to Calcutta, arriving after the outbreak of the Indian Mutiny. The older Havelock was commanded to relieve Cawnpore and Lucknow, which were besieged by the mutineers. At Cawnpore, the younger Havelock bravely rode in front of the infantry towards a 24-pounder gun, which was firing first roundshot and then grapeshot. The gun was captured by a gallant charge. For his courage Havelock received the Victoria Cross.

In succeeding battles, Havelock again showed his gallantry, especially at the attack on the Charbagh Bridge of Lucknow, during which he was badly wounded. Managing to enter the town, the British relief troops also found themselves besieged and as soon as he recovered from his wounds, Havelock took part in the defence until the siege was raised by Sir Colin Campbell. Wounded again in a later battle, Havelock continued to mark himself out for his bravery. Later involved in campaigns against the Maoris in New Zealand and serving in Canada and Ireland, Havelock moved into politics and became MP for the south-east division of Durham County. He died 1897 when he visited the Afghan border and was shot by Pashtun tribesmen on the North West Frontier. It is ironic, that today there is a large population of Pashtuns in Saltley and Alum Rock.

Hawthorn Road, Kingstanding

Going down hill from the Kingstanding Road to Perry Common Road, Hawthorn Road was called **Short Heath Road** until the area was developed as a council estate in the 1930s. It takes its name from the Hawthorn Brook that used to provide the boundary between Perry Barr and Witton. In 1317 a mill was mentioned in Witton and Erdington, and it is likely that this was on the Hawthorn Brook. Then in 1338/9 Giles de Erdington granted to Sir Roger Hillary a piece of waste called Colldfeld (Sutton Coldfield) and the rights to the water of the Hawthorn Brook to build a mill. By the early sixteenth century, it seems that there were two mills on the brook, Over Mill and Nether Mill. A third mill emerged in the early 1700s. Like the other two, it became a blade mill. All three mills had gone by the late 1880s.

Hawkesley Road, Turves Green

Close to the modern Culmington Road stood the moated house of Hawkesley Farm. It lay in that part of Northfield which is now on the borders of Longbridge and Turves Green.

Hawkesley Square, Hawkesley.

First mentioned in the Subsidy Rolls of 1275 as Hauckslowe, this estate in King's Norton had become Hawkslow in 1565 when a bond was recorded between John Myddlemore of Hawkeslow, gentleman, in favour of Richard Hawkes. The name itself may signify it was the hill belonging to a family called Hawkes or that it was a place where hawks gathered. For the Middlemores see Middlemore Road.

Hazelwell Street, Stirchley

Like the nearby **Hazelwell Road** this street comes off the Pershore Road and suggests that once there was a hazel well or spring nearby. The name is an old one for Haselwell was mentioned in the Patent Rolls in 1325.

Hawkes Street, Small Heath

A short street off Grange Road, Hawkes Street calls out to us of one of the leading Radicals and public figures in nineteenth-century Birmingham, Henry Hawkes. Born in 1815, in Easy Row, he was the son of William Hawkes, a gun maker, and in 1840 married Emily, daughter of Mr. Joseph Griffin, a limestone merchant of Walsall. After an education at King Edward's School and a private boarding school, Hawkes entered the office of Mr. Joseph Parkes, an prominent attorney. In the agitation that forced through the Great Reform Act of 1832, Parkes was a confidential adviser to the Government. Hawkes was drawn in to the political atmosphere of the office and was instrumental in forming a debating society. In 1833, Parkes left Birmingham and Hawkes became a pupil of an uncle, Mr. Richard Painter, who was a respected surgeon in London. Soon after, he came back to Birmingham to work as managing clerk for William Sextus Harding. Hawkes now became involved in politics, campaigning for the abolition of the Church rates. In 1835 he began to write for the *Birmingham Journal,* and after that for the *Pilot*, which was started by Joseph Sturge as a weekly newspaper (for Sturge see Saint John's Road). In a series of leading articles, Hawkes criticised the actions of the Whigs on the Town Council. Living in Vauxhall Grove, he became the organiser of the Radical party in Duddeston Ward, and through his energy secured an unbroken succession of victories.

Always seeking ways to improve the conditions of working-class folk, Hawkes formed a Working Man's Society to build a 'People's' Hall' on the corner of Loveday Street. It later became a factory. After eleven years, Hawkes left Harding's practice and was admitted as an attorney. That year, 1846, according to *Birmingham Faces and Places*, 'he commenced his remarkable municipal career in the Town Council. In those days he was no doubt the ablest member of that body; for he possessed the exact qualifications which make a typical and valuable Town Councillor. A clear and incisive speaker, a close reasoner, a ready and finished debater, – a marvellously precise, orderly and accurate marshaller of intricate details, requiring infinite care and patience in their arrangement before embodied in speech.'

Made an Alderman after four years, in 1852 Hawkes was unanimously elected Mayor. He abolished the Mayor's Court of Record, 'a costly and dilatory tribunal' and also the 'obnoxious system' of paying the magistrates' clerks by fees. By now the Radicals and Whigs had come together in the Liberal Party, and the Birmingham Liberals elected Hawkes as president of their association in 1867. Eight years later he resigned as Alderman and by forty votes to one was elected Coroner. The Council passed a glowing resolution of his services and placed his portrait in the Corporation Gallery.

As Coroner, Hawkes reduced the number of inquests by twenty per cent, encouraged the Council to erect mortuaries in various parts of the town, and established a central coroner's court. These measures meant that he reduced his income because he was paid by fee. From the late 1870s, Hawkes became a vehement opponent to the way the Liberal Party ran Birmingham through its own select band of politicians and officials. This led him to split with the party in 1881 and join the Conservatives. A strong Churchman and ardent enthusiast for Women's Suffrage, Hawkes was also keen on the theatre. Hawkes Street was cut out of the Small Heath Estate belonging to the Birmingham Freehold Land Society (see Franchise Street). The adjoining streets were named after George Dawson (see Dawson Road) and John Skirrow Wright (see Wright Street).

Hay Road, Hay Mills

Just a short street off George Road, Hay Road calls out the rural origins of Hay Mills. In Anglo Saxon, a 'gehaeg' meant an enclosure. Over time, the 'ge' part of the word was dropped and haeg developed into hay or hey. The name is a prominent one locally. Before 1327, a Robert de le Hay was living on the site which would become Hay Hall, Tyseley – hence **Hay Hall Road**; whilst across the River Cole in Bordesley, between 1367-70 there was mention of Haybarns, meaning the enclosure with barns – and thus leading to **Heybarnes Road**, going from the Coventry Road to Newbridge Road, Small Heath. Victor Skipp suggests that the farm of the Hays emerged with others in Yardley during the twelfth or early thirteenth centuries when agricultural land was expanded in the parish.

Looking up the Coventry Road, Hay Mills from the bridge over the River Cole.

Headley Croft, West Heath

A small road off Grange Farm Drive, Headley Croft recalls the Headley Yield (district) of Kings Norton. It was mentioned first in 849 as 'Headlage'.

Heath Street, Winson Green

Both Heath Street and the shorter **Heath Street South** come off the Dudley Road and emphasise that once much of Birmingham was heathland. This wasteland covered a large area. It stretched from what became the Dudley Road in the west to the Hockley Brook in the east – across which lay Handsworth Heath. Its northern limit was about where Winson Green Road, Lodge Road and Bacchus Road would run, whilst to the south its border approximately followed the line of the modern Clissold Street and All Saint's Street.

High Street, Harborne, formerly Heath Street, in the 1930s. The Mason's grocery is at number 169, with a van outside being filled up with deliveries.

In 1529, the king's supervisor John Daunse carried out a survey 'of the Lordship or Manor of Byrmyngehame, of the Lord of Byrmynghame, Esquire, now in the King's hands'. This examined those lands still held by the lord in the foreign. This was that part of the manor that was not part of the borough, the built-up area that could be classed as the town of Birmingham. Focused upon the Bull Ring locality, Edgbaston Street, Park Street, Moor Street and Deritend, the borough was smaller but more populated; whilst the foreign covered the greater part of the manor. Part of this foreign was cultivated, but much of it was not. The wasteland of Birmingham Heath was mentioned in a memorandum to the Survey: 'It'm ther ys Comon belonging to the same Manor callyd Byrmygehame heth. whych ys nere aboute a myle in circuyte & the Free Tenants & Gens's of the Borough, done comon there alman'r of beste at all tymes, when they wyll. w'tout any thyng payeinge therefore.' As this indicates, animals were grazed on the common by free tenants. These were burgesses, people who had plots of land in the Borough and thus had certain privileges.

Interestingly, the Survey of 1553 mentions that a William Symonds held by indenture 'a rabbit warren lying upon the "Hethe" of Birmyngham aforesaid, with its appurtenances . . .' By the end of that century, the northern section of Birmingham Heath had become known as Gib Heath, whilst part of its southern reaches around the forthcoming Crabtree Road were drawn into Brookfields. The rest of the heathland was pulled into Winson Green. Originally this was that area which bordered

Smethwick and through which the **Winson Green Road** would be cut. This district is noted first 1327 when a William de Wynesdon was taxed. In the Warwickshire volume of the English Place Name Society it is suggested that this indicated the hill, 'don', of a man called Wine. Joe McKenna feels that a better explanation is that it derives from the Old English word 'winn' meaning a meadow. Thus Winson Green would be meadow hill green. Certainly, the land drops quite sharply to the north of Winson Green Road and as the **Handsworth New Road** it runs down towards the valley of the Hockley Brook. This topographical feature supports both interpretations as far as the 'don' element of Winson Green is concerned. It remains debateable as to which case is the stronger for the origin of 'Win'.

Locally Bordesley was pronounced with a barely discernible 'd' so that it became Bor'sley. Similarly, it is most likely that Wynesden was spoken as Wynes'n. This shift is indicated by two documents separated only by 30 years. In 1592, John Barebon of Wynsdon Greene leased land from Ambrose Phillips; whilst in 1622, Sir Walter Erle, knight, and Anne his wife, conveyed to Edward Bests of 'Wynson greene' in the parish of Birmingham, smith, premises and lands at Winson Green and Smethwick, 1622.

By the end of the eighteenth century, the rabbit warren on Birmingham Heath was owned by Sir Thomas Gooch. He leased land to George Whitehouse, a brickmaker, who was sued by Lord Archer, then the lord of the manor, for digging and carrying away the soil of the Heath. The land itself had been sold by the Marrow heiresses, who had succeeded to the estates of the lords of the manor, but Archer claimed the right to the soil. He won his case. In the following few years, the Archers allowed encroachments of cottages, ponds, plecks and much else upon the heath. Then in 1798, an act of Parliament allowed this common land to be enclosed and divided amongst the landowners of the manor. Gradually the old heath disappeared as Birmingham marched outwards, although as late as 1884 Till's Map showed fields between Winson Street and the Winson Green Road, and between the Handsworth New Road and Bacchus Road; whilst the King's Norton Map of 1899 still gave Birmingham Heath Farm as by Cavendish Road on the Dudley Road.

Interestingly, the built-up area of Winson Green was largely upon land which had been cultivated. By comparison, the old heathland was mostly dominated by major buildings: the Borough Gaol was opened in 1849; the Borough Asylum, later All Saints, followed a year later; and the workhouse opened in 1851. Finally, in 1883-4 the Borough Hospital for Smallpox and Scarlet Fever was in use. Until 1870, **High Street**, **Harborne** was called Heath Street, after the Harborne Heath which lay to the east of the street.

Heath Mill Lane, Deritend

Now famous because of the 'Old Crown', one of the oldest buildings in Birmingham sited on its corner with Deritend High Street, Heath Mill Lane takes part of its name from the 'Heth Feld Pasture' of which Roger Foxall became tenant in 1524 at a rent of twenty shillings. Two years later Heath Mill was mentioned as leased to Gilbert Webb; and later that century, the widow and children of John Prattye or Pretty claimed the

Heath Mill, by virtue of a lease said to be signed by Edward Byrmyngham whilst a prisoner in the Tower, and dated 11 October, 1532. The original course of the Rea had probably been diverted to create the necessary power for this mill.

By the middle years of seventeenth century, the Heath Mill was in the hands of John Cooper. In 1673, he was accused of raising the height of the water above the mill so that wagons could not pass through the ford of the River Rea by the bridge. This continued to be a problem and in 1726, William Cooper undertook to rebuild the mill within two years and not to raise the level of the water to the damage of the Town Mill (see Mill Lane). Six years later the mill was named on Westley's Map. As late as 1756, Heath Mill was still grinding corn, but soon after it became a blade mill. The name Cooper was well known in Birmingham, and there was a John Cooper, also spelled Couper, mentioned in the early 1400s. Originally coopers, as the name suggest, some of the Coopers became smiths at an early date. In the early nineteenth century, the mill was in the possession of a sword cutler, James Woolley, and it was known as Wooley's Mill or Deritend Forge. By 1828, Whitmore, had reverted to grinding corn and called the place Deritend Mills. It disappeared soon after and its buildings became part of adjacent factories. The Mill House itself stood at what is now the junction of Heath Mill Lane and Lower Fazeley Street. Heath Mill Lane was also called **Heath Lane**, **Mill Lane**, and **Coopers Lane**.

David Cox, the famed landscape painter, was born in Heath Mill Lane in 1783. His father, Joseph, was a blacksmith and whitesmith; whilst his mother, Frances, was one of fourteen children of Aris Walford, a farmer and miller of Small Heath. From an early age, Cox showed an interest in painting and drawing, and unsuited to work in a smithy, he was taught by Joseph Barber, Birmingham's only professional drawing-master. After an apprenticeship with a miniature painter, Cox worked as a scene painter at the Theatre Royal, Birmingham. Here he met the actor–manager William Macready (the elder) and was taken on for provincial tours. From there, Cox, still nineteen, became a scene painter in a theatre in Lambeth.

Cox then developed as a landscape painter of talent. He returned with his wife, Mary, to live in Birmingham in 1841. Their home was in Greenfield Road, Harborne, which boasted 'a large willow-bush, of which [he] was immensely proud, having been originally a cutting from *the* willow which grew over Napoleon's tomb at St Helena'. Cox died in 1859 and was buried beside Mary in Harborne churchyard. His obituary in the *Birmingham Daily Post* hailed him as 'the contemporary of Turner and Girtin, and one of that small band of artists who have made the English school of water-colour painters the finest in the world'. A memorial stained-glass window by Hardman & Co. was placed in the east end of St Peter's Church, Harborne, in 1874. Some of Cox's most important paintings are in Birmingham Museums and Art Gallery, including Crossing the Sands (1848), and what is regarded as his masterpiece, Rhyl Sands (1854–5). However, for Brummies he is best-known for his wonderful, vibrant painting of the Bull Ring on market day and of the Crescent Wharf at the back of Broad Street.

Heaton Street, Hockley

Named in 1880 and off Lodge Road, Heaton Street brings to the fore a noteworthy man called Ralph Heaton III. In a biography of him in *Birmingham Faces and Places* it was stated that 'whenever and wherever the name of Mr. Ralph Heaton ismentioned — and in what part of the civilized world has it not been heard? — the association of it is naturally with the Mint in Icknield Street. He is the head and guiding spirit of that great manufactory, where, everyday in the year, vast piles of metal are converted into current coin, not only for this, but other countries.' Indeed, the Birmingham Mint supplied coins 'to the English, French, Italian, Canadian, Ecuador, Bulgarian, Servian, Tunisian, Haytian, Paraguayan, Uruguayan, and numerous other governments and manufacturers of metals or blanks and machinery'. Praised as a citizen whose 'kindly-expressed face, bright and cheerful to look upon, and strongly reflective of a gentle nature and a warm and generous heart has been familiar to us all for very many years', Heaton had been an active public figure and a councillor.

The business of which he was the head was a most important one for Birmingham and survived until the turn of the twenty-first century. The founder was his grandfather, Ralph Heaton I, who was regarded as an 'inventive genius', some of whose inventions in machinery 'have never been superseded and survive to this day'. Ralph Heaton I was the originator of the shot used at the siege of Gibraltar in 1783. As General Elliot, Lord Heathfield had been in command at the time of the siege and when he visited friends in Birmingham he declared of Heaton that 'This is the man who saved Gibraltar'.

The All Saints Mission Hall in Heaton Street in 1961, looking down to Whitmore Street.

Ralph Heaton III was born in 1827 and was educated by Mr. Thomas Aston, of Rose Hill School, Handsworth and then by Mr. E. Jackson, of Aldridge Free Grammar School. In 1839, he began work with his father, Ralph Heaton II, as a brassfounder, stamper, and metal tube manufacturer. Then when Matthew Boulton's historic mint at Soho was dismantled, Heaton the younger purchased the coining apparatus 'and from that time turned his attention to coining and similar processes. The first important commission his firm were entrusted with was from the British Government, and was for a considerable quantity of copper " blanks," to be converted into coins at the Royal Mint, London.' This was soon followed by an order for 500 tons of finished coins of copper, consisting of pennies, halfpennies, farthings, and even half and quarter-farthings. So rapidly were these coins required that Heaton had to bring in new machinery to his manufactory that was then in Shadwell Street in the Gun Quarter.

Trade picked up swiftly, both from the British and foreign governments. The orders frpm India alone amounted to many thousands of tons and as a result of the need for bigger premises The Mint in Icknield Street was built. An 'enormous structure, covering an area of over 10, 000 yards' it was fitted with 'machinery of almost phenomenal power, calculated, as a writer has happily put it, to supply all the monetary wants of the world'. In 1861, soon after the new works was completed, The Mint gained a contract from the Italian Government, which led Heaton 'to fit up the Royal Mint at Milan, and fix quite an astonishing number of coining machines; while they supplied from Birmingham many millions of " blanks," for receiving the impression at Milan of the Royal effigy.' For this and other work, Ralph Heaton III was made a member of the order of the Cross of St. Maurice and St. Lazarus.

Heeley Road, Bournbrook

A long road running parallel with the railway line from Raddlebarn Road to the Bristol Road, Heeley Road recalls John Heeley, a gunmaker whose company occupied the blade mill on the south of the Bourn Brook and just off the Bristol Road. This Bournbrook Mill had been built as a blade mill on part of Gower's Farm by Henry Cambden the elder, a knife cutler, in 1707. Heeley is mentioned there in 1816. Previously he had the tenancy of the Speedwell Mill, on the west of the River Rea and just above the Balsall Heath Road in Edgbaston. Later the mill was occupied by James Kirby as a rolling mill. The mill pool then became known as Kirby's Pool and later in the 1800s it was used as a boating pool, by which time the mill and its buildings had become industrial premises. Heeley Road emerged in the later nineteenth century from a farm track.

Hemlingford Road, Kingshurt

A hundred was a sub-division of a county and as a unit it emerged during the tenth century in that part of England that had not been conquered by the Danes, that is, Wessex and West Mercia – which included Warwickshire, Worcestershire and Staffordshire. By the late Anglo-Saxon period, the term a hundred was applied to that area which a team of eight oxen could plough in a year and which was sufficient to support a family, and probably it consisted of 100 hides of land. Normally a hide was 120 acres, but its size varied according to the quality of the soil and the landscape.

A unit of taxation, each hundred also had military, judicial and administrative functions, some of which survived for centuries. For example, the militia records for the eighteenth and nineteenth centuries were arranged by the hundred. Each hundred took its name from its original meeting place. Usually these were remote settlements by a river crossing or a highway. By the Domesday Book of 1086, there were ten hundreds in Warwickshire, the largest of which was Coleshill. In the twelfth century its name changed to Hemlingford Hundred after a crossing place on the River Tame below Coleshill. Birmingham belonged to the Hemlingford Hundred.

Henns Walk, City

More like a passageway, Henns Walk used to run off the southern side of Dale End, just before Newton Street and Masshouse Lane. In 1707, a conveyance for a year was made from Henry Pratt and John Hopkins to John Hen of premises in nearby Bull Street; and then in 1725, Joseph Scott and John Henn made a similar lease in the same street to Susanna Boyce. Later in the eighteenth century, Henry Henn was one of the two auditors of the General Hospital accounts, and he was a merchant who lived in Old Square. John Henn is a descendant of this family and 'my father once told me when he was young there was a public house in Milk Street and they would give you one shilling for every one in the pub who was not named Henn.'

Henns Walk from Moor Street in 1961.

Henshaw Road, Small Heath

Running into the Coventry Road, Henshaw Road like **Henshaw Grove** off Fast Pits Road, Yardley is a tribute to the painter Frederick Henry Henshaw. He was born in Edmund Street in 1807, in a house which was on the front of the site later occupied by Mason College – itself demolished to make way for the present Central Library. Educated at Severn Street, Henshaw's schooling was finished at King Edward's in New Street, where his drawing-master was the celebrated Mr. J. V. Barber. He was then apprenticed to Barber, who specialized in art for manufacturing, especially japanned ware. After a time in London, Henshaw had his first exhibition at the Royal Birmingham Society of Artists, now based in Saint Paul's Square, with a view of Handsworth Old Church. He completed his apprenticeship in 1829 and went to London and elsewhere, gaining attention. Four years later he returned to Birmingham, although he continued to exhibit in London. He then travelled widely in Europe before finally settling back home in 1841.

However, as was recorded in *Birmingham Faces and Places*, Henshaw 'continued his practice of painting out of doors; an excellent habit which he kept up to 1872, never spending less than half of each year in this method of work. Being painted from the scenes themselves, all his pictures for exhibition were full of freshness, vigour and intense realism. During winter and spring the out-door sketches were reserved for his own studio . . .' At times Henshaw 'was urged to fix his residence in London, but he has resisted all such solicitations. His love for his native city is too strong for him to leave it; his wish to increase its art reputation too fervent for him to sever his connection with it. So he remains at his residence in Green Lanes …'

How he came to live here is a romantic story. It was said that as a poor young artist he was passing by and he asked a widow who lived at the cottage permission to paint it. She did and brought him out cups of bohea – fragrant, milkless tea. Love bloomed and they married. Henshaw's Cottage, Green Lane, Small Heath was then on the edge of the country (see Green Lane), surrounded by green and well-wooded fields. One of Henshaw's favourite haunts nearby was Hob Moor Lane. According to the *Birmingham Post*, Henshaw's painting of the great oaks at Packington Park, Warwickshire 'stamped him as amongst the foremost of English tree painters'. Two of his paintings are in the Birmingham Museums and Art Gallery, one of which is 'A Forest Glade, Arden, Warwickshire', 1845.

Henshaw died in 1891 and was buried at Yardley Parish Church. Soon after his death, builders developed the seventeen-acre estate he and his wife had owned around their cottage. Henshaw would not have approved. When plans had been mooted to cut down the trees locally he had prevented that action by buying the land, for he looked upon the trees 'in the same light as children, having them over fifty years'.

Hermitage Road, Edgbaston

Coming off the Hagley Road up from Norfolk Road, Hermitage Road and **Westfield Road** were named **Grindstone Road** or **Grindstone Lane** until 1866.

High Street, Birmingham

High Street is part of the original street line of Birmingham and was on the route from Coventry to Wolverhampton that went through Bordesely High Street, Deritend High Street and Digbeth. According to Joe McKenna it takes its name from the fact that it was on the King's Highway from London. However, the main London Road went via the Chester Road to the north of Birmingham, and it seems more likely that High Street was so-named either because it was on the higher part of the town, above the Bull Ring, or else because it was the main street of Birmingham that led to other places.

High Street, Birmingham in the 1950s before the coming of the Inner Ring Road swept away this part of the street. The Times Furnishing building in the background is now Waterstone's Bookshop. Prominent on the right is the Army and Navy store of Oswald Bailey at numbers 1, 2, 3 and 4, just up from where the street the Bull Ring ended at Park Street. The shop next to Bailey's is Woodley's house furnishers and it is advertising that 'the building's coming down', and so it soon would. Then comes the famous Devoti's sweet shop, the Bull Ring Café, Pimm's the noted animal and bird dealer, Lush's upholsterers and Brooke Brothers the tailors.

High Street, Aston in the 1950s, showing the 'Malt Shovel' at number 42 and the well-remembered 'Orient' picture house, with Jack Carter's betting shop next to it. Just by the bus stop is Parker's, the horse butcher's and A. G. Andrews, jig maker, then Murray's record player shop and the local branch of the Birmingham Musicial Bank.

Given as le High strete in 1551, on Joseph Hill's Conjectural Map of 1553, High Street is indicated as beginning at Moor Street and ending at New Street. This section fell beneath the Inner Ring Road after the Second World War. The middle part of the High Street (now its bottom end) was known as the **English Market**, whilst that space approaching Bull Street was called the **Welch Market**. It is likely that this is the spot where drovers from Wales sold their cattle in the later Middle Ages and it highlights the importance of the Welsh to Birmingham (see also Sampson Road).

By Westley's Map of 1731, the English Market had become the **Beast Market**, whilst High Street itself was called **High Town**. Nineteen years later, Bradford's Map indicates that the name High Street now applied to the whole route from the Bull Ring to the Welsh Cross. This spot itself had faded away by the end of the eighteenth century. There are a number of other High Streets within Birmingham, bringing to attention places that once were independent, as with **High Street Aston**. Until the mid-nineteenth century Aston was largely rural with a small village based around the parish church. Then in 1848 much of the 327 acres of parkland of Aston Hall was

High Street, Kings Heath in the early twentieth century.

High Street, Erdington in the 1920s.

sold off, hence **Park Lane** and **Park Road**. According to Tomlinson's Plan of 1758 this was just over a third of the total area of Aston Manor (943 acres). Within a few years, new roads had been cut in the pentagonish-looking area bounded by Park Lane, High Street (Aston), Witton Road, Frederick Road/Sycamore Road, Church Road, and the Lichfield Road. This led to the disappearance of Potter's Farm, recalled in **Potters Hill**, the house of which had been sited in what became Bevington Road. South west of the former parkland, Aston New Town had emerged by 1860. Bounded by Alma Street on the west, its boundary with Birmingham was below Phillips Street and Inkerman Street. The urbanisation of this neighbourhood led to High Street Aston becoming a major shopping thoroughfare until it fell before the onslaught of road widening in the 1960s.

High Street, Erdington, **High Street, Harborne** (see also Heath Street), **High Street, Kings Heath**, **High Street, Northfield**, **High Street, Quinton** and **High Street, Saltley** are all the main streets of mostly-agricultural areas that joined Birmingham between 1891 and 1911. For High Street, Bordesley and High Street, Deritend see Bordesley and Deritend.

Highgate Road, Sparkbrook

Known as **Highgate Lane** until 1893, Highgate Road brings to mind the toll gate on the Alcester turnpike – now the Moseley Road – which halted travellers at the junction with Skirt's Lane, or Kyrwicks Lane as it would be called later. The Lane was formed in 1807 to connect the Alcester and Stratford turnpikes. From 1831 until 1897, the section of Highgate Lane from the Ladypool Road to the Stoney Lane was called **Thomas Street**, after Thomas Mole – who is still remembered in **Mole Street**. A wealthy attorney, Mole may have been associated with the Moles involved in brass founding in Bartholomew Street. He died on 7 February 1831 and his will directed that his real and personal estate should be put in trust for his children, and that when the youngest, Harriet, achieved her majority, the residue unsold should be auctioned. In preparation for the auction, the trustees had instructed that Thomas Street and Mole Street be cut out 'at very considerable cost'. Lots for building along these roads were offered in 1834. Development, however, was slow. By the mid-1840s, only eighteen houses had been erected in Thomas Street and many of the plots were in use as gardens. Indeed as late as 1890 the odd garden lingered in Mole Street, by then an otherwise heavily-built up street.

Highters Heath Lane, Highters Heath

Named as **Whorstock Road** in 1774 in the Enclosure Awards for the Manor of Kings Norton, Highters Heath Lane strikes back to the Tudor period. The Patent Rolls of 1549 mention Halers Heth, but by 1650 it had become Hayter's Heath. It would seem to be called after someone named Hayter – from which the word Highter developed.

Hill Street, City

As its name suggests, Hill Street runs down the slope from Victoria Square to Smallbrook Street Queensway. It was called **Tonk Street** and sometimes **Tunkses Street** until 1879, which suggests it was then called after someone named Tunks or Tonks. The line of Hill Street was apparent by the mid-eighteenth century.

Hill Street in 1959, looking up towards Victoria Square from Navigation Street.

Hingeston Street, Brookfields

Dave Morris, now living in Southampton, was raised in Brookfields and recalls that many of the yards in Hingeston Street had names of places in India. His father told him that 'there was a Major or Colonel Hingeston in one of Kipling's stories of India.

The 'Rose and Crown' at 126, Hingeston Street in 1968.

I have never sought to verify this but my father thought there might be some connection here, however tenuous.' Given that Hingeston Street had emerged by the mid-nineteenth century and that Kipling became famous decades later, it is unlikely that the builder could have been influenced by the writer. Still, there is something intriguing about Hingeston Street and its yards calling out to India. Dave Bicknell provides an explanation. He states that 'regarding the Indian place names for groups of buildings like Serringapattam, Streepmoitore and Poonmallee, these are names of places where battles were fought between the East India Company's regiments and local Indians during the establishment of the Raj on the Indian sub continent'.

Hinckley Street, City

Lying between Hill Street and Dudley Street, Hinckley Street recalls the Old and New Inkleys. It is thought that the two streets followed the line of narrow lanes called the **Upper Inkley** and **Nether Inkley**. On Westley's Map of 1731, the Hinkleys appear to be covered with gardens, bounded by a **Hinkly Row** running from Dudley Street to Tunkses Street (Hill Street). The open outlook of the locality was changed drastically in the late eighteenth century with the appearance of Swallow Street, Navigation Street, the **Old Inkleys**, the **New Inkleys**, Tonk Street, Green's Village, Myrtle Row and others.

According to William Hutton, the Inkleys were so named because the smoke from the welding of gun barrels in Smallbrook Street made the air as black as ink over the leys, the grazing fields hereabout; however, John Edward Langford supposed that Hinkley Street was associated with the Hinckley family. He noted that in 1783 'the land now occupied by some of the worst class of houses in the town was open ground, or enclosed gardens, with fruit trees and flowers; and there was a Hinckley Hall!' On 15 November that year an advertisement offered to let 'A substantial Messuage or Dwelling-House, situate in the New Hinckleys, consisting of Three Rooms on a Floor with three good Cellars, a Stable for *Two Horses, a large Garden and Summer-house, all entire,* late in the Occupation of Mr. John Taylor, deceased. The House will be very convenient for a Manufacturer, as there is some vacant Land adjoining the said Garden, upon which the Proprietor has no objection to build any Quantity of Shopping that may be required for a responsible Tenant.'

John Taylor was the Brummagem button king who was praised by Hutton as one of the men responsible for Birmingham's rise to pre-eminence as a manufacturing town. The mention of shopping relates to small workshops built off the street. It was this infilling of gardens by shopping that led to the rapid urbanisation of the Hinckleys. Indeed, in December 1783 another advertisement offered the lease of 'A House, with a large Quantity of Shopping behind the same, situated in that part of the New Hinckleys leading up to Hinckley-Hall.' Langford felt that Hinckley had belonged to Dr Hinckley or some member of his family. This Dr John Hinckley was rector of Northfield between 1662-95, and 1690 he bought a large part of the Rotton Park Estate from Humphrey Perrott. The purchase included 53 acres at Birmingham

Heath, twelve acres near the Sand Pits, 30 acres and a good barn at Ladywood, and another 49 acres in Ladywood.

The name Hinkley was long established in Birmingham. In 1300 the Rector of Saint Martin's was a Thomas de Hinkeleigh – and he is the first rector whose name is known; a list of inhabitants of Birmingham, Edgbaston and Aston from 1327 named an Elena de Hinkeleye; and an Inquisition of 1425 mentions a Hynkley Field. It is plausible that Hinckley Street is named after the family, which later became associated with Harborne, although there is a tradition that the street recalls the leys, open land, of a family called Hinks, who were tenants of the Smallbrookes.

Another story proposes that the ink part of the name came from the black characters of the local people, because by the early 1800s the Inkleys had gained a fearsome reputation as a rookery – a place filled with tottering, decrepit dwellings in which lived criminals, rogues and roughs and through which the police only ventured in pairs. This terrible image was made clear in 1882 by a writer in the Town Crier.

Where are the peaceful Inkleys fair?
Where I did roost at night
And murder and manslaughter were
Among its pleasant sights.

By this date, the old buildings of the Inkleys had been thrust from the face of Birmingham by the building of New Street Station between 1846 and 1853. A section of the New Inkleys became part of **Station Street** in 1884; whilst the Old Hinckleys is now Hinckley Street.

Such a negative view of the Inkleys was exaggerated, but it was also applied to the nearby **Green's Village**. This seems to be derived from a colourful character called Beau Green. A dandy and eccentric, he once lived in Hinckley Hall, also called Rag Castle. According to John Thackray Bunce, the emergence of New Street Station and later John Bright Street did away with 'a series of narrow streets, close courts and confined passages, shut out from fresh air, imperfectly lighted, fetid with dirt, ill-supplied with water, and so inhabited that at one time – in the flourishing days of the Inkleys and Greens Village, and the like – the police could not venture into them single-handed; while no family could dwell there without destruction to the sense of decency, or peril to health and life'.

Greens Village was a collection of decrepit houses that had inadequate drains, overflowing miskins, tumbledown privies and a polluted atmosphere, but to those who lived it there was a place of refuge and support. Like the Inkleys, it was the setting of close county and kinship networks of emigrants from the west of Ireland. In 1851 Greens Village had 189 people who were born in Ireland. They formed 51% of the population and if their English-born children were added to the total then the Irish community in the street rose to well over 60%. The places of birth of forty-one of these folk are recorded: twenty-six were from Roscommon – five of whom originated in Strokestown; eight came from Mayo; and three had roots in Galway. Strokestown was a place whose people suffered grievously in the famine. It is likely that two couples in Greens Village, Birmingham had lived through the trauma that beset Strokestown. They were William Graham, a thimble maker, his wife Honorieth, a servant and their four-year old child who was born in Birmingham; and Patrick Gannon, a young blacksmith and his nineteen-year old wife, Margaret, a warehouse woman. Dorothy Greary was also from Strokestown. She worked as a servant and her husband, Patrick, was a metal roller from Loughrea in Galway.

Councillors were unaware or unmindful of the reality of Greens Village, that it was a neighbourhood in which the poor Irish supported each other. Determined to create a fashionable city centre, they had already fastened upon clearing the narrow streets between New Street and Bull Street (se Corporation Street). Greens Village and the adjoining **Myrtle Row** did not escape their gaze. Concerned that such a disreputable spot was so close to the Council House, councillors decided to clear some of the worst passages, yards and alleys and in the process connect Edgbaston, via Bristol Street and the Horsefair, with the civic centre of Brum.

In 1880 sixty-eight houses and a number of workshops were knocked down and a new thoroughfare was laid out at the cost of £31,000. Going downwards from Navigation Street and across Greens Village and the New Inkleys to Smallbrook Street, it was called **John Bright Street** after the man who was a Member of Parliament for Birmingham for thirty-odd years from 1857. A Quaker and a cotton manufacturer from Rochdale, Bright became a household name in the 1840s during the agitation against the Corn Laws. This legislation ensured that imported wheat was charged heavily, thus making the price of bread dearer than it needed to have been. Because the cost of English wheat was high the income of English landlords was supported by this form of protectionism.

Bright played a leading role in the successful campaign to repeal the laws and was elected a Liberal MP for Manchester in 1847. Ten years later his Quaker beliefs led him to oppose the Crimean War and the voters turned against him. Manchester's loss was Birmingham's gain. Bright was a major influence on Joseph Chamberlain and held the Cabinet offices of President of the Board of Trade and then Chancellor of the Duchy of Lancaster. Rightly John Bright Street recalls one of the most prominent politicians ever to be associated with the city. Yet when walking along its length or looking at its sign, none of us should forget those thousands of poor Brummies who once lived hereabouts. They never benefited from fame but like John Bright they too played their part in the making of Birmingham.

Until the 1960s and the building of the Inner Ring Road and the huge Holloway Circus, John Bright Street stretched as far as Smallbrook Street and looked across at the Horsefair. It now goes southwards from the top of Hill Street to its present-day junction with Station Street. Part of Greens Village survives as **Beak Street**, just off John Bright Street.

Hob Moor Road, Small Heath

Known as **Hob Moor Lane** until 1881, this is one of the most fascinating of Birmingham's street names. In English mythology, hobgoblins were part of the fairy world and were unearthly or supernatural beings that haunted woods or other solitary places. Unlike goblins who were grotesque looking and malicious towards humans, hobs on occasion could be better disposed towards people. Thus Hob Moor was a place frequented by hobgoblins. It was included in the Rental of Bordesley Manor in 1511-12 as Hob more; whilst Tomlinson's Map of 1760 shows a Hobb Leasowe (meadow) and a Hob Close. Hob Moor Lane itself was mentioned in 1702 as Hobmore Lane in a list of property settlement upon marriage of Clement Fisher of Birmingham and Ann Jarvis. It was later described as having 'no house from beginning to end, narrow and rutted without a footpath and deep between high hedgerows'. It stopped at the River Cole and ran for a few hundred yards alongside its bank.

The area was developed in the inter-war years. Beginning at the junction of Green Lane and Yardley Green Road, Hob Moor Road now crosses the Cole at the new bridge, hence **Newbridge Road**, Small Heath and carries on through Yardley to the Yew Tree. The new bridge itself is not new. A Rental of Bordesley Manor from the early sixteenth century indicated a 'Newe bridge and the torrent called Cole Broke'.

Hob Moor Road, Small Heath in 1910.

Hockley Hill, Hockley

Running south and upwards from the bottom of Soho Hill to Great Hampton Street, Hockley Hill takes its name from the brook which divides the two hills and which for centuries separated Birmingham from both Handsworth in Staffordshire and Aston in Warwickshire. The Hockley Brook itself is now culverted but it used to run openly south eastwards from Rabone Lane by the Smethwick Gas Works, past Gib Heath and over Factory Road. From there it went along the old tramway depot off Whitmore Street, along the top end of Farm Street and through Lozells to cross Summer Lane by its junction with Alma Street. By now it was known as Aston Brook, running on between the street of the same name and Philips Street and then over the Aston Road North. The last part of its journey took it north across Rocky Lane to its junction with the River Tame at Salford Bridge.

Hockley Hill was one of a number of banks rising either side of the brook, and amongst the others were Soho Hill, Key Hill, Potters Hill and Holborn Hill. It was part of the old turnpike road from Wolverhampton to Birmingham, formed in 1727. This route was owned by a company which maintained the road through charging travellers a toll at gates placed strategically along the way. But the 'one grand Obstacle to the carriage of Coals on that road has been the Sands or Ice at Hockley Brook, and the Ascent there from'. Accordingly in 1764 a subscription list was started to raise funds to erect a bridge over the stream and lower the hills on either side.

Hockley Hill from the corner of New John Street West in 1964. The newsagent's of the Misses Coleman, Violet and Elsie, is next to the television shop in New John Street West. Down below the shops end at Hunters Road and Farm Street, across from which is the imposing structure of Goodlass House, the paint manufacturer's.

Meaning Hucca's woodland clearing, the name Hockley appeared first in 1529, leading Joe McKenna to believe that an incoming family brought it with them. This may be so, or it may be that it is an older name but there are now no records to so prove. **Hockley Street** is another that takes its name from the brook and the area.

Hodge Hill Road, Hodge Hill

A rental dated 1569 mentioned Hidgehyll, after which Hodge Hill Common and thus the road was named. Hodge was the diminutive for Richard.

Hodge Hill Common in the early 1900s.

Holder Road, South Yardley

The name Holder was long associated with Yardley. In 1373, Alan le Holder of Yerdeley granted to William de Bradewell all his lands and tenements of the parish of Aston juxta Bermyngham; however, the modern name relates to Sir John Holder. Born in 1838 he was the son of Henry Holder, the man credited with opening Birmingham's first music hall in Coleshill Street, which later became the 'Gaiety' picture house. Building on the family business, Sir John headed the Midland Brewery based in Nova Scotia Street. A successful and wealthy man, he was noted in *Birmingham Faces and Places* for his benevolence, of which 'the poor of the district in which the brewery is situated and the parishioners of Bishop Ryder's can bear eloquent testimony to it all. Round about that neighbourhood, which is one of the poorest in Birmingham, his name is a household word for everything that is kind and generous.' In his public life, Sir John was active on behalf of the Blue Coat

School and the General Hospital. Indeed as chairman of the Committee of the General Hospital he was a strenuous advocate for the removal of the hospital from its insanitary surroundings in the Summer Lane neighbourhood to Saint Mary's Square by Corporation Street.

Always prepared to give large sums of money to good causes, Sir John lived in Moor Green, Moseley where he is recalled in **Holders Lane**. He died in 1923 and four years later his house was knocked down to make way for the Ideal Benefit's building at Pitmaston. He also owned the Redhill Estate – hence **Redhill Road** – in South Yardley, close to Hay Mills, and lying alongside the Coventry Road – hence **Redhill Road**. **Gladys Road**, **Kathleen Road**, **Geraldine Road** and **Flora Road** were also cut out of the estate and were named after his daughters. Holder Road itself was called **Workhouse Lane** until 1898. **Sir John's Road, Selly Park** brings to mind another estate owned by Holder and which is notable for its Avenues: **First Avenue**, **Second Avenue**, **Third Avenue** and **Fourth Avenue**.

Sir John's Road, Selly Park.

Holdford Road, Witton

In the later Middle Ages there were two fords on the River Tame: one was at Hamstead, close to the modern Hamstead Station; and the other was Old Ford, also known as Hol Ford and Hold Ford, meaning the old ford or the ford in the hollow. The Roman Road, Icknield Street, crossed the Tame at this point. (See Icknield Street). Just south of the ford lay Oldford or Holdford Mill, mentioned in 1654 in a lease from Sir John Wyrley to William Edwards and John Crooley. The Wyrleys were associated with Holford for centuries. In 1358, John of Wyrley was granted Holford Mill and a fishery in the Tame by the lord of the manor of Handsworth (see Wyreley Road). The mill was used for fulling. In the later sixteenth century it was a hammer mill and by 1654 it was a blade mill. By the mid-twentieth century, the mill was on the site of IMI and was used as an office and store. Although historically part of Handsworth and separated from Witton by the Tame, the Holdford locality is now seen as part of Witton.

Hole Lane, Northfield

The word hole refers to a hollow or low place and gave its name to Hole Farm, the building of which survives still in Hole Lane. For much of the twentieth century, the farm was associated with the Garland family. Miss Dolly Garland died in 1963 aged 85. In her lifetime, she supplied local people with milk, fruit, eggs, vegetables, chrysanthemums and bedding plants, and was noted for riding on her bicycle to worship at Saint Laurence's. In 1926, two 'all-electric' houses were built in Hole Lane to show off the advantages of electricity over coal.

Holland Road, Aston

Coming off the Aston Road North close to Aston Cross, this may be named after Alfred Holland Emery who was a metal roller of Aston Village in 1850s. However, an alternative explanation is that it recalls a Mayor of Birmingham, Henry Holland. Mayor in 1868, Holland was a leading Liberal and a staunch advocate of a free and compulsory state education. During his term of office the influential National Education League was founded, which was partly responsible for the passing of the Education Act in 1870 (see Dixon Road). Holland was also prominent in pushing for Birmingham to have a public library.

The 'Glassmakers Arms' on the corner of Holliday Street and Granville Street in the 1950s.

Holliday Street, City

William Holliday was mayor of Birmingham in 1863-4. In 1836 he had founded Warwick House in New Street, the largest drapery and general furnishing business in Birmingham. He was described by Eliezer Edwards as ever-youthful and along with Joseph Chamberlain, George Dixon and others he was regarded as one of the leading citizens who believed passionately in civic renaissance and municipal activity and who helped transform Birmingham for the better from the 1870s. Holliday Street runs off Suffolk Street.

Hollier Street, Highgate

A short street off Darwin Street that is no longer there, Hollier Street brings to attention a generous woman. By her will of 1790, Elizabeth Hollier left land in what is now Highgate in the parish of Aston to trustees who were to use the income from the property to buy coats, gowns and shifts for twelve or more poor men and women of Birmingham and eight or more of Aston. From 1862, there were appeals by public bodies that the charity's land be used for a park. It was situated on the slope leading down from the Moseley Road and in 1873 Birmingham's town clerk explained that it 'commands an extensive prospect over the town and neighbourhood'. The Council was concerned that the charity might sell the land for commercial development and the only open space in this 'densely populated neighbourhood' would be lost for ever to 'exercise and recreation'. Fortunately, the charity sold most of the land to the Corporation for £8,100 and the greater part of it became Highgate Park.

Holloway Head, Attwood Green/Lea Bank

Holloway Head was literally that – a way that had been hollowed out by the passage over centuries of innumerable people and animals. In the 1553 Survey of Birmingham, a lane leading from 'Birmyncham to Edgebaston and Horburn' was mentioned. This was Holloway Head, and a conveyance from Richard Danks the elder to Richard Danks the younger in 1690 included premises in Holloway Head. Part of the way was called Exeter Row until 1883 as it was on the old route from Birmingham to Bristol (see Bristol Road). The head refers to the fact that the hollow way went across a high piece of land. Other hollow ways were below Camp Hill, Constitution Hill, and the high causeway at Gosta Green – where the pavement was higher than the road.

Holt Street, Gosta Green

Although without the final 'e', Holt Street is named after the Holte family (see Holte Road). It was the site of the Holt Brewery started in 1887, but based on the brewing and malting business of H. C. Fulford which had begun locally in 1819. In 1934, Holt's became part of Ansell's, which adopted the squirrel logo of Holt's. Beer production at the Holt Brewery, behind the 'Pot of Beer' and now the 'Gosta Green', was ended in 1972.

Holte Road, Aston

Just off Serpentine Road and close to Witton Lane, Holte Road reminds us of the former lords of the manor of Aston. With a surname spelled either Holt or Holte, the first member of the family to come to notice was Sir Henry Holte, who would seem to have lived in Edgbaston Street. Certainly the 1553 Survey of Birmingham indicated that the Holtes owned 'one burgage and one tenement, with their appurtenances, in Edgebaston Stret and Malte Mille Lane'. Sir Henry's son, Sir Hugh, was married to Matilda, the daughter of Sir Henry Erdington and in 1327 she was living as a widow in Edgbaston Street. Three years later her grandson, Simon, gained the manor of Nechells from his mother's sister, Alice de Castello.

The Holtes were now set upon becoming landed gentry and a family of power locally. In 1366, Maud de Grymersawe conveyed the manor of Aston to John atte Holte, a great nephew of Simon Holte. Upon John's death, Aston was inherited by Simon's son, Walter. There then followed some dispute over the ownership of the manor. Walter was married to Margery, daughter of Sir William Bagot and their youngest son, William, successfully held off challenges to his lordship from both the Bagots and his older brother's son, Aymer – who was involved in a wrangle with the Greswoldes over Greethurst (see Greethurst Drive). From William, Aston was passed to John, son of his other brother, Simon.

It would seem that the manor of Duddeston went with that of Aston and so by the late fourteenth century the Holtes had become substantial landowners to the north and east of Birmingham. Their holdings increased substantially in the reign of Henry VIII because of the cunning of Thomas Holte. A 'learned' lawyer, in 1525 he farmed the tolls to the market and two fairs of Birmingham, along with the rents for the borough, the built-up part of the town, from Edward Bermingham, the last of his line. In effect, for receiving one lump sum, Edward sold his income as lord of the manor for less than it was worth, allowing Thomas to make his profit on the difference. The enterprising Holte also became steward of Birmingham, receiving forty shillings a year – small beer compared to the wealth he would gain from Henry VIII's dissolution of the monasteries.

When the king broke with the Roman Catholic Church he dissolved the religious houses. This brought their property into the hands of the crown, and looking for a swift return on his new estates, Henry sold them at competitive prices. This gave his henchmen an unparalleled opportunity to increase both their lands and their influence. Amongst them was Thomas Holte, probably one of the Visiting Commissioners appointed by the king to oversee the dissolution. In Birmingham, the lands of the Priory of Saint Thomas (see Bull Street), the Guild of the Holy Cross (see King Edwards Road) and the Deritend Guild of Saint John the Baptist were confiscated. Many of them were bought by Thomas Hawkins, who was married to a sister of Thomas Holte. It is reckoned that he gained 150 acres of land. According to Joseph Hill, 'Fisher' Hawkins as he was called was a notorious figure who was the 'creature' of the powerful Duke of Northumberland. Fisher sold his Birmingham properties to the father of Holte's wife, Margery. Holte himself died in 1545 and his wife then inherited her father's estates which were passed on to her son Edward Holte.

In 1572 Edward sold to Thomas Rastell, a Birmingham draper, two pastures, 'commonlie called Pryorie Croft, lying between other land of Holte, the lane called Pryors Conyngrey Lane, the Quenes hygheway, leadinge from Birmingham towards Aston, and the croft called Scythewell Croft'. Twelve years later, Holte disposed of a tenement, with three closes and a meadow, 'near unto a certayne ryver or brooke comonlie called borne brooke', to William Colmore, mercer (see Colmore Row). Although this and other parcels of land in Birmingham were sold, the Aston, Duddeston and Nechells estates remained intact.

The Holte family reached its apogee under Edward's grandson, Sir Thomas Holte. A wealthy and powerful man, he was well read, versed in several languages and knowledgeable in the law from his time at the Inns of Court. One of the biggest and most prominent landowners in the Birmingham region, Sir Thomas also had a home in London. Yet for all his intelligence and prosperity, his name was blackened by his reputation for having a vile temper which led him to violence. In particular, it is said that his hand was bloodied by the murder of one of his servants. According to old stories, the only person who received a tender word from Sir Thomas was his cook, John, for he 'had found the only way, To reach his master's heart, Was via his esophagus, And ably plied his art'.

Then one day, Sir Thomas was out hunting deer when one of his companions, Richard Smallbroke (see Smallbrook Street) wagered his swiftest horse that if they rode back unexpectedly to Holte's home they would find his cook unprepared. Sir Thomas accepted the bet with alacrity, declaring 'I'd sooner doubt the sun, To keep his accustomed time, Than doubt my good cook John'. Unhappily, when the hunting party arrived at Duddeston Hall, where the Holtes then lived, the table was unspread. Enraged because he had lost the wager and had been shown up, Sir Thomas 'seized a cleaver keen and cold' and cleft the skull of his cook in twain. The story may well be based on truth, for in 1606, Sir Thomas sued for slander a William Ascrick of Birmingham, who had recounted the tale. Awarded just £30 damages, Sir Thomas lost even this when the verdict was overturned on appeal.

Still, the rumours of murder did not stop Sir Thomas from rising socially and in 1611 he paid the great sum of £1095 to buy a baronetcy. The money raised was to have gone towards the cost of the Army in Ulster which was keeping down the Irish population. This is reckoned to explain the fact that the red hand of Ulster was taken as the Holte's coat of arms, although less kindly folk proposed that in reality it signified the bloody hand of Sir Thomas. Keen to flaunt his new status and power locally, Sir Thomas decided to leave his ancestral home at Duddeston Hall, close to the banks of the River Rea and which later became part of Vauxhall Gardens (see Vauxhall Road), and build a new home on a hill overlooking Aston Church. This prominent position would allow him to look across his wide lands, which included

Duddeston and Nechells as well as Aston, and to proclaim to the world his success and significance.

Sir Thomas paid John Thorpe, a well-respected land surveyor, to design his house and then engaged masons, carpenters and other craftsmen to build it. The foundations were made of big bands of iron slag, most of which probably came from the Aston Furnace which was to give its name to Furnace Lane in Lozells. Similarly, the bricks for the shell of the hall were made from local clay and were dressed with soft grey sandstone. The rest of the house was made of timber and for this purpose, several hundred oak trees were cut down on the Holte estates.

Work on Aston Hall – hence **Aston Hall Road**, Aston – began in 1618 and Sir Thomas was able to move his home there in May 1631, although construction was not completed for at least another four years. It was a spectacular building and amongst its rooms on the ground floor were a Great Hall (now the Entrance Hall), a Great Parlour in which Sir Thomas dined, and kitchens. A superb cantilevered oak staircase ran round a square well up to the floors above. On the first was the Great Dining Room; the Best Lodging Chamber, where King Charles I slept on 18 October, 1642; the Withdrawing Room; and the Long Gallery. Originally this was about 125 feet long and was used for a variety of purposes, such as for music and pictures. Up on the second floor is where the servants slept and here is to be found 'Dick's Garrett, a low attic which was called this name from at least the later 1700s.

During the English Civil War, Sir Thomas was a lukewarm Royalist, but even so Aston Hall was attacked by Parliamentarians from Birmingham in 1643. After a three-day siege and bombardments which damaged the balustrade of the Great Stairs, Sir Thomas surrendered. Imprisoned he was fined the huge sum of £4,491 2s 4d by the Parliamentarians after they won the Civil War. Sir Thomas died in 1654, by which time he was also the lord of Erdington and Pype (see Pype Hayes Road).

He was succeeded by his grandson, Sir Robert, who was faced with clearing substantial debts. He was unable to do so, and despite a reputation as charming, intelligent and amusing man he was imprisoned for debt – even though he was an MP. Sir Robert's son, Sir Charles slowly paid of what his family owed, partly by selling Holte property in Birmingham. This included 'various closes, lands, and a moor, including the round hills lying between Walmer Lane and Aston Road' and through which Pritchett Street and New John Street were cut. Between this estate and Gosta Green lay the Crossfields Estate which had already been sold by Sir Robert to Robert Whittall, yeoman and through which Fisher, Moland, and other Streets, were to be cut (see Whittall Street, Fisher Street and Moland Street).

Sir Charles died in 1722 and his lands were passed on to his son, Sir Clobery Holte. He married Barbara Lister, whose maiden name was given to their son, Sir Lister. He and his mother are recalled in **Lister Street** and **Great Lister Street**, Duddeston. Sir Lister was nine when his father died. Ten years later he married Lady Anne Legge, daughter of the Earl of Dartmouth, who lived at Sandwell Park and was the major landowner in West Bromwich. He is recalled in **Dartmouth Street**, Duddeston. Sadly

Great Lister Street in the late 1950s, looking down to Rupert Street, shortly before these shops were demolished in redevelopment. Number 194 was the grocer's of Fred and Mary Hemingway and on the left is Pardoe's home made bread and cake shop. Then comes Alexander's florit's and a host of other shops shouting out the vitality of a street that should not have been cleared. Thanks to the Evening Mail.

Anne Holte died of smallpox after eight months of marriage. Sir Lister was distraught and never recovered from his loss, and for the rest of his life he wore a diamond ring that contained a lock of his wife's hair. His grief did not stop him in his search for an heir and he went on to marry Mary Harpur who died of apoplexy ten years later.

Sir Lister's third wife was Sarah Newton, supposedly a 'haughty, cold and selfish woman'. She fell out with Anne, the wife of Charles Holte, Sir Lister's younger brother. This couple had a daughter, Mary. Apparently out of spite, Sarah persuaded Sir Lister to exclude their niece from the settlement of his estate. This will was a strange thing. Sir Lister left his real estate to his own sons if he had any, and if not to his brother, Charles, and his male heirs. However, if Charles had no sons then the Holte lands were to go to Heneage Legge, a nephew of Sir Lister's first wife – thus **Heneage Street**, Duddeston and **Legge Street**, Gosta Green; and if he had no successors then everything would be passed on to Lewis Bagot, Bishop of Saint Asaph, thus **Bagot Street**, Duddeston. If Bagot's line failed, the properties were to be given to Wriothesley Digby of Meriden and his heirs. He was recalled in **Digby Street**, Duddeston, now gone (see Digby Walk). Finally, if he had no issue then the Holte estates would revert to Mary, the daughter of Charles. William Hutton expostulated that this was 'one of the most unaccountable assignments that ever resulted from human weakness'.

Sir Lister died in 1770 and his brother suddenly became a wealthy landowner. He died twelve years later and Heneage Legge inherited the Holte lands. With Birmingham marching outwards and seeking space for building houses and workshops, the Duddeston area especially rose in value. Legge Street and others began to appear, whilst development also took place in Ashted – which Dr John Ash had bought from Sir Lister Holte. Legge was a sound custodian of the Holte estates, but it became apparent that neither he, or Bagot or Digby would have an heir.

By now Mary Holte was married to Abraham Bracebridge of Atherstone, passed on in **Bracebridge Street**, Aston and **Bracebridge Road**, Erdington. He was spectacularly irresponsible and unsuccessful in his business affairs. In anticipation of his wife inheriting the Holte property, Abraham Bracebridge used them to raise mortgages. By 1798, he owed the massive sum of £55,000 and oblivious to his shortcomings he continued to make disastrous financial decisions. Because of his business failures he was unable to discharge his loans and in 1818, he finally secured the support of Heneage Legge to obtain an act of Parliament allowing the partition of the Holte lands. This led to the sale of Aston Hall and Park and other properties to meet the demands of Bracebridge's creditors; the passing on to Legge of the most of the manors of Duddeston and Nechells; and to his nephew, Wriothesley Digby, of the manor of Erdington and lands in Bordesley (Small Heath, see Digby Walk) and Sutton Coldfield. Even after the sale of so much land, Bracebridge was unable to clear his huge debts. His 'poor' wife died the year after the profligacy of her inept husband had destroyed her ancestral estates which had stretched from Gosta Green to beyond Erdington Hall and from Nechells and Saltley to Hay Mill Brook.

Their son, Charles Holte Bracebridge, proved the antithesis of his father. A clever and caring man, he was involved in prison reform and he and his wife played a vital role in helping Florence Nightingale in the Crimean War. He was delighted when Aston Hall and Park was opened to the public of Birmingham, and bearing no resentment only generosity of spirit, because he was childless he left what Holte heirlooms he owned to the Corporation of Birmingham when he died in 1872.

Holly Lane, Erdington

The bottom end of Holly Lane was also known as **Factory Lane** after the brace factory that once was there. The rest of it had been called **Ashold Lane**, and a document from 1651 noted it leading into Ashall Meadows. Like the word Ashold, the meadows recalled a wood of ash trees.

Homer Street, Balsall Heath

Henry Homer was a tanner whose business stood where the 'Castle and Falcon' was later built. He died in 1802, by which time he owned a large tan yard with barns and store rooms, a mansion house, and 700 acres of 'rich arable land'. The firm was continued by his son, Avery, until 1833. The following year a sale notice declared that 'the situation is inferior to none in the kingdom for the purchase of hides and bark, and the never failing supply of water'. Avery's brother, Henry, married Anne Chambers of Yardley and started a tannery which survived until 1966.

The Horsefair, City

The outdoor sale of horses took place at two annual fairs that dated to grants made to the lords of the manor of Birmingham in 1251. The first was originally held for four days and began on the eve of the Ascension; the other was held over three days, starting with the eve of St. John the Baptist. With the change in the calendar in 1752, the first fair was moved to the Thursday and two following days in Whitsun week; and the second to the last Thursday in September. Known as the Michaelmas Fair, this became the Onion Fair that survived well into the twentieth century.

Selling horses at the Horse Fair in 1901.

In 1778 Birmingham's Street Commissioners moved the selling of horses at these fairs from its previous site in Ann Street, which was also called Mount Pleasant and Hay Market at various times and was later to become part of Colmore Row. The new location was in **Brickiln Lane** at the upper end of Smallbrook Street. The order of the commissioners stated that Brickiln Lane was spacious and that it boasted 'exceeding good riding Ground, and every other Accommodation will be provided for the Encouragement of Horse Dealers, &c.' In 1825, William Hawkes Smith explained that

> the quantities of horses, cattle, sheep, *&c.* brought to each fair is considerable; but excepting in these, the Whitsuntide fair is one of little business. It is however a time of great mirth and hilarity. Falling on a week which is universally held as a holiday, and in the gay season of the year; it is frequented by unnumbered crowds of visitants from the surrounding country; is enlivened by the presence of numerous itinerant exhibitors, who find its duration present an ample harvest to their exertions; and thus preserves entire, the true characteristics of the country assemblage, with all its excitement and qualification;—mixed, it must be confessed, with the more boisterous mirth and vicious indulgence which are apt to prevail at such times, both, in town and in country.

The open sale of horses survived into the early twentieth century and is harked back to in the short street called The Horsefair at the top of Bristol Street.

The Horse Fair in 1953. The international restaurant on the corner of Windmill Street was run by Michael Nicholas Angelides, then comes Matthews's radio supplies shop and the dining rooms of Cecil Andrew Penny. The big premises further along are Gordon and Munro Ltd, coffin furniture manufacturers and then comes the Roman Catholic Church of Saint Catherine of Sienna.

Hospital Street, Summer Lane

On 4 November 4 1765 Dr John Ash (see Ashted Row) put an advertisement in *Aris's Birmingham Gazette*. It read:

> A GENERAL HOSPITAL, for the Relief of the Sick and Lame, situated near the Town of Birmingham, is presumed would be greatly beneficial to the populous Country about it, as well as that place. A Meeting therefore of the Nobility and Gentry of the Neighbouring Country, and of the Inhabitants of this Town, is requested on Thursday the 21st Instant, at the Swan Inn, at Eleven in the Forenoon, to consider of proper Steps to render effectual so useful an undertaking.

In his important work on *Old and New Birmingham*, Robert K. Dent pointed out that 'the rapid increase of the population of Birmingham, and the danger attached to many of the occupations which they followed, rendered it necessary that some provision should be made to supply, in case of sickness and bodily injuries, competent medical assistance, which the majority were too poor to provide for themselves'. Unfortunately this worthy aim was objected to by those who, whenever any useful measure was projected, were ready to cast a wet blanket on the enthusiasm of the projectors of the hospital. Like their prototype, Ebenezer Scrooge, they reminded the philanthropic doctor that an infirmary was attached to the workhouse and 'what more could the sick poor need?'

Hospital Street in the early 1900s. Thanks to Birmingham Library Services.

Undaunted, Ash persisted in his task and gained the support of leading people such as Sir Lister Holte, the Earl of Bradford, Sir Henry Gough, Charles Adderley, Matthew Boulton, John Baskerville, Sampson Lloyd and others. With a committee formed and money beginning to come in, Ash fastened upon a spot in the Summer Lane neighbourhood owned by a Mrs Dolphin. The Committee paid £120 per acre for 'all those four closes, pieces, or parcels of Land, Meadow, or Pasture Ground, situate, lying, and being together near a place called the Salutation, in Birmingham aforesaid, containing, by estimation, eight Acres or thereabouts, be the same more or less, adjoining at the upper end or part thereof into a Lane there called Summer Lane, and at the lower end or part thereof unto a hue called Walmore Lane' (Lancaster Street). William Hutton was unimpressed with the location, declaring it to be 'very unsuitable and 'in a narrow dirty lane, with an aspect directing up the hill, which should ever be avoided'.

Unhappily the project moved slowly, and although work was begun on the hospital it was stopped through lack of funds in 1766. Matters improved two years later when a Music Festival was held to raise funds. Still, the necessary sums to finish the building and equip it were not forthcoming, although money had poured in to pay for a new theatre in Birmingham after the old one had burned down. In 1774 this 'disgraceful contrast' aroused the ire of a young clerk in a mercantile house who was also a member of the Baptist Church in Cannon Street. He was Mark Wilks, afterwards a famous minister of Lady Huntingdon's Chapel at Norwich. As Dent stated, he was determined to arrest the attention of the public by writing a biting poem.

Even this failed to improve matters immediately. Still by 1777, fundraising had improved and the next year another Music Festival was put on. This proved so successful that it became a triennial event and the need for a proper concert hall for it would lead to the building of the Town Hall in the 1830s. At last the Hospital was opened on 20 September 1779. Its doctors included Ash, George Freer, founder of the Orthopaedic Hospital, Joseph Hodgson, founder of the Eye Hospital, and William Withering, who was a member of the Lunar Society. Withering found fame as the discoverer of digitalis and lived at Edgbaston Hall, the former home of the Goughs. Because of the financial problems only 40 beds were provided for patients, less than half the number planned for. In the ensuing years, the hospital grew. A burns ward was built in just three weeks after several factory disasters and eventually 235 beds were provided. However, by the later nineteenth century the Hospital was regarded as 'a dear, dirty, dismal pile' and it was moved to Steelhouse Lane in 1897 to new premises that were the most modern in Europe.

Hubert Road, Bournbrook

This may be named after Reverend Hubert Arnold Gem who was involved in a number of land transactions in the area. Indeed an Edward Gem owned Raddlebarn Farm and Bournbrook Farm just prior to their development.

Looking towards Hubert Road from Exeter Road, Bournbrook in the 1930s,

Hunton Hill, Erdington

Previously this was called **Hillaries Road** and then **Station Road**.

Hunters Road, Lozells

Hard on the border with Handsworth, Hunters Road was **Hunters Lane** until 1866 and was named after Hunter's Nursery, hence **Nursery Road** and also **Hunter's Vale**, Lozells.

Hurst Street

Hurst Street takes its name from the Old English word 'hyrst', meaning wooded hill and when the road first appeared at the end of the eighteenth century it was known as Hurst Hill. At that time it was just a passage way which went through an arch at the side of the 'White Swan' pub in Smallbrook Street. Down this entry was a knacker's yard, a shop for the dyeing of felt hats and a few cottages. The passage which became Hurst Street is shown but not named in Bradford's map of 1750, and it continues as a lane down to the River Rea. By the time of Hansons' Map of 1778, the nearby Thorp Street has been cut but gardens dominated the area between the future Hurst Street and the back of Edgbaston Street and Jamaica Row. Ten years later, an advertisement offered a building lease for 'a spot of land' on Hurst Hill, and by the time of Pye's Map of 1795 Hurst Street itself is shown.

The corner of Hurst Street and Bishop Street in the late 1940s.

Hutton Road, Washwood Heath

William Hutton was Birmingham's first historian. He came here first in 1741 as an eighteen-year old apprentice stockinger who had run away from his master – his uncle – in Nottingham. Hoping to make his way to Ireland, he slept in barns and arrived in Lichfield, where his few possessions were stolen. Distraught and down hearted he met a man who advised him to move to Walsall where it was market day. By the time he got there his feet were badly blistered and he had to rub them with beef fat cadged from a butcher. Another chap told him that he ought to carry on to Birmingham as he would be sure to find work there.

Coming down through Hamstead, he struggled past St Mary's Church, Handsworth, to Soho Hill. Standing on the shrubland above the Hockley Brook, he gasped at the sight before him. Thrown into relief by the setting sun, his eyes were drawn first to Saint Philip's Church. It stood alone on the top of Bennett's Hill, for apart from New Hall (the home of the Colmores) there was no other main building north of the town. With no other houses hemming it in and no smoke from the manufactories enveloping it in a haze, the recently finished place of worship charmed Hutton with its beauty.

Crossing the brook he came up Hockley Hill and along the Wolverhampton Road to Snow Hill. He was impressed with the difference to the outskirts of the other towns he had visited, 'which seemed to be composed of wretched buildings, visibly stamped with dirt and poverty'. Not so the edges of Brum, for here the buildings 'rose in a style of elegance' while 'thatch, so plentiful in other places was not to be met'. Surprised by everything he saw, Hutton was amazed at the people of Birmingham. He exclaimed they possessed a vivacity he had never beheld. It was if he had been among dreamers and now was amidst men awake. Even the briskness of their steps appeared to show their cheerful readiness. Asking around, he found out that there was three stockingers in Birmingham. He tried his luck at each – but it was no use, the bosses soon worked out that he was an apprentice on the run and would not take him on.

By seven o' clock in the evening he'd traipsed all over Brum and was wearied and despondent. Sitting down by the Old Cross near Philip Street he'd just about had it when a couple of working chaps in aprons came up to him. Striking up a conversation, the one mentioned that he knew what it was to be distressed and seeing William's dusty shoes and forlorn face, they were going to cheer him up. They did, by taking him to the 'Bull' pub in Philip Street. Buying him a pint, bread and cheese, they also sorted him out with some lodgings for three ha'pence.

Hutton was unwilling to leave Birmingham, but he had no choice as there was no chance of work locally in his own trade. Unable to find a position he reluctantly returned to his position with his uncle. Nine years later, Hutton had packed up as a stockinger and was now selling all kinds of Bibles, Common Prayers, and school books in all arts and sciences, both new and second hand. Keen to do well, he was drawn back to Birmingham – as while it was crowded with inhabitants it had only three booksellers. On 11 April, 1750, once again he strode the streets of the town, but this time with more success as he was able to rent a shop in Bull Street.

The first couple of years were hard, but things started to pick up when he moved his business to High Street where William soon gained a 'smiling trade'. Although he ventured into other businesses and had his fingers burned, Hutton's bookselling and later his paper mill business brought him prosperity – so much so that in 1769 he and his wife could afford to buy half an acre of land at Bennett's Hill in Washwood Heath – hence **Bennetts Road** – and build a grand house. In the succeeding years Hutton was involved increasingly in public life but he is best remembered for writing the first *History of Birmingham* in 1782. In his preface he captured the essence of his work, for it was addressed to the inhabitants of the town: 'Birmingham, like a compassionate nurse, not only draws our persons, but our esteem, from place of our nativity, and fixes it upon herself... I might add, I was hungry, and she fed me, thirsty and she gave me a drink; a stranger and she took me in. I approached her with reluctance, because I did not know her, I shall leave her with reluctance, because I do.'

At the age of seventy-five Hutton characterized the predominant activity of his life from twenty-nine to fifty-six as reading; thereafter it was 'writing history'. He never lost his faith in Birmingham or its people – even in 1791 when his home was burned down by rioters who targeted wealthy Non-Conformists such as himself (see Priestley Road). Hutton wrote that the riots 'totally destroyed that peace of mind which can never return, nearly overwhelmed me and my family, and not only deprived us of every means of restoring the health of the best of women, but shortened her life' He continued to write, walk long distances and involve himself in the affairs of his adopted town. In 1811, when 'sensible of decay', he claimed that at the age of eighty-two he had considered himself a young man and could without fatigue walk 40 miles a day.

At eighty eight he still walked twelve miles with ease, and in 1812, in his ninetieth year, he walked from Bennett's Hill into Birmingham for the last time. He died in 1815 aged 92. Today he is recalled in Hutton Road, which like Bennets Road goes from the Washwood Heath Road to Arley Road. Sixty-odd years after his passing R.K .Dent wrote another history of Birmingham and declared that she had 'utterly forgotten or ignored her first historian'. He raised the question 'ought not this man to have a statue or other memorial in our midst?' Surely it is now time to have some other tribute to William Hutton, the immigrant who became a Brummie and who gave us our first history.

Renamed Streets

Present Name	Former Name
Featherstone Road, Kings Heath	Hollyoakes Road
Fernley Road, Sparkhill	Fox Street (1891)
Frankfort Street, Summer Lane	Macdonald Street (1881)
Frederick Road, Edgbaston	Frederick Street (1870)
Hancock Road, Alum Rock	Fulford Road (1910)
Holly Lane, Erdington	Holly Road
Hunton Hill, Erdington	Pritchett's Road
Garland Street, Bordesley	Green Street (1911)
George Road, Edgbaston	Frederick Road (1870)
George Street, Handsworth	Charles Street
Gosford Street, Balsall Heath	Princess Street (1898)
Grasmere Road, Handsworth	Slade Lane (1911)
Grosvenor Street West, Ladywood	Mill Street
Harborne Park Road, Harborne	Park Road (1898)
Hylton Street, Hockley	Richard Street (1884)
Ivy Road, Handsworth	Summer Road

Further Reading

Michael J. Arkinstall and Patrick C. Baird	*Erdington Past and Present* (Birmingham: 1982 edition)
Geoff Bateson	*A History of Castle Vale* (Birmingham: 1998)
A. H. Bevan	Birmingham Street Names (City Surveyors Department, unpublished manuscript no date)
W. B. Bickley (translated) and Joseph Hill (introduction and notes)	*Survey of Birmingham in 1553* (Birmingham)
Vivian Bird	*Portrait of Birmingham* (London 1970).
Vivian Bird	*Streetwise. Street Names in and about Birmingham* (Oldbury: 1991)
J. G. Hammond (publisher)	*Birmingham Faces and Places 1888-92. Volumes 1-4* (Birmingham: 1888-92)
Birmingham Library Services	*The Changing Face of Pype Hayes* (Birmingham: 1994)
H. A. Botwood	*A History of Aston Manor Past and Present* (Birmingham: 1889)
John Thackray Bunce	*History of the Corporation of Birmingham with a Sketch of the Early Government of the Town. Vol. I.* (Birmingham: 1878)
Simon Buteux	*Beneath the Bull Ring. The Archaeology of Life and Death in Early Birmingham* (Studley: 2003)
William Fowler Carter (introduced)	*The Records of King Edward's School, Birmingham. Vol. 1. The Miscellany Volume* (London: 1924)
Philip B. Chatwin	*A History of Edgbaston* (Birmingham: 1914)
Linda Chew	*Images of Stirchley* (Birmingham: 1995)
Ronald E. Crook	*Kingstanding Past and Present* (Birmingham: 1968)
Kathleen Dayus	*Her People* (London: 1982)
Christopher Dingley	'F. H. Henshaw. A Birmingham Landscape painter, *Birmingham Historian*, 5 autumn/winter 1989,

G. Dowling, B.D. Giles and C. Hayfield	*Selly Oak Past and Present* (Birmingham: 1987)
William Dugdale	*Antiquities of Warwickshire* (1656)
Jerry Dutton and Colin Green	*Castle Bromwich. – 1066 to 1700* (Castle Bromwich: 1999)
English Life Publications	*Aston Hall* (Derby: no date)
Henry John Everson (Birmingham: 1896)	*Everson's Moseley, King's Heath and Balsall Heath Directory and Year Book*
Oliver Fairclough	*The Grand Old Mansion. The Holtes and Their Successors at Aston Hall 1618-1864* (Birmingham: 1984)
Alison Fairn	*A History of Moseley* (Birmingham: 1973)
William Fowler	*A History of Erdington* (Birmingham: 1885)
J. Newton Friend	*Forgotten Aston Manor in Birmingham* (Birmingham: 1965)
F. W. Hackwood	*Handsworth: Old and New* (Birmingham: 1908).
Joseph Hill and Robert K. Dent	*Memorials of The Old Square* (Birmingham: 1897)
Michael Hodgetts	*Midlands Catholic Buildings* (Birmingham: 1990)
George Jacob Holyoake	*Sixty Years of an Agitator's Life* (London: 1906)
F. E. Hopkins	*Cotteridge and its Churches before 1911* (Birmingham: 1986)
William Hutton	*History of Birmingham to the end of 1780* (Birmingham: 1780)
John Morris Jones	*The Manor of Handsworth. An Introduction to its Historical Geography* (Birmingham: 1983 edition)
John Morris Jones	*Manors of North Birmingham* (Birmingham: 1984)
John Morris Jones	*The Swanshurst Quarter* (Birmingham: no date)
J. A. Langford	'Birmingham Names' in Birmingham and Midland Institute Archaeological Section *Transactions* (Birmingham: 1870)

John Alfred Langford   *A Century of Birmingham Life or a Chronicle of Local Events, from 1741 to 1841. Volumes I and II* (Birmingham 1868)

John Alfred Langford   *Modern Birmingham and its Institutions. A chronicle of Local Events from 1841 to 1871 Volumes I and II* (Birmingham: 1873-7)

Francis W. Leonard   *The Story of Selly Oak Birmingham* (Birmingham: 1933)

Arthur B. Lock   *The History of King's Norton and Northfield Wards* (Birmingham: no date)

Joseph McKenna   *Birmingham Street Names* (Birmingham: 1986)

Joseph McKenna   *Birmingham Place Names* (Birmingham: 1988)

Bob Marsden   *ABC of Small Heath and Bordesley Green Past and Present* (Birmingham: 1987)

H.W. Mason   *Austin Village Preservation Society* (Birmingham: no date)

Norman Meacham (put together by Kenneth A. Jones)   *A Historical Tour Around Erdington* (Birmingham: 1987

Rita Morton   *The Building of the Elan Valley Dams* (Birmingham: no date)

Northfield Society   *Recollections of Victorian and Edwardian Northfield* (Birmingham: 1983)

Alma Organ   *Aston During the Nineteenth Century* (Unpublished manuscript: no date)

Ian Piper (compiled)   *We Never Slept. The Story of 605 Squadron* (Tamworth: 1996)

Valerie A. Preece   *Duddeston and Vauxhall Gardens* (Birmingham: 1990)

Mary and Walter Reynolds   *Memories of King's Heath* (Birmingham: 1989)

Anthony N. Rosser   *The Quinton and Round About. A History. Volume 1* (Birmingham: 1998)

L.F. Salzman (editor)   *The Victoria History of the County of Warwick. Volume IV. Hemlingford Hundred* (London: 1947)

Walter Showell   *Dictionary of Birmingham* (Oldbury: 1885)

Sketchley and Adams   *The Streets and Inhabitants of Birmingham in 1770*
                                 (Birmingham: 1770)

Pearson and Rollason   *The Birmingham Directory* (1777)

Victor Skipp   *Medieval Yardley* (London: 1970)

Victor Skipp   *A History of Greater Birmingham – down to 1830*
                                 (Birmingham: 1980)

Toulmin Smith   *Memorials of Old Birmingham. Men and Names*
                                 (Birmingham: 1864)

William Hawkes Smith   *The Picture of Birmingham* (Birmingham: 1825)
(Printed by James Drake)

W. B. Stephens (editor)   *The Victoria History of the County of Warwick.
                                 Volume VII. The City of Birmingham* (London:
                                 1964)

Will Thorne   *My Life's Battles* (London: 1925)

William West   *The History, Topography and Directory of
                                 Warwickshire* (Birmingham: 1830)

Francis White   *History, Gazeteer and Directory of Warwickshire*
                                 (Sheffield: 1850)

Frances Wilmot   *The History off Harborne Hall* (Birmingham:
                                 1991)

Donald Wright   *Bygone Bartley Green* (Birmingham: about 1977)

Donald Wright   *An Account of Harborne from Earliest Times to
                                 1891* (Birmingham: 1981)

R. Wrightson   *Wrightson's New Triennial Directory*
                                 (Birmingham: 1818)

Maps

John Bartholomew	*Bartholomew's New and Revised Plan of Greater Birmingham* (about 1904)
John Bartholomew	*Bartholomew's Pocket Atlas and Guide to Birmingham* (1954)
Samuel Bradford	*A Plan of Birmingham Surveyed in 1750* (1751)
Bradshaw	*Plan of Birmingham* (1840)
J. W. Brown	*Street Map of the Manor of Aston* (1883)
Ebenezer Robins	*Plan of Birmingham* (1820)
W. Augustus Davies	*Map of the District of Aston Manor (1894)*
James Drake	*Plan of Birmingham* (1832)
James Drake	*Map of Birmingham Divided into Wards* (1835)
W. Fowler	*Aston Manor in 1833* (1835)
J. A. Guest	*Plan of Birmingham 1834* (1837)
Kelly	*Kelly's Directory Map of Birmingham (1896)*
J. Kempson	*To the Commissioners of the Street Acts, this map of Birmingham shewing the boundaries as perambulated by them in 1810 (1811)*
J. Kempson	*Town of Birmingham* (about 1818)
King's Norton Joint Committee	*Map* (1894)
T. Hanson	*Plan of Birmingham* (1778)
T. Hanson	*Plan of Birmingham* (1781)
Ordnance Survey Office	*Edition of 1914* (scale of 1 to 2,500)
Ordnance Survey Office	*Edition of 1916* (scale of 1 to 2,500)
J. Pigott Smith	*Map of Birmingham engraved from a minute trogonometrical survey made in 1824 and 1825* (1828)
J. Pigott Smith	*Street Map of the Borough of Birmingham* (1855)
C. Pye	*Plan of Birmingham Survey'd in 1795* (1795)

Society for the Diffusion of Useful Knowledge	*Birmingham* (1839)
William S. Till	*Street map of the Borough of Birmingham* (1884)
J. Tomlinson	*Plan of Aston Manor* (1758)
J. Tomlinson	*Plan of Duddeston and Netchells Manors* (1758)
J. Tomlinson	*A Map of Little Bromwich Manor* (1759)
J. Tomlinson	*A Map of Bordesley Manor* (1760)
J. Tomlinson	*A Map of Saltley Manor* (1760)
W. Westley	*The Plan of Birmingham Survey'd in 1731* (1731)

Letters

All letters are in the BirminghamLives Archive, **www.BirminghamLives.co.uk**., developed through South Birmingham College.

INDEX

Index note: page numbers printed in italic refer to photographs